MARRIAGE
FOR THE
EVERYDAY

365
Conversation Starters
Designed to Deepen
Couple Relationships

BOBBYE AND BRITTON WOOD

T0126466

MARЯIAGE
FOR THE
EVERYDAY

© 2017 by Britton and Bobbye Wood
Couple Growth, Unlimited
Fort Worth, Texas

All rights reserved. No part of this book may be reproduced or transmitted in any
form or by any mans, electronic or mechanical, including photocopying,
recording or by any information storage and retrieval system,
without permission in writing from the copyright owner.

Published by Carpenter's Son Publishing, Franklin, Tennessee
Cover and Interior Design by Debbie Manning Sheppard
Special Thanks to photo contribution from Haley Nicas
Printed in the United States of America

ISBN # 978-1-942587-93-4

DEDICATION

To our grandchildren

and great grandchildren,

with hope for quality relationships

for the future

MARRIAGE FOR THE EVERDAY

ACKNOWLEDGEMENTS

We are grateful for the many contributions to our lives and ministry over the years. Among them:

- ❦ Drs. David and Vera Mace, mentors, pioneers, and founders of the Association for Couples in Marriage Enrichment (ACME), currently known as Better Marriages

- ❦ Our three wonderful daughters and their husbands for their encouragement and love

- ❦ MK and Jesse Larson and the Hudson Foundation for their support in writing this book

- ❦ Healthy Marriage/Healthy Families Coalition of Tarrant County for the development of the Marriage Education Projects, The Parenting Center of Fort Worth, Texas and

- ❦ Other educators who have made great contributions of instruction and insight: Sherod and Phyllis Miller, David Olson, Scott Stanley, John Van Epp and Joe and Michelle Hernandez

MARRIAGE FOR THE EVERDAY

BRITTON'S INTRODUCTION

Writing this book is the result of the accumulation of experiences, trainings, goals for living and the hopefulness of healthy couple relationships.

In my early ministry, I was a youth minister and led the church's music. When I finished seminary, I moved into campus ministry with college students. It was there I learned how to lead and deal with people who were on the new edge of their independence. After an exciting ten years (during the entire decade of the 1960s), I noticed that many of our former university students kept coming back to our campus retreats. They could not find a church that addressed their needs. It was that realization that led me to move to a local church in the heart of North Dallas to create a viable ministry for adults who were single.

As I ministered to single adults, I soon learned that many were coming out of a marriage that could not be held together. Others tended to delay marriage due to their fear of failure in relationships. It was during this time that I saw the need for dealing with relationship training for single adults. I felt we needed to better equip them for marriage.

It was during these single adult ministry days that I thought Bobbye and I needed some training to help those still married to stem the tide of divorces. In January of 1978, Bobbye and I were trained as couple leaders in Marriage Enrichment. It was in that training where we met our mentors, Drs. David and Vera Mace. The Maces were the founders of the Association for Couples in Marriage Enrichment (ACME). It is now known as Better Marriages.

The skills we learned and the progress we have made in our marriage is because of the training. At the time, we had been married for 19 years and had a good marriage, yet we had not learned to deal well with disagreements. Part of that was due to our different family backgrounds. The new training helped both of us to see the need for dealing with conflicts. Our mentors had said that we 'should never waste a conflict.' When we worked through our initial conflict after the training, it brought a brand-new hope for the success of our marriage. It showed me that we can work through anything. The only regret I have had is that two of our daughters were out of high school when we learned better ways to relate to each other.

Our marriage has continued to grow through the years. At this writing we are in our 60th year of marriage, because we daily practice the skills learned in that training back in 1978. As we see it, we have been in three different phases in our marriage. The first was all the years prior to our marriage enrichment training. It was a time of rearing our three daughters and striving to get along well with each other even though we lacked some skills we could have benefitted from during those years.

The second phase of our marriage came after our marriage enrichment training. We chose to utilize the skills we were introduced to in the training and we helped organize a Marriage Enrichment Group (MEG). The MEG is a group of five or six couples who meet monthly to work on each marriage. We started this MEG in 1984 and it continues till this day. Regular sessions each month with couples who want their marriages to grow as well has been one of the highlights of our lives.

The third phase has taken place as we entered our 60th year of marriage. Through conversation, expressions of affection, and commitment of time with each other every day, we have had a new discovery of lovemaking and energy that was missing from our lives. It was not that we were acutely aware of what was missing, but when we shared honestly about what we were thinking and feeling, we began to feel like newlyweds. It has been and is exhilarating.

So, why write this book? We want other couples to enjoy on an everyday basis some of the joy we feel every day. We have learned from other couples that one of their most difficult things to do is to take the time to talk with each other each day about topics that enhance their marriage. They talk about what they need to do, where they need to take their children, what needs fixing, and other daily tasks and chores. Couples need to talk about who they are becoming together, who they want to be, and even who they are as lovers. So, we have created a simple way to help couples talk about relevant couple issues and grow closer together through doing it daily. After all, the first marriage enrichment training children get is watching how their parents interact and love each other. When the children grow up, the couple remains. How the couple has grown through the years will make a great deal of difference when the children are gone from the home.

We hope each couple will use this book in whatever manner is appropriate for you. You may wish to go from page to page in each section or you may choose to skip around through the book. We have chosen the themes for the sections based on our experiences and hope they become useful to you in your marital growth.

EMANUEL BRITTON WOOD, JR.

MARRIAGE FOR THE EVERDAY

BOBBYE'S INTRODUCTION

The genesis for this book began in January of our 60th year of marriage. Britton and I came together with a joyful and emotional impact, with all the subtlety of a hand grenade. Over the next few weeks the continuing impact led to some general questions, such as, "What in the world is happening to us?" We tried to preserve the closeness we felt for each other by claiming a space every day which we called "our time" in which we gave each other all the things we believed married couples need but sometimes don't get around to—affection, attention, intimate talking, physical connection, affirmation, and shared laughter.

"Our time" conversations led to an examination of our years of teaching marriage education classes, participating in a local Marriage Enrichment Group, speaking on marriage in other countries, attending marriage conferences of all kinds, and reading books on marriage. What had we learned from decades of work and from the difficulties of our own relationship? It was as if we were mountain climbers who had climbed to one enormous peak, only to see that that there were other peaks above, peaks we had not seen when we first started to climb. So here are some of our beliefs about marriage.

Marriage is the best institution for individuals to grow socially, emotionally, spiritually, and personally. Marriage allows couples to reach astonishing levels of joy. Marriage trains the families of the future by equipping them with healthy interaction skills. Marriage gathers up all the divergent strands of individual talents, personality, and hopes and weaves them into an intricate, beautiful, and historic tapestry-for-two.

MARRIAGE FOR THE EVERDAY

Marriage deserves a celebration everyday. At its core, that is what this book is about.

BOBBYE NELSON WOOD

TABLE OF CONTENTS

MARЯIAGE FOR THE EVERDAY

THE CONCEPT OF "US-NESS"

"And now let us welcome the new year,

Full of things that have never been."

RAINER MARIA RILKE

THE CONCEPT OF "US-NESS"

A vital marriage is composed of a strong "you" and an equally strong "me." Both are essential for the marriage to flourish. Often couples overlook the idea and value of the "us," the relationship itself. Yet that relationship, that concept of "us-ness," is what ultimately brings about the happiness of the couple.

As an anniversary present one year, Bobbye and Britton bought a painting of an old-fashioned couple holding a heart over their heads. On the heart was the number 3. Although they did not know what the artist intended, they thought the 3 would be a daily reminder of the fact that the relationship itself was important, at times more important than just pleasing the "you" or the "me."

That bond, the relationship, the "us," needs to be nourished and paid attention to. After all, if divorce comes, the "you" does not die, nor does the "me." But something dies between the two. It is the "us," the relationship itself. This is something the couple may not have considered when they first started their marital journey. Protecting the "us" means that together or apart the couple is aware of its value and its power.

DAILY COUPLE TALK:
(EACH PARTNER RESPONDS TO THE OTHER)
What is one quality that you value in yourself?
In your partner? In the relationship?

THE CONCEPT OF "US-NESS"

"A cord of three strands is not easily broken." (Ecclesiastes 4:12) This statement from the Bible's Wisdom Literature may speak of the fact that in marriage the "us," added to the "you" and "me," makes an enduring and dependable bond.

This "cord" of three strands keeps relevant the vows and promises we make to each other. It protects our independence as humans but also moves us toward interdependence as a loving couple. It makes significant our daily choices and actions. Paying attention to the way that the "us" works causes a new awareness of possibilities for interaction. In this way the "us" begins to speak and to claim a place as essential as a strong "you" and "me."

❤❤

DAILY COUPLE TALK:
(EACH PARTNER RESPONDS TO THE OTHER)
What is one thing I can do
to build a stronger relationship with you?

THE CONCEPT OF "US-NESS"

Creating a win/win/WIN in times of disagreement is difficult. Often in the heat of an argument one person wants to win more than he or she wants to protect the relationship, the "us."

Practice arguing fairly so that both persons' ideas and feelings are equally heard. This is one small step toward insuring that the outcome is a "win" for both "you" and "me." Both "win" by feeling respected and listened to, even though on some subjects only one can be right. (And it should not be the same person every time there is a disagreement.) One partner may be louder, may gather ideas more quickly, and may control emotions better. But if the other partner does not feel good about what happens during this time, the outcome will not be workable for the future, no matter what is said. Both "win" when there is the met expectation that while arguments may be inevitable, equitable standards for conducting the argument are just as important as the outcome.

The relationship itself wins if both "win" in a disagreement. Figuring out how to do this one action pays the greatest of dividends in closeness and intimacy.

DAILY COUPLE TALK:
(EACH PERSON RESPONDS WITH AN IDEA)
How can we argue more fairly?

THE CONCEPT OF "US-NESS"

Recently we traveled to Australia to speak at a Marriage Enrichment Conference and saw an advertisement for a couple's meeting. The sign said, "Putting Back into Your Relationship What Life Takes Out." It sounded very practical for the average time-challenged, two-job, stressed out couple. We cannot prevent life-stressors—health issues, job changes, money shortages, family problems—but focusing on the "us" in our daily lives can give a dependable and strangely powerful resource for dealing with them. With too many couples the individuals struggle with life's issues without learning to rely on the help and aid that their relationship can offer.

Balance is achievable when both lean on each other in honesty and openness, sharing daily concerns just as easily as discussing schedules and vacation plans. Putting some feeling talk into the sharing also helps the partner know where you are on the issue. For example, merely reminding your partner that you are meeting with your boss that afternoon is different from saying, "I am really anxious about meeting with Mr. Smith today." One way of talking is imparting schedule information; the other way conveys feelings as well and helps the partner know that the "us" is being asked to pay attention.

DAILY COUPLE TALK:
(EACH PERSON RESPONDS)
Try to use a feeling word as you discuss information about your day, such as "I am so relieved to have found my contact lens" or "I am frustrated that I didn't get the photos to the developer before they closed."

THE CONCEPT OF "US-NESS"

PREP, a program for improving couple relationships developed out of the University of Denver, is heavily into research. One thing they have learned about many couples in long-term, stable relationships is that the number one reason they give for their success is that they like each other and like to have fun together. They have stayed together happily through the years because they are good friends, and they regularly have dates to do the things they enjoy with each other. Their success is not due just to having good communication, important as that is, not just to resolving their issues in a fair way, not just to parenting responsibly, not just to great sex, not just to receiving support from family and friends. Their success is due to having fun together.

No one wants to work and bargain and compromise all the time, even if those actions pay the bills, smooth out the rough spots, and produce a peaceful home environment. There must also be play times whose purpose is just to relax and have fun. A strong "us" is a de-stressed "us." Occasionally you have to put issues "on the shelf" for a space of time, setting an appointment for getting to them later. Reserve the time for joint relaxation.

A date night would be good, but make sure it includes things that both of you like to do—AND take turns planning the agenda. It does not have to be costly; a picnic at the park with music from the radio works too.

DAILY COUPLE TALK:
(EACH PERSON RESPONDS)
Name one thing you would like to do (or to do again) with your partner.

THE CONCEPT OF "US-NESS"

As the song says, "You and me got a whole lot of history." That history includes births, deaths, family events, vacations, moves, illnesses, thrilling connections and discoveries, or shared jokes. It is the history of "us," which we share with nobody else.

The good memories of our early relationship can be drawn on in lean times or difficulties. They should be discussed from time to time by both of you so that they remain as vivid as a photograph in a scrapbook. The painful memories between you do not need to be constantly on your minds, lest you hang on to resentment or keep score on slights and inconsiderate actions. Every day has enough problems without storing up past injustices.

Freeing ourselves for loving actions today sets the "us" on a steady course.

DAILY COUPLE TALK:
(EACH PERSON ANSWERS)
What is one piece of your history together that brings you joy to think about?

THE CONCEPT OF "US-NESS"

In Jan Karon's <u>Come Rain or Come Shine</u>, Father Tim is performing a wedding. The bride has asked him for the meaning of the word "cherish" in the line of their vows "to love and to cherish." He tells the bride that cherish means to "outdo." It is the practical idea, he says, that each partner seeks to "outdo" the other in kindness, in sweet surprises, in loving actions, in honor. In this way the partner knows that he/she is being cherished.

"Outdoing" each other is not done just to insure the partner's happiness. "Outdoing" each other often leads to our own happiness. All three entities are winners: "you," "me" and "us."

If cherishing is expressed by "outdoing," we are on a high level of interaction. We may feel vulnerable, yes, but the rewards are also generous.

DAILY COUPLE TALK:
(EACH PARTNER ANSWERS)
What do you think of Father Tim's active definition of "cherish"?

THE CONCEPT OF "US-NESS"

A sign hangs on the wall where Bobbye goes to Weight-Watchers. It says, "If you always do what you always did, you'll always get what you always got." Reminding us to break out of old ruts and eating habits if we want to be slimmer and healthier, this sign suggests something about relationships as well.

Trying new ways of talking to each other, new ways of arguing, or new ways of showing affection may feel awkward at first. After all, no one learns a new sport or a new skill without some initial practice time. But many people are astonished to discover new aptitudes in themselves that they did not know existed. They say that it is like walking through a door into a whole new room.

Sharing in the conversation starters at the bottom of each page of this book is possibly a new and innovative activity. It invites us first to discover our own feelings and opinions (always a useful project), to share them with a trusted companion, and to really listen to what the other person says. Further discussion may or may not follow, and it is important not to challenge or disagree with the other person. Their feelings and opinions come from their own point of view, and even if they differ from yours, they are helpful to know.

DAILY COUPLE TALK:
(EACH PERSON RESPONDS)
What new relational skill would you like to develop with your partner? What steps could make that happen?

THE CONCEPT OF "US-NESS"

Making assumptions about another person's meanings or motivations is sometimes called mind-reading. Often without ever checking if the assumptions are correct or incorrect, and proceeding as though there is only one possible point of view, that person takes action and makes plans.

The habit of mind-reading is hard on a relationship because only one person is really needed. That person assesses the situation, makes a judgment, and acts independently. Often the partner does not even know that his/her words or actions are being weighed, measured, and defined.

Checking for clarification or confirmation of a problem situation helps eliminate misunderstandings and promotes mutual responsibility for sharing information about daily activities. It reduces the times when one partner assumes he/she knows what the other is thinking or feeling. It honors the "us-ness" in our lives.

DAILY COUPLE TALK:
(EACH PARTNER RESPONDS)
Think of a time when one of you assumed he/she knew what the other was thinking. What happened?

THE CONCEPT OF "US-NESS"

Everyone likes to be complimented on a job well done. If we compliment others on what they did well instead of harping on what they did not do, we should not be surprised that they behave warmly toward us. Criticism (particularly if it is delivered often) is not usually well-received, even if it begins with, "I'm sorry, but." It is especially poorly received when it is from someone we love and whose opinion we value.

Learning to look for the ways our partner is trying to please us focuses our attention in a different place than looking for the shortcomings or slights. Feelings follow actions, and looking for the sweet, the funny, and the endearing usually puts us in a better mood because that's what we see.

All of us are consistently short of compliments. That's just the kind of world it is. Getting them from someone we love is not only helpful to our self-esteem but nourishes the "us" that is the living connection between us.

DAILY COUPLE TALK:
(BOTH RESPOND)
Name one thing you really
admire about your partner.

THE CONCEPT OF "US-NESS"

The growth and celebration of our "us," our relationship, can happen every day. Two things make it possible. In the first place, it needs to be a mutual goal. In the second place, there needs to be a daily performance of a loving action requested by your partner. This keeps awareness sharp and central.

One of you may want more joy for your relationship, more honest, intimate conversation, more sex, more fun, or more closeness. But you alone cannot make it happen. Expressing to your partner your interest in a certain goal for your relationship is a good place to start. Listening with an open mind to the other's desires and goals is also instructive.

When both are interested and can agree on a specific goal or need, plan actions that can make it a reality. Do these actions often enough that they begin to feel comfortable and not awkward or forced. Any new skill or task takes some time to learn. No one gets on the tennis court for the first time and is immediately eligible for the Davis Cup. At first, make sure your partner understands what you are trying to do for them, especially if it is not an ordinary action for you.In this simple way the "us-ness" unique to every couple knits together with the hopes and needs of the "you" and "me."

DAILY COUPLE TALK:
(EACH PARTNER ANSWERS)
What is a goal that you think would enliven your experience as a couple?

THE CONCEPT OF "US-NESS"

So often it is about me. Name the topic, I am more concerned about how I fit into that topic or what I get out of the situation. I want to feel good about "me." When does the "us-ness" kick in? We must choose to have a different attitude. If I am grateful for the relationship with my life partner, then why am I so wrapped up in how I benefit? Unless my thoughts shift to "us" along with what I want for me, I cannot successfully join the "us-ness" of the relationship.

When Britton was a 10-year-old boy visiting his Grandmother Cooper's farm in Louisiana, he noticed that the family often came out on the front porch to watch and listen to a car or truck shift into first gear in order to come up the steep hill to their farm. The family could also tell when it shifted into second gear as it gained speed at the top of the hill. That is what we need to do in our closest relationships. We need to get out of first gear. Shift into second and gain speed into the "us" relationship. It really is about "us." If I am only concerned about "me," I will stay in first gear and struggle, but if I shift to caring about "us," I will gain momentum in our relationship.

DAILY COUPLE TALK:
(BOTH PERSONS ANSWER)
What is something you can do to show you are thinking more about "us" than about "me"?

THE CONCEPT OF "US-NESS"

An announcer on sports radio said that it takes hearing something three times before we remember it. Perhaps this is why commercials annoyingly repeat a telephone number. But in case this statement is true, here is a reminder of a sure-fire way to build (and keep) an "us":

1. Have a couple talk time every day. Make sure the conversation is about the two of you—your day, your hopes, your concerns.

1. Have a couple talk time every day. Listen attentively to what your partner is saying, perhaps even repeating back what you hear, especially if there is even a hint of an emotional message being conveyed.

1. Have a couple talk time every day. Staying current and knowing where you are and where your partner is leads to the kind of cooperation that builds the "us," the relationship.

DAILY COUPLE TALK:
(EACH PARTNER ANSWERS)
Which of the reasons for having a daily couple talk do you best understand? Why?

THE CONCEPT OF "US-NESS"

Flower gardening and relationship-building are a lot alike. Both take work and planning. Both can produce joy and satisfaction when plants bloom and others notice the colors and shapes. Bobbye's family even sends pictures of their successes: roses, peonies, hydrangeas.

It takes a while for planted flowers from the nursery to get established on their own. The same is true for transplanted flowers from other sites. Their root systems under the ground, not visible even to the gardener who planted them, need time to develop. Once rooted and drawing in nutrients, however, the plants are ready to bloom.

Close relationships are the same. When we pay attention to them and give them what they need for health, they reward us with beauty and color. It is the nature of a healthy relationship to provide pleasure and satisfaction to the persons involved, whether or not they are aware of what is going on under the surface. One bonus of a healthy relationship is that family and friends also enjoy the beauty.

❤❤

DAILY COUPLE TALK:
(BOTH RESPOND)
What is one thing about your relationship that brings you satisfaction?

29

THE CONCEPT OF "US-NESS"

Our son-in-law Bill recently posted a message on Facebook on the occasion of our daughter's birthday. It drew many responses, one even asking him to write more, since the words were so sweet and sincere.

It tells of 23-day-old Billy N., looking around his crib, suddenly aware that something extraordinary had just happened in the world. He would someday discover that it was the birth of his "best friend, partner, helper, and soul mate," Leigh Ann.

Now, he says, older and much more experienced, he feels "grateful, humbled, and awed. Still comforted at the thought that she is here. Still prone to wild excitement at the thought of her."

This beautiful expression of love reveals a husband content in his relationship with his wife. It shows a strong "us," as well as some of the ways each touches the other. The world is always in need of these kinds of testimonies and enriched by their simple profundity.

DAILY COUPLE TALK:
(EACH PARTNER RESPONDS)
Name one reason you love your partner.

THE CONCEPT OF "US-NESS"

In close relationships, each partner needs to be able to express his/her dreams, ideas, hopes, flashpoints, regrets, and concerns. He/she needs to do it honestly and often. This will not happen, however, if the partner does not listen or does not seem receptive to these personal expressions. Hearing "You shouldn't feel that way," getting a snort of laughter, or receiving a curt dismissal does not make further sharing easy.

The need is still there to speak aloud personal goals and events. The need still exists to clarify ideas and opinions by stating them in words and objectifying them just enough to test their accuracy or relevance. They now will be shared with someone else—a trusted friend, a colleague at work. But the partner will not hear them. The "us" will not be privileged to learn this important information.

All it takes to become the recipient of intimate verbal sharing is some kind of acknowledgement that you want to hear it and that you are listening. You don't have to agree with what you hear. You don't have to "fix it." Just listen.

DAILY COUPLE TALK:
(EACH PERSON RESPONDS, CONCENTRATING ON GOOD LISTENING SKILLS)
Describe an important event in your life before you met your partner. Why was it important?

THE CONCEPT OF "US-NESS"

Dealing with differences between you can be a challenge. Sometimes the differences in preferences and personalities lead to laughter and tolerance. Sometimes they cause friction, even anger.

Britton and Bobbye had been married for many years and knew each other well—including many differences—when they went to see the movie "Pearl Harbor." Beside each other in the theater Bobbye heard Britton say, "Look at that!" She looked attentively at the screen. She saw nurses coming ashore in Honolulu all dressed up for a party. Britton whispered, "That's a '40 Ford." Bobbye did not even see a car on the screen. Differences.

Not all differences make you smile. Bobbye does not like clutter and tends to throw things away in order to reduce it. Britton likes to hang on to everything, just in case he might need it someday. This has led to bitter arguments over piles of "National Geographic" in the garage or a discarded piece of mail that had a check in it.

Coming to terms with differences, amusing or annoying, is a step toward a stronger "us." The differences probably can't be changed; the attitudes leading to compromises can.

DAILY COUPLE TALK:
(EACH PERSON ANSWER THE QUESTION)
What is a difference between the two of you that you can laugh about? What is a difference that has caused trouble? How did you work it out?

THE CONCEPT OF "US-NESS"

Routine is sometimes the enemy of a growing relationship. Eating the same meals, watching the same TV shows at the same time, never varying schedules or habits—this can lead to boredom without ever thinking about it. Routine calls for minimal effort and almost no thought. We can even keep important rules, such as fidelity or good manners, without engaging our minds or hearts. It's just routine.

Putting our minds and hearts into new ways of loving our partner not only pleases him/her but quite often refurbishes our own interest. Take turns arranging for entertainment that you think your partner will like. Go dancing, if one of you likes it. Play a new board game. Take in a local museum's latest exhibit. Order a pizza and eat it outside under the stars. Sing each other love songs. Leave Post-it notes on a toothbrush or in an underwear drawer with sexy suggestions. Kiss and touch in the kitchen.

Seek new ways of connection and never settle for "I guess this is as good as it's going to be."

DAILY COUPLE TALK:
(BOTH PERSONS RESPOND)
What is an activity you would like to do with your partner?

THE CONCEPT OF "US-NESS"

Recently Bobbye and Britton heard a TED Talks sex therapist who was quoting statistics about the reasons couples had affairs. In analyzing their reasons for an extramarital relationship, many people said they just wanted to feel "alive" again. They wanted joy, they said, and they wanted to be wanted. They never meant to hurt anyone, and they almost always intended to stay with their spouse as a life-partner.

Affairs cause great and sometimes irreparable damage to a relationship. But there IS an important statistic here. Keeping a relationship fresh and exciting, whether you've been married seven years or 57, is one way of keeping each other's attention. Dig in on the "us-ness" of your time together and enjoy the variety of pleasure and mutual fulfillment.

Relying on laughter, having honest and intimate conversation, showing affection, and exploring new ways of showing appreciation can absolutely rejuvenate a relationship drifting into routine and sameness.

DAILY COUPLE TALK:
(BOTH PERSONS RESPOND)
Choose one word from the last sentence (laughter, open conversation, affection, or appreciation) and discuss how that might be used in your relationship.

THE CONCEPT OF "US-NESS"

When your child takes his first math course, it won't be trigonometry. He/she will be starting simply, with a study of how to add. Next he/she will learn to subtract. It is a logical process that will lead to the performance of more complex skills at a later time. But the complex skills will only be reached by mastering the simple ones.

Think of some goals you have for the future. What do you want for yourself regarding health, income, retirement, family, marriage, and "us-ness"? Think in increments of five years. Do you need to make any changes now? Keeping your eyes on long-term goals is important if these goals are going to be accomplished.

But realizing long-term goals also needs daily practical actions that keep us on the right path. As Teddy Roosevelt once said about accomplishment, "Keep your eyes on the stars, and your feet on the ground."

DAILY COUPLE TALK:
(EACH PERSON RESPONDS)
What is a goal you have for the future? What could you be doing today that would make reaching that goal a possibility?

THE CONCEPT OF "US-NESS"

The creativity we bring to loving not only entertains and benefits the loved one but also enhances our own lives. Eighty-one-year-old Sophia Loren speaks to this point by calling creativity "a fountain of youth."

If we brought to our close relationships just a portion of the time, energy, and cooperation we bring to our jobs, we might be astonished at the response. If we added creativity and imagination to our loving, we might feel the difference even in our outlook on the world. I don't know if Sophia Loren is right about the "fountain of youth" found in the perspective of honoring close relationships with attention and joyful giving. But I am sure that such creativity makes us happily "young at heart."

DAILY COUPLE TALK:
(EACH PERSON RESPONDS)
What special surprise could you do that
you know would really please your partner?
Shh! Think about it, don't tell him/her, and do it soon.
Even anticipation is a part of the process.

THE CONCEPT OF "US-NESS"

When Bobbye was growing up, there was an old saying used by snickering children when they saw a couple holding hands. It said, "First comes love, then comes marriage, then comes _____ with a baby carriage." That saying may not fit with modern sequences of events, but it does suggest that love and sex are meant to be bound up in the unique relationship called marriage.

Time, energy, and health circumstances may change sexual engagement from the way it once was, but the need for physical touch and closeness never changes and defies time. Many wedding ceremonies quote the Bible about the "reason" brides and grooms leave behind their families of origin. It is to "cleave" to each other in a special way. "Cleave" is an old-fashioned word that still packs a punch. It suggests that as human beings our deepest needs for closeness and thrilling physical union are met in marriage—one of life's most wonderful relationships.

DAILY COUPLE TALK:
(EACH PERSON ANSWER)
*What physical love expression from your
partner do you enjoy most?*

THE CONCEPT OF "US-NESS"

Britton's growing up years were not filled with affection. His was not a hugging family. He does not remember a full embrace from his Mom or Dad. He says that he usually fought or teased with his older sisters. So, when Bobbye came into his life, he discovered that he enjoyed the hugs and kisses they had in their dating days. To say that he was a quick learner is an understatement. Demonstrated affection was so different from Britton's upbringing, but today he prefers the "us" they have developed.

How fortunate it has been to enjoy becoming a part of an **"us"** that not only kisses and hugs but celebrates almost everything. As we rejoice with each other and other family members when something good takes place, we demonstrate that we care and we are thrilled for some victory, achievement or success. Rather than bemoan the fact that good things happen to others, we are delighted with any good news about people we love. This is a good attitude for us to have. We rejoice with those who rejoice and celebrate with them.

DAILY COUPLE TALK:
(EACH PARTNER RESPONDS)
Discuss what kind of home situation you experienced growing up regarding affection and celebrations.

THE CONCEPT OF "US-NESS"

Many couples struggle with keeping their "us," their relationship, close and satisfying. They work hard, raise their families, pay their bills, and try to be responsible neighbors and citizens. There is not much energy or time for anything else, they often feel.

It is exactly these couples that can most benefit from the Couple Talk in this book. It is exactly these couples who need a simple formula for establishing a new bond that feels much like being newlyweds again. Take the time to look at each other as you share your thoughts and feelings. This small but significant action goes a long way toward intentionally creating connection, even when you are apart. It builds the "us" while it gives the information that clearly reveals the "you" and the "me."

If life circumstances don't make every day's Couple Talk possible, do it as often as you are able. Enjoy the experience. As a wise counselor once said about prayer: Keep it honest, keep it simple, and keep it up.

DAILY COUPLE TALK:
(EACH PERSON ANSWERS)
What is one important thing you want to say to your partner? Say it now.

THE CONCEPT OF "US-NESS"

Britton and Bobbye have been involved in a Marriage Enrichment Group for decades. This is a group of five couples who meet once a month to work on our marriages. They credit it for keeping them on track and growing as a couple, even in times of adverse circumstances.

COUPLES NEED SUPPORT. Parents and other family members would be very upset if the couple separated or divorced, but they seldom if ever provide the couple with necessary time to be alone or offer the economic means to make that possible from time to time. Children experience much distress (at any age) if parents split up, but they naturally want all the parents' time and attention. Our society cries out for more models of loving couples of every age, race, and economic circumstance. Yet even many churches, an agency that performs weddings, seldom offer their young couples courses or programs that show how to enhance relationship.

So it is up to the couple to find the motivation for doing the things that build relationship and develop intimacy. Seldom can couples grow (and stay) close if they make little effort to maintain a strong "us."

DAILY COUPLE TALK:
(EACH PARTNER PARTICIPATES)
What is one change you could make in your schedules that would allow some couple time? Discuss.

THE CONCEPT OF "US-NESS"

Recently Harvard University published the results of a 25-year study regarding what makes people happy. They followed freshmen students through their academic careers and through their subsequent jobs, marriages, births of children, and achievements. Although it was a complex study, one researcher sums up what they found out about happiness by saying it was supported by Two Pillars. One pillar is "Love," and the other is "Find a way of coping with life that does not push love away."

The first pillar—love—must be an active verb, suggesting that in the end it's what we DO that brings our own best feelings and sense of emotional well-being. The other supporting pillar tells us that hurtful behavior and negative attitudes matter because they undermine our own efforts to be happy.

Two pillars, simple and relevant, that not only help in the building of a stronger "us" but give us a direct reason for doing it.

DAILY COUPLE TALK:
(EACH PERSON ANSWERS)
What do you think about the two pillars regarding your relationship?

THE CONCEPT OF "US-NESS"

In baseball the batter who gets a hit must touch one base before he can run to the next one. If he fails to touch the base, he is automatically out. Those are the rules of the game.

In life it is necessary to focus occasionally on the values and goals we find important in the world. Scoring runs of achievement sometimes comes down to touching the "base" of our dreams to make sure they are still what we want.

Take a moment to think of some goals or values that you find important. Consider family, health, job, housing, politics, travel, or religion. Pick one or two that you find important enough to spend money on. What would you want to accomplish in a year, in five years? (Perhaps writing your goals would help to clarify them.)

DAILY COUPLE TALK:
(EACH PARTNER RESPONDS)
Share some of your goals for the future, and listen carefully as your partner does the same. How can you help each other to accomplish some of these goals?

THE CONCEPT OF "US-NESS"

One beautiful (but possibly unexpected) side effect of working toward a strong "us" is the healing of old hurts. There simply is not room in our hearts and minds for rehearsing former grievances or reviewing injustices when we are concentrated on the ways we can give and receive love.

Trust, hope, and understanding begin to flourish, and with them a new awareness of a happier "me" whose needs are being met by someone consistently in my corner. This awareness can even go on while daily dealing with life's strains and stresses. It sometimes even extends to childhood events and disappointments. On the surface it is hard to explain to anyone else, but in the heart's core a deepening satisfaction lets us know that we are doing something important.

○○

DAILY COUPLE TALK:
(EACH PERSON ANSWERS)
What is a positive side effect you have experienced while feeling a new connection with your partner?

THE CONCEPT OF "US-NESS"

A sign recently appeared in the Weight Watchers studio Bobbye attends which really caught her eye. It says, "Keep your WHY close by." The sign is of course referring to one's motivation for losing pounds, but it also works for relationship-building.

If both partners want the benefits of growing stronger relationally and both feel good about what can happen between them, staying close to their motivations and expectations can be very helpful.

Our WHY stays on our minds and helps us avoid damaging words and actions. It makes "I'm sorry" easier and more sincere. It allows us to look for ways to demonstrate affection and kindness to our partners. It makes us more aware of our partner's efforts to be cooperative and loving.

Keeping the Why close by helps us define our love and be hopeful about our future.

ⵉ⎯ⵔ

DAILY COUPLE TALK:
(EACH PARTNER RESPONDS)
What was one reason you were attracted to your partner when you first met?
Why are you attracted today?

THE CONCEPT OF "US-NESS"

The Garden Guru in his column in our Saturday newspaper spoke of "pops of white flowers" in his yard, making a big impression against dark green foliage. A list of his favorite white flowers followed this statement. Couples need "pops of joy" fairly often just to keep their relationship, their "us," running smoothly. No pharmaceutical, these "pops" come from intense couple appreciation. They may come physically or emotionally. They may be simple or have many layers of experience. They may even come from a long, hearty laugh over a shared ridiculous occurrence that strikes both partners as funny.

The "pops" relieve individual stress, while at the same time drawing the couple together. They not only lead to a healthier "you" and "me" as the couple experiences a happy moment together but they also help confirm that our "us" is in good shape and worth maintaining. And just as the Garden Guru thought the white flowers stood out in a dark environment, these experiences and the pleasure they produce are often noticed and celebrated by others.

DAILY COUPLE TALK:
(EACH PARTNER SHARES)
Think of a joyful time recently when you felt especially close to your partner. Get in touch with the details and describe them aloud. Perhaps your partner remembers the time also. Share what made it so joyful for you.

THE CONCEPT OF "US-NESS"

It was a surprise to learn recently that celery, spinach, and kale have the highest percentage of healthful nutrients of all the vegetables. These nutrients and the vitamins and minerals they provide are meant for the health of our bodies when we eat and digest these vegetables.

The same is true of the emotional nutrients available to those in a close, growing relationship, the exact place to process those nutrients. A sense of identity and belonging is one nutrient available; another is the joy of being affirmed by someone whose opinion matters. For some it is the relaxed sharing of an honest conversation; for others, it is a sense of security. For all couples, it is the invaluable treasure of feeling loved AND known.

DAILY COUPLE TALK:
(EACH PERSON RESPONDS)
Name three ingredients in your relationship that nurtures you in a special way.

COMMUNICATION

"Dialogue is to love, what blood is to the body. When the flow of blood stops, the body dies. When dialogue stops, love dies and resentment and hate are born. But dialogue can restore a dead relationship. Indeed, this is the miracle of dialogue: it can bring relationship into being, and it can bring into being once again a relationship that has died. There is only one qualification to these claims for dialogue: it must be mutual and proceed from both sides, and the parties to it must persist relentlessly."

REUEL L. HOWE
THE MIRACLE OF DIALOGUE, 1963

COMMUNICATION

On a recent trip to Virginia Britton and Bobbye informally interviewed many people with one question: "What do you think makes a strong marriage?" We talked to college students, relatives, hairdressers, mechanics, waiters, teachers, businessmen, even those who were retired—a big variety. Some were married, some were divorced, some were single. Almost half of them said that the most critical element in a strong marriage is communication. Although they defined communication differently, they agreed as to its importance.

Tim defined it as being honest with each other. "Tell the first lie and it's over," he said. Monica said it meant sharing feelings. Carol said it was "hearing each other with open minds and a willingness to think what the words might mean." Leslie quoted a line from a movie called "We Bought a Zoo" where one character says that "the key to talking is listening." They each focused on a part of communication but each was aware of its relevance in helping a couple develop a style of talking that leads to understanding and reduces friction and distance.

DAILY COUPLE TALK:
(EACH PERSON ANSWERS)
How would you answer the question
of what makes a strong marriage?
Why is your answer important to you?

COMMUNICATION

Bobbye was recently reading a story in which a man was grieving for his wife, who had been killed in a random, drive-by shooting. He decided that one of the things he missed most was the sense of "connection" with his wife during their late afternoon conversations as they talked about their day. It was such a simple activity, but it was one that had given meaning and perspective to his day. Now suddenly it was gone and he keenly felt its loss.

Shared words with someone we love and know well are often profound. They connect us through experience and feelings. They allow us to discover new ideas in ourselves as we objectify the events or occurrences by saying them aloud. Sharing our experiences and opinions with someone else also offers us THEIR responses, which sometimes gives new and different ways of looking at them.

The Daily Couple Talk is one level of conversational connection. Answering the questions and discussing our answers and ideas allow us to learn new (or forgotten) things about ourselves and about each other.

DAILY COUPLE TALK:
(EACH PARTNER RESPONDS)
Describe the best thing that happened to you yesterday.

COMMUNICATION

Words spoken to us as children can be carried with us throughout adulthood. Some of those remembered words have given us courage and direction at critical times; some have undermined our confidence in ourselves and caused us to struggle.

Several years ago Britton and Bobbye spoke at a couple's conference in New Mexico. Included in each evening's program was a couple who dramatized typical couple scenes. One night the scene was of a husband coming home after work to hear his wife ask if he had remembered to pick up milk and bread. He said no. She asked, "Can't you ever get anything right?"

The husband went over to the edge of the stage and got down on his knees in order to look smaller. Over the sound system came a booming voice saying, "Son, you should know that in the ninth inning of the ballgame with the bases loaded and two outs, you do NOT bunt. Can't you ever get anything right?"

Then the husband got up and told his wife that when she said those words, he heard his father's voice reminding him of all his failures. They began to discuss the common issue of remembered words which labeled us: klutz, loser, screwup, clown. They planned together what they might do to help each other.

DAILY COUPLE TALK:
(EACH PARTNER RESPONDS)
Are there some words you remember from the home you grew up in that still intrudes into your life today? Explain. Do you need to make any changes in dealing with it?

COMMUNICATION

Some words have become famous historically, like "Give me liberty or give me death" or "Remember the Alamo." A current favorite of Bobbye's is "Let's Roll," the statement made by some brave passengers aboard United Airlines Flight 93, as they attacked the terrorists that had high-jacked their plane on September 11. Their courageous actions caused the plane to plunge into a field near Shanksville, Pennsylvania, instead of hitting its likely target, the dome of the U.S. Capitol.

The marriage ceremony also has important words couples say to each other: "I do," "to love and to cherish," "as long as we both shall live." Couples all over the world at the time of their ceremonies are promising things to each other that are solemn and sometimes personalized, sanctioned by church and state.

Just as these promises and pledges we once made to each other, some words continue to inspire and smooth our daily interactions with each other.

DAILY COUPLE TALK:
(BOTH PERSONS RESPOND)
What are some important or encouraging words that you have said to me lately?

COMMUNICATION
PART 1

Many communication programs these days have a strong emphasis on the power of listening. PREP (Prevention and Relationship Enhancement Program) calls theirs the Speaker/Listener Technique. It is designed for use in a couple's serious discussion when clashing points of view need to be clearly identified.

The Speaker has the "floor" and if necessary holds an object to give him/her the visual right to state his message without interruption or challenge. He/she is to be brief and pause often. This is because the Listener also has a definite task. He/she is to paraphrase what he/she hears the Speaker saying, and it's hard to do that if the message is too lengthy. He/she is not to edit or rebut the Speaker's message, although he/she may ask for clarification. When the whole message has been stated and paraphrased, the "floor" is exchanged and the roles are switched. The former Listener now gets a chance to express his/her point of view as the Speaker, and the former Speaker becomes the Listener.

Sometimes our arguments are over issues about which we have made assumptions or mis-interpretations. They can be cleared up simply by being forced to listen closely to what is being said. Putting the partner's message in our own words and saying them back allows us to make sure the partner knows that we heard them. Agreement is never the goal; understanding is.

DAILY COUPLE TALK:
(BOTH PARTNERS RESPOND)
Discuss the advantages of this technique of communication.

COMMUNICATION
PART 2

The Speaker/Listener Technique has other names used by other communication teachers. Some call it "mirroring," some "active listening," some "reflective listening." Bobbye even recently heard it called the "drive-by technique," referring to fast-food ordering where a voice over a speaker repeats our food order and adds the price.

Britton and Bobbye should have practiced this listening technique at a football game on a hot September afternoon. By the 4th quarter, Bobbye had had enough of the lop-sided game and told Britton, "I'm going to the bathroom and then to the car." That's what she did, standing under a big tree in a shady neighborhood where they had parked.

Britton heard half of Bobbye's message, waited impatiently outside the ladies' room after the game was over, and finally came angrily to the car. A spirited discussion further heated up the September afternoon.

That scene could have been prevented following the initial statement in the stands. Bobbye should have stated, "Tell me what I just said." If she had asked, "Did you hear what I said?" Britton would have answered yes. It is important that both persons know that the WHOLE message was heard or not heard.

DAILY COUPLE TALK:
(BOTH PERSONS PARTICIPATE)
Speaker will answer the following questions: Would you rather be rich or famous? Why? Listener will paraphrase what he/she heard. Switch roles.

COMMUNICATION

Words can bless or wound. For some reason we tend to remember the wounding words longer.

PREP has designed what they call a Time Out for adults. It simply means that rather than staying in an angry scene (when it is becoming increasingly clear that damaging words will be said that can't be taken back) both partners take a break and calm down. Some couples even have a signal or a buzzword that they can use to alert the other one that emotions seem to be running high and Time Out might be helpful. Damaging words spoken in anger tend to wound, and the wounds can last a long time.

The subject of the argument can then be more profitably resumed when both partners are able to discuss it calmly and rationally. If the timing does not allow for a meeting right away, set an appointment so that both know you are not going to avoid the subject.

DAILY COUPLE TALK:
(EACH PERSON RESPONDS)
*Time Out is one way to limit the effect of
damaging and wounding words.
Short of the unrealistic choice of never getting angry,
what else might we do to prevent
hurting each other with words?*

COMMUNICATION

David and Vera Mace were pioneers in the field of working with couples who wanted a better relationship. In 1973 they founded the Association for Couples in Marriage Enrichment (now called Better Marriages). The Maces advocated the Daily Sharing Time, a deliberately planned meeting for the couple to connect verbally by not only sharing their experiences but also the feelings they have about those experiences. An early riser, David would make tea in the mornings and bring it to Vera in bed. Then they would have a shared time of discussing the coming day, with ample time for feelings. If the early morning is not a possibility for this intimate conversation time, pick another time. It can even be done by phone.

Couples who regularly schedule some intimate talk time report that it has made a difference in the quality of their relationship, especially in keeping things current. Sharing and discussing the pages of this book can go a long way toward producing a feeling of closeness. That feeling helps counteract the annoying and debilitating issues of daily life.

DAILY COUPLE TALK:
(EACH PARTNER RESPONDS)
Get in touch with 3 feelings you currently have about this day. Express the feelings as adjectives (I am frustrated, I feel amused) and avoid statements such as "I feel that you," which is not really sharing a feeling. Then listen to your partner do the same thing.

COMMUNICATION

Even though a couple may know several excellent communication techniques, if they do not practice these skills regularly with each other, the skills are of little value to the couple. One may even have a profession such as psychiatry or law or teaching and practice certain communication skills daily in his/her work, but in relationship-building both need to understand AND USE the same skills.

Britton agreed to paint the outside of a patio door in order to save money when it was installed in their home. Time and choices and forgetfulness kept him from completing (or even beginning) the task. Then one Saturday he returned home to find Bobbye painting the door. Britton was upset. He told her she was doing it wrong. She needed to put masking tape around the glass panes and use a cloth to catch the drips. Bobbye was upset because he did not appreciate her efforts to complete a task.

After a few moments of poor interaction and loud talk, both began to use the Couple Communication technique where a person shares what he/she feels, wants, thinks, and will do. Britton learned that he felt embarrassed for having stated he would do a task which he did not do. That is why he was free to criticize Bobbye's work. Once they understood each other better, they decided to do the completion of painting the door together. The work did not look very professional, but both still remember the pride in using skills that led to cooperation.

DAILY COUPLE TALK:
(BOTH PARTNERS RESPOND)
Share with your partner a time when you felt misunderstood while doing some work together, even driving a car. What could you have done differently?

COMMUNICATION

There is a big difference between these two statements: "I'm feeling angry" and "You are making me mad." The first is a personal announcement of the flavor of emotions. The second is a charge that the other person has deliberately done an action to affect my emotions.

Phyllis and Sherod Miller, in their helpful program called Couple Communications, call these two kinds of statements Straight Talk and Control Talk. Straight Talk, with its key word "I," gives information about feelings. It levels the playing field by honestly presenting an emotion to a listener. Control Talk, with its key word "you," seeks to manipulate the partner by cleverly blaming the argument on him/her. The pronouns are the means by which the disagreement can become weighted or directed.

Straight Talk can become an aid to both partners, even in the most ordinary conversations. It states where each person stands and lets the partner in on interior thoughts and feelings. It defines what exists, in the opinion of the speaker. It makes no attempt to ascribe blame. Control Talk, on the other hand, covertly brings into the discussion other actions and motivations, often blurring the issue at hand. Seldom does a person like to feel manipulated or controlled—and especially not by someone in an intimate relationship. Choosing to let the partner know what we are thinking or feeling pays astonishing dividends in our investment of relationship-building. It is light years away from lecturing, nagging, and blaming.

DAILY COUPLE TALK:
(EACH PERSON ANSWERS)
How can we make better use of Straight Talk?

COMMUNICATION

Happiness is often a by-product of an activity or experience that engages our hearts and minds (and sometimes our bodies). It is more than pleasure, for it involves moving us toward some goal that we value.

The outcome of happiness, according to Happiness Expert Sonja Lyubomirsky, is that we become "healthier, more creative, and have better relationships." She also states that happiness is partly "genetic" and partly determined by "life circumstances." The rest, she says, lies within your control because it is made up of "attitude and how you think and behave."

Regarding relationship-building, that statement of what makes happiness is good news. If our attitudes are hopeful about the value of a growing "us," and if our words and actions are lovingly consistent with that hopeful goal, success is within our reach. Everyone wins.

DAILY COUPLE TALK:
(EACH PERSON ANSWERS)
What are three things I feel happy about? How do these things relate to a goal that I find meaningful?

COMMUNICATION
PART 1

In Dr. Gary Chapman's famous book called The Five Love Languages, the number one language discussed is called Words of Affirmation. Perhaps Dr. Chapman chose to begin here because affirming words are so helpful in counteracting the stresses of the day and in building self-confidence. They can even affect the climate of our social environment.

There were six of us (two parents, three teen-age daughters, and Bobbye's mother) heading by car to California on a hot July day. Less than 250 miles from home the car's air conditioner went out. This led to delays, sweat, and frustration. By the next morning, it also led to a car of cranky people.

Bobbye suggested that they play a "game" as they drove, each one in sequence telling other family members something he/she liked about them. They would take turns and Britton could be the first recipient. After some initial reluctance, they completed the first round and the compliments got longer. Then there were statements like "I didn't know you thought THAT!" Then there were tears and hugs and an enthusiastic request to play again.

Bobbye learned two important lessons. One was that although this was a family that loved each other, it hadn't taken the time to do the essential task of sharing appreciation for each other. The second thing she learned was that the climate in the car changed from complaints and accusations to a spirit of cooperation and courtesy. And it changed fast.

DAILY COUPLE TALK:
(EACH PARTNER RESPONDS)
Tell your partner three things you appreciate about them.

COMMUNICATION
PART 2

Somewhere around each grandchild's 12ᵗʰ birthday, Britton and Bobbye take him/her on a trip with the two of them. At South Padre Island one summer Britton made a speech at a church and told the anecdote on the preceding page.

When they got in the car after the speech, grandson Christopher said, "Let's play that game." "What game?" Bobbye and Britton asked. "The one where you tell me what you like about me," he said.

Covering the surprise that he had even been listening, we agreed to "play that game." Christopher wanted to be the first to hear compliments, so we told him the things we appreciated about him. When it was his turn to compliment, he said, "I like you all because—because you are active." That was it.

Here was a third-generation response to hearing about the value of words of affirmation. Christopher was intrigued enough to initiate the "game" with his grandparents, not knowing at that time that this particular Love Language has the power to warm our hearts and affect our attitudes.

DAILY COUPLE TALK:
(EACH PERSON RESPONDS)
If you were to tell a friend about your partner, what two positive things would you say? Tell them to your partner.

COMMUNICATION

If we stand back to back with our partner and describe to each other what we see ahead of us, it may be interesting but it will not be the same. He sees a wall with four framed diplomas and a table with a computer. She sees a door opening into a further room where there is a washing machine and shelves. Both then make interpretations of what each sees, the visible data from which each one forms conclusions. The only way to understand what the partner sees is to turn the head and look over his/her shoulder. Now both of you have seen two different scenes, with two different sets of data and two different sets of conclusions.

In a discussion with your partner over some disputed subject, this process is called "empathy," symbolically looking over the partner's shoulder at what he/she "sees," letting words describe the point of view as it is perceived, including the conclusions about the visible data. We do not change our point of view—we are certain that we have "seen" it clearly—but we begin to have a greater understanding that there is room in a growing relationship for more than one point of view.

Keeping in the forefront of our awareness this one idea of "empathy" not only gives us a different perspective on arguments but frees us up from the determination to be right.

DAILY COUPLE TALK:
(EACH PERSON RESPONDS)
What is a troublesome difference between you that you are willing to talk about? Get in touch with the details of what you "see" and the conclusions you have drawn from those details. Tell your partner. Discuss the different views.

COMMUNICATION

All of us come to adulthood with a style of talking firmed into habit. We seldom analyze the effect of our style; it is simply the way we talk. Some people grew up in homes where sarcasm and lecturing were everyday staples. Some people grew up with little conversation and long periods of silence. Some people were expected to have dinner every night as a family, without cell phones and with something specific to say about their day. The homes we grew up in helped shape our styles of talking and will continue to if we never think about them or the role they play in our lives.

Entering an intimate relationship calls for an examination of talking styles. Intimidation and witty put-downs may have worked as a teen-ager, but they do not help build adult relationships, especially if the partner has (and likes) a different style. Moody silences do little to bring closeness. Avoiding difficult issues may SEEM to prevent arguments and thus keep harmony, but soon the relationship's rooms are so cluttered with "things we cannot talk about" that there is little freedom of movement for fun and romance.

DAILY COUPLE TALK:
(EACH PARTNER PARTICIPATES)
Think about the ways people talked in your family of origin. Do you need to improve on any of these styles that you sometimes imitate? Are there some styles of talking that now seem more productive to you? Discuss this with your partner.

COMMUNICATION

Bobbye saw a tee-shirt today that said, "I need Vitamin Sea." She responded to it enthusiastically because time on a beach is a great motivator for her sense of well-being.

Some days all of us need special motivation just to get out of bed, go to work, get exercise, pay our bills, or give to a worthy cause. So here is some motivation for building a long-term relationship with a loved person (besides the joy of closeness or the exhilaration of innovative sex).

In the July 13, 2016, issue of Time magazine an interesting article called "How To Stay Married" discusses some practical motivations. Simply put, the article quotes several studies on marriage that show married people have more money, have better health and better sex, and have children who do the same when they grow up (avoiding on the whole poverty, addictions, mental illness, dropping out of school, and getting divorced). The article by no means suggests that the marriage relationship is not difficult, but it does show that society is better off when a couple is motivated to have many conversations about maintaining a satisfying experience together.

DAILY COUPLE TALK:
(EACH PERSON ANSWERS)
If you were choosing today from a "marital buffet of satisfaction," what items would end up on your plate?

COMMUNICATION

Several years ago, Britton and Bobbye were some of the Family Wellness speakers at a university in Taiwan, during its 50-year anniversary celebrations. They spoke to many classes, often lecturing on the value of listening as an important part of communication. At the end of the one-month lecture series, the secretary of the department gave them a laminated poster of the Mandarin word for listen, "ting."

Mandarin is an ancient Chinese language which in its written form is full of characters made from former picture-writing. "Ting" embodies an ear, an eye, and a heart. It implies that all three need to be engaged when we really listen to others. Britton and Bobbye were both struck by the complexity of "ting."

Listening with our eyes implies looking at the speaker, always a help toward understanding but not always used in these days of multi-tasking. Looking at the speaker gives us the added non-verbal messages that go with facial expressions and postures. An accompanying wink, for example, goes a long way in helping us determine the spirit in which something is said. Listening with our ears adds the interpretive tones of irony, frustration, or humor. Listening with our hearts suggests that speakers sometimes have thrilling emotional meanings easily understood by loving recipients.

DAILY COUPLE TALK:
(EACH PERSON ANSWERS)
How can we improve our listening skills?

COMMUNICATION

In the marriage relationship, we unveil our hearts with words to each other, just as we unveil our bodies. This unveiling allows our partners to see us as we really are, physically and emotionally. It is in some ways a terrifying prospect, but it is the only way to achieve the fullness of the marriage experience—to be both known and loved. This knowledge is what every adult human heart needs for wholeness, but one special place to find it is in the intimacy and honesty of the marriage relationship.

Using words along the way to affirm and reveal makes our journey together more comfortable and secure. It also allows us as a couple to measure our accomplishments and to set goals to accomplish even more. It can also help to heal old wounds and to feel the psychological approval some persons did not get from their families of origin, what some professionals call "a blessing." Some people even assert that persons feel closest to those with whom they practice self-disclosure.

Words are both guides and revelations and some of the ones which matter the most are from the heart.

DAILY COUPLE TALK:
(EACH PERSON PARTICIPATES)

I love it when you _____.

I feel appreciated when you _____.

I don't want us to _____.

COMMUNICATION

At a recent marriage conference Bobbye and Britton met a couple who did not take advantage of the hotel's free, bountiful breakfast. They ASSUMED it was merely a continental breakfast and chose to have coffee in their room with snacks that they brought from home. When they learned of the made-to-order omelets, counters of fruit, shelves of pastries, and chafing dishes of eggs, bacon, hash browned potatoes, sausage, and beans, they immediately came to breakfast. But it was unfortunately the last day of the conference.

Many couples assume their relationship is as good as it's going to be. Others assume that adding anything to their good relationship is unnecessary and maybe even counterproductive. One couple even used the common adage, "If it isn't broken, don't fix it."

But like the couple who missed out on sumptuous breakfast choices, they might be missing chances to add new skills and new information about each other that could lead to more closeness and excitement.

DAILY COUPLE TALK:
(EACH PERSON ANSWERS)
Celebrate your relationship, wherever it is currently. State the things that make you happy about it. What is one thing that each of you could do to make it better?

COMMUNICATION

The fast-track to deepening couple growth is by means of communication. Couples who come to value their skills in speaking and listening to each other are also the same couples who feel new affection and awareness of each other in a variety of ways. Here are two suggestions of communication skills for those who want to hurry the process of a growing "us."

1. <u>Be responsive</u>. Dr. John Gottman, professor at the University of Washington, calls this action "turning- toward." When the partner shares something about his/her day or his/her ideas, show that you have heard not only the words but the emotion and interest behind them. Doing so begins to build trust and assurance in each person that the partner will be "there."

2. <u>Have at least a 15-minute conversation with each other every day.</u> Recommended by counselors, sex therapists, and relationship coaches, this one habit keeps a couple current, does wonders to bring about closeness and reduce friction, and often leads to increased sexual intimacy.

DAILY COUPLE TALK:
(EACH PARTNER ANSWERS)
What three words would you use today
to describe your relationship?

COMMUNICATION

It is often said that we cannot NOT communicate. A slammed door, a big smile, a deep sigh—all are saying something, and sometimes it is something important. But we cannot be sure just what the exact message is and are forced to make our own interpretations and assumptions.

One early morning as Bobbye got out of her car in her school's parking lot, she saw her principal standing by his car with an angry scowl on his face. It was the day of Bobbye's annual review of her performance as a teacher, so she mentally said good-bye to a merit raise, assuming that the scowl meant that she had done something wrong. What she did not know was that the principal's young daughter was kneeling on the ground on the other side of their car, rummaging in her backpack and reporting that some necessary homework had been left behind at their house. The scowl had nothing to do with Bobbye.

This episode illustrates the need to suspend judgment in assumptions. The scowl was a kind of communication but additional information was needed.

DAILY COUPLE TALK:
(EACH PERSON RESPONDS)
Design a non-verbal signal that says to your partner,
"I love you and I am thinking of you at this moment."
Talk about how you might use this agreed-upon signal.

COMMUNICATION

All relationships with a strong "me" and a strong "you" will have disagreements. Most couples will also have times where one has hurt the other by thoughtless, harsh, or hasty words or actions.

Renowned worldwide for his research into improving couple relationships, Dr. John Gottman invented what he calls the 5:1 Ratio. This means that for every negative or hurtful word spoken to the partner, there must be five positive words spoken just to keep the relationship stable and on an even keel. It is interesting research and often borrowed by counselors and teachers. It demonstrates clearly both the power of damaging words in a relationship and a path to overcoming their effects.

When negative words have been spoken and the partner has reacted with signs of emotional distress, it may be familiar but it is counterproductive to say something like, "get over it" or "I was only kidding." Gottman's 5:1 Ratio offers a sensible way to deal with painful episodes and still stay close as a couple.

DAILY COUPLE TALK:
(EACH PARTNER ANSWERS)
What do you think about the 5:1 Ratio?
Is there a recent time when the two of you
could have used it? Explain.

COMMUNICATION

Intrigued by a suggestion in one of Dr. John Van Epp's lectures, Bobbye and Britton started leaving Post-it notes in surprising places for each other. The notes they chose to use were bits and pieces of familiar songs they knew. Britton got a note in his underwear drawer saying, "I have got a crush, my sweetie, on you." Bobbye found a note attached to her bedside lamp that said, "You light up my life." The notes have unexpectedly appeared in the pages of a current book, in a suitcase being unpacked in a hotel room, on a toothbrush, and in gardening gloves.

Post-it notes can be whimsical, sexy, or inspirational. Their purpose is simply to let the partner know we are thinking of him/her and to do so in a novel way. It also brings a smile to the one who finds the surprise communication. It brightens up the day and reminds each partner that there is more to life than work and worry.

DAILY COUPLE TALK:
(EACH PERSON PARTICIPATES)
Think right now of two "messages" you could give your partner that express your feelings when you are in a romantic mood. Tell one of the "messages" at this time. Save one of the "messages" to leave in a surprise place.

COMMUNICATION

The packaging of most products from the grocery store contains a list of the nutrition you will be getting: protein, sugars, fats, fiber.

The nutritional health of a couple can also be labeled and measured when each person begins to get the things that each one needs. Carefully examine the following items for what they contribute.

1. Intentionality (choosing to be proactive in growing a happy marriage)

2. Communication (talking and listening to each other for better understanding)

3. Conflict management (finding a successful way to deal with disagreements)

4. Humor (using laughter and play to relieve stress and have fun together)

5. Respect (Honoring our differences)

6. Intimacy (expressing our love in many ways)

DAILY COUPLE TALK:
(EACH PARTNER RESPONDS)
Choose two items which in your opinion give the relationship the most nutritional health. Communicate your reasons to your partner.

COMMUNICATION

Every couple has an "us," a relationship. Some are stronger and more satisfying than others, but every couple has one. Furthermore, other people notice the quality of the relationship. Like relationships, some city streets have cracks, pot holes, and uneven old repairs.

City budgets are usually stretched to meet the demands of street repairs. Often, city officials turn to coal-tar pavement sealants because those are cheap and easiest to acquire. That those sealants also may be toxic and harmful to the environment must be overlooked in the interest of budgets.

The cheapest and most common method of dealing with relationship repair is either to ignore the problem altogether or to attempt to "fix it" with occasional gifts or trips. Direct communication about the troubling issue (old or new) seems at first to be too "costly," especially if it has not been our habit, rather like turning to the familiar coal-tar sealants in order to get street repairs done quickly and with a minimum of cost. For the long term, however, the use of a frank, fair, and respectful dialogue starts the process of relationship repair that brings the most benefits. Like city streets, relationships with neglected potholes eventually affect other drivers.

DAILY COUPLE TALK:
(EACH PARTNER ANSWERS)
Choose some issue that needs talking about by the two of you. Focus only on THAT issue, exchange information, and listen to each other's point of view.
Set an appointment to revisit the subject as you move toward a better understanding.

COMMUNICATION

Many city streets have potholes, cracks, and rough evidence of old repairs. So do many relationships. The couple is the major entity in any family, and keeping its relationship street running smoothly and in good repair is essential.

One way to mend minor relationship potholes (and begin to repair major ones) is to acknowledge them. Ignoring issues in streets and relationships not only eventually gets to be costlier and affects others.

A second way to mend minor relationship potholes is to focus on only one pothole at a time, which makes it easier to stay on task. Speak to each other with "I" messages and no blaming. Listen to each other attentively, giving summaries of what you are hearing. You are at this point aiming at understanding, not agreement.

Finally plan together how this pothole might be resolved. All ideas are welcome. Choose an idea that BOTH think has a chance to work, or take parts of several ideas. Many marriage-builders also suggest setting a time to review the agreed-upon solution in order to see if both of you are still satisfied. Make any needed changes at this time.

DAILY COUPLE TALK:
(EACH PARTNER RESPONDS)
Name one minor relational "pothole" you would like to repair. Set a time to talk about it. Remember that building an "us" is just as important as repairing the "pothole." Be fair.

COMMUNICATION

None of us would go into a department store and expect a clerk to "just know" what we want. It is unreasonable and unrealistic. But it often happens with our partners.

Once after teaching school all day Bobbye came home from the grocery store with the car's trunk loaded. The noisy garage door opener gave the signal that she was home. Britton was already there, watching the news on television in the living room. Bobbye carried in one heavy sack and no expected help arrived from Britton. She rattled the sack and slammed a few doors as a "hint." Before she got MORE indignant, Bobbye went to the edge of the living room and said," I need some help with the groceries." Britton left the TV and carried the rest of the sacks. He had not heard the garage door and did not know she was home. The "hints" had been wasted.

Saying what we need does not guarantee the action we want. But that action can never happen if the partner does not "just know." Saying what we need gives us a better chance of getting it.

DAILY COUPLE TALK:
(EACH PERSON PARTICIPATES)
On a scale of 1 to 10 (with 10 being highest) how do you measure your current communication method of saying what you need? Explain.

COMMUNICATION

Several years ago, Bobbye and Britton worked for a month in an international church in Madrid, Spain, teaching marriage education. There they encountered many couples who had come from other countries to work or study in Madrid. Some of these couples had fallen in love, married, and started to raise a family while struggling with the issue of daily conversation. Theirs was a unique issue of speaking together in a language that was not their birth language or as they frequently expressed it, "the language of the heart." Learning to relate to each other as a couple while integrating traditions, food, music, religion, and of course language was an exciting but frustrating experience.

Although not as dramatic as these couple's experiences, we all must negotiate the minefields of having different backgrounds, different educations, and different experiences in growing up. Some even have the differences of other marriages prior to this one. Putting it all together into a new "us" can be a formidable experience, since sometimes you are in the midst of a situation before you realize it is a "situation." Holding frequent honest conversations about where you are and what you want is one way to smooth out the differences between you and establish boundaries that help define the couple you want to be.

DAILY COUPLE TALK:
(EACH PARTNER PARTICIPATES)
Devise a statement of two things you value as a couple and one function you want to achieve as a couple.

COMMUNICATION

The discouraging news today regarding marriage in the U.S. is that almost half of all couples will divorce or legally separate. More than half of second marriages do not last (some statistics show figures as high as 60%). Couples who have formerly co-habited have even more depressing results.

The encouraging news supported by the latest research and enthusiastically quoted by marriage educators is that 80% of all couples who DO something to improve their relationship report that they are happier than before and have fewer arid and stressful times. They begin to feel once again the joy of being together, joy that they believed had gone.

The improving actions may be as big as going on a marriage retreat or as tiny as fulfilling a cooperative request such as putting the cap back on the toothpaste after using it. Gaining and maintaining trust is one goal you are striving for, as is building and re-building the relationship toward mutual fulfillment. Relationships are dynamic not static, and every bit of progress deserves celebration.

DAILY COUPLE TALK:
(EACH PARTNER RESPONDS)
Describe your relationship today in terms of a weather report. What is one thing that you can celebrate, no matter what the weather?

COMMUNICATION

Shakespeare said, "To err is human, to forgive divine." He must have known how easy it is for couples to say and do the very things that hurt each other the most. Since couples know each other well, they know where the weak and vulnerable spots are and how to exploit them. Add the deliberate insults to the inadvertent mistakes, and it's quite a formidable list to overcome. In fact, many couples sink under the weight of intended and unintended pain.

Forgiveness releases couples from the hold this list has on them. Keeping score and nursing grudges sounds on the surface to be practical, even efficient. We may tell ourselves, "I will keep track of this insult so that I can pay it back with interest; THEN he/she will not dare to say or do it again."

One problem with scorekeeping and grudges is that they can take over. One partner is unable to notice the other partner's 5:1 Ratio efforts, should they be offered. Apologies become hypocritical. There is no awareness of one's own need to practice loving behaviors with those we love.

Forgiveness takes courage and willingness. It takes saying "I forgive you" to the partner and repeating those same words to ourselves until we can see once again through the lenses of love.

DAILY COUPLE TALK:
(EACH PARTNER RESPONDS)
What words about forgiveness and acceptance need to be said today to each other?

COMMUNICATION

Friedrich Nietzsche once said, "When marrying, ask yourself this question: Do you believe that you will be able to converse well with this person into your old age? Everything else is transitory." Whether you agree with Nietzsche's bold assertion, he is right about the importance of couple talk.

Spending time in conversation is an absolute MUST for any healthy marriage. It affirms the "us"; it gives information for the Love Map (what Dr. John Gottman has named the data we know about our partner). It is good for relaxation and mental health. It is what Bea and Jim Strickland (Marriage Enrichment friends from California) call "the pathway to relationship."

Quoting a book called <u>Conversationally Speaking</u> by Alan Garner, the Stricklands recommend using "open-ended questions" to keep dialogue going. "Open-ended questions" promote answers of more than a word or two. They ask for explanations and elaboration. There is a difference between asking "What was your first car like?" and "What brand was your first car?" "Open-ended questions" typically begin with "How?" or "In what way?"

For some couples conversation has slowly begun to disappear under the relentless pressure of a hectic lifestyle or a full TV schedule. "Open-ended questions" can bring back the easy give and take that once led to satisfying dialogues.

DAILY COUPLE TALK:
(CHOOSE ONE OF THE FOLLOWING AND BOTH ANSWER)
How would you describe the perfect age for a person to be? OR What was the best surprise you've ever received?

CREATING A CLIMATE FOR INTIMACY

"Sex is about the

quality of your entire love life,

not just the alignment

of your bodies."

KEVIN LEMAN

CREATING A CLIMATE FOR INTIMACY

Different cultures define marriage differently. Traditions, expectations, customs, goals, language—all may lead to differing expressions of the marriage covenant. One thing crosses all cultural boundaries. That is the physical and emotional need for closeness and connection with one special person.

When we come together in the rites and ceremonies of marriage, we come with this need. Even if the marriage was arranged or forced, even if we had little understanding of or interest in what would be required of us over time, this need was present in our hearts. When couples have lived together for many years through both distress and enjoyment, they still have this need.

Love songs, fairy tales, and Disney movies give one kind of presentation of this need. An elderly couple walking through a mall holding hands gives another kind of testimony of the same need. Getting and maintaining the intimacy our psyches long for is a shared goal. Marriage is simply the best place in the world to achieve it.

DAILY COUPLE TALK:
(EACH PARTNER RESPONDS)
When are we at our best as a couple?
Explain.

CREATING A CLIMATE FOR INTIMACY

One of the joys of modern living is that we can change the climate of temperature and humidity within our homes, businesses, and public buildings. In the summer, we can cool buildings; in the winter we can make them warm and comfortable.

Couples can also change the climate of their intimacy relationship, as long as both want to. They need to talk together about the desired temperature and decide what would be pleasing to each one. Couple dialogue is the place to start, defining what kind of intimacy climate would feel pleasurable and safe. Next, they should proceed on the level of the one who wants change least. Add playfulness, lots more talking, loving behaviors, and relaxed expectations. Give it time.

There is no such thing as instant intimacy, just as the temperature in our home does not immediately jump from 48 to 72 degrees. But it is a goal worth working toward and an achievement noticeable to family, friends, and even to work colleagues. An intimate, close relationship is heart-warming, unpredictable, and absolutely worth working for.

DAILY COUPLE TALK:
(EACH PARTNER ANSWERS)
What is a term of endearment
you have enjoyed from your partner?
Why?

CREATING A CLIMATE FOR INTIMACY

Attitude affects our perception of the quality of our lives. It cannot control what happens to us, but it can order and arrange how we personally handle what happens.

No one accuses a baseball team manager of having an overly optimistic attitude or being lucky just because he hopes to win a game by putting his batters in the order that he thinks gives the team the best chance for scoring runs and winning the game. Yet couples often get a cynical response from others when they express a hopefulness about getting more out of their marriage.

If couples mutually want more intimacy—more sex, more sharing, more loving behaviors, more expressive affection--a hopeful attitude helps them be more aware of the actions and choices that can bring this about. Luck in life may be a factor in our happiness but so is attitude. Motivational speaker Zig Ziglar might just be right when he said, "If you aim at nothing, you'll hit it every time."

DAILY COUPLE TALK:
(EACH PARTNER RESPONDS)
Perhaps this is a good day to set some couple intimacy goals. What do you want (or want more of) regarding intimacy? What could you personally do to help achieve this? What could your partner do?

CREATING A CLIMATE
FOR INTIMACY

Think of your relationship not as a thermometer but as a thermostat. The thermometer merely records the temperature. The thermostat controls it. How close you get (and stay) to each other lies largely within your control.

Many therapists say things like, "Sex begins in the kitchen." By this they mean that sexual awareness can happen anywhere, and that caring behaviors need to go on all day and in every room. A jointly unloaded dishwasher just might be a turn-on to someone used to working alone on kitchen tasks. A cool drink of water delivered unasked to one partner mowing the lawn on a summer's afternoon might produce unexpected feelings of desire.

Bobbye and Britton's new granddaughter-in-law Grace put it this way. "Don't be so worried about getting. Think more about giving." Grace is a new bride, and she was responding to a question of what advice she would give to a friend who is getting married. But the idea is true for a relationship of any length. When couples are alert to the ways they can share in each other's lives, AND when they consistently take the time to warm the other person with help and unexpected assistance, the result is often a change in the thermostat of intimacy.

DAILY COUPLE TALK:
(EACH PERSON PARTICIPATES)
When is a time your partner helped you with something
that made a big difference to you? Describe.

CREATING A CLIMATE
FOR INTIMACY

Babies come into the world with a need for intimacy. They need to be cuddled, held, stroked, talked to, rocked, and given skin-on-skin time with someone. Because this is true, hospitals arrange for volunteers to come into their nurseries just to hold and cuddle new-born babies whose parents are not available. Babies' brains cannot begin to develop properly otherwise.

Adults, too, have intimacy needs, and this is true whether or not sexual intercourse is a possibility. Snuggles and cuddles, pats and soft kisses, strokes and hugs—these are some of the ways our bodies let us know we are welcome in the world and secure. Widows and widowers in assisted living facilities often struggle with the fact that there is no longer someone to touch and be touched by.

Marriage is one of the best places to have these intimacy needs met. Too many married adults let time go by without savoring the benefits of intimate touch.

DAILY COUPLE TALK:
(EACH PARTNER PARTICIPATES)
Describe a nourishing touch that you receive from your partner that you especially enjoy.

CREATING A CLIMATE FOR INTIMACY

Family Wellness gurus, Joe and Michelle Hernandez, remind us that from "we" to "wow!" is a short distance. That means that when we feel really close to our partners, when our "us" is strong, we are then creating a climate in which affectionate expressions happen more often and are more enjoyable to both partners.

The skills needed in creating a climate for intimacy are some of the same skills needed for an athletic team to succeed in sports:

1. The team will have rules, called "values in action" by Michelle Hernandez. Those rules will help to keep the couple team on track to accomplish what they want most—showing the very best individual efforts toward playing as a team, supporting each other off and on the "playing field."

2. Practice. Practice good communication skills. Practice loving behaviors. Practice forgiveness and encouragement. Practice the plays and strategies that can lead you toward a WIN/WIN/WIN. Practice being a strong and responsible "me." Practice loving a strong and responsible "you." Practice moving the "we" to "wow!" as often as possible.

DAILY COUPLE TALK:
(EACH PERSON ANSWERS)
What are some "values in action"
that can help our couple team?

CREATING A CLIMATE FOR INTIMACY

Intimacy is one prime, proud specimen of what humans can achieve together. It often comes after decades of living together through storm and shadow. It sometimes peeks out of a shared tragedy or adventure. It can arrive during a joint project or a team effort when partners are striving to reach a desired goal. It is not bound by age, race, monetary status, or education. Everyone can have it who is willing to risk loving another person and revealing to that person how we want to be loved. Light as feathers and warm as a summer day, intimacy moves the heart to want what is best for ourselves and for those we love.

Intimacy means different things to different people, and it is crucial to understand each other's definitions. To some it just means a special touch. To some it is a vulnerability that leaves us exposed. To some it means closeness and cuddling with a childlike trust. To some it is only activity that leads to orgasm. Recently at a marriage workshop Bobbye saw a sign announcing the subject to be presented, "Into-me-u-see."

Whatever intimacy means to you, this is a subject where both partners profit from being honest with each other. Only in this way can you deal with skills that are mutually wanted and mutually satisfying.

DAILY COUPLE TALK:
(EACH PARTNER RESPONDS)
If you were describing your current intimacy experience in terms of seasons, which would you pick?
Winter, spring, summer, autumn? Why?

CREATING A CLIMATE
FOR INTIMACY

All of us struggle with external and internal issues through-out every day. Those struggles affect most facets of our lives, even the facets we value most. Job issues, migraine head-aches, business decisions, allergies, depression, family crises of various kinds—all take a toll on our health and sense of well-being.

One wonder of intimacy in a growing relationship with some-one we love is that there is a deep consciousness that there is someone on our side, someone consistently in our corner.

Recently Bobbye read about a French frigate that had been re-stored and put on display at a museum in Austin, Texas, for the public to see. Shipwrecked in 1686, the frigate still bore witness to a way of life more than 300 years old, when the French ex-plorer La Salle had been on board. That restoration, however, is no more exciting that the rejuvenation of a long-term relation-ship that one or both partners had assumed was "shipwrecked."

When both partners begin to see in each other glimpses of the possible revival of old sparks and old romantic interests, they also begin to feel the comfort of having a partner in the true sense of the word. When both begin to use skills and tools to reach out to each other, the restoration of intimacy begins to be visible to others. The stresses and issues may still be there, but so is a new strength.

DAILY COUPLE TALK:
(EACH PERSON PARTICIPATES)
Name and describe one of your biggest struggles—
internal or external. How can you draw closer to each
other, in spite of that struggle?

CREATING A CLIMATE
FOR INTIMACY

Considered scandalous in her day, the Wife of Bath in Geoffrey Chaucer's <u>Canterbury Tales</u> was really a modern woman. She knew what she wanted: to FEEL loved and respected. She would settle for nothing else, marrying four times on her quest for a man who could meet her standards.

The Wife of Bath even tells a tale to the other pilgrims which illustrates her point. In her story a knight is being punished for mistreating a woman, but his sentence will be reduced if in one year he can find out what a woman wants most. When he finally learns (and shows that he has learned) the correct answer, he not only goes free but meets the beautiful love of his life.

The Wife of Bath's tale is from the 12th century but modern research gives us supporting data about her ideas. Studies by Dr. Nicholas Long, Pediatrics professor at the University of Arkansas for Medical Sciences, show that children grow up to deal more successfully with life when they have a mother who feels loved and nourished and in turn loves and nourishes her children. Significantly less instances of smoking, alcohol abuse, drug use, and suicide attempts as adults prove that these children profit from the mother's feelings. Loving, respectful behavior from both partners apparently casts a long shadow.

DAILY COUPLE TALK:
(EACH PARTNER PARTICIPATES)
What is something your partner does that makes you feel loved? What is something your partner does that makes you feel respected?

CREATING A CLIMATE FOR INTIMACY

Warmth, welcome, and a wonderful shimmer of passion—that is many couples' ideal of something to come home to, something to counteract the dreariness of job/commuting/the daily grind.

Dreams are important, but so is a steady hand on the steering wheel of the everyday. Marriage is where Romance and Reality can meet and have a picnic. Romance can bring the rose-colored glasses. Reality can bring a strong light to see exactly where you are. Romance sings about what "can be." Reality sings harmony about what "Is." Both are important and in the folds of the warm blanket of intimacy often lies the motivation for keeping the relationship going.

All of this is to say that in a climate of intimacy there is room for playfulness AND serious examination of facts. There is time for jokes AND plans for the future. A couple can pay bills AND dance together in the kitchen. The jobs and obligations of life get done, but the sheer beauty of a close couple connection is never lost in efficiently performing those duties.

DAILY COUPLE TALK:
(BOTH PARTNERS ANSWER)
Describe a romantic moment the two of you have shared. What made it memorable?

CREATING A CLIMATE FOR INTIMACY

Here are Seven Deadly Sins against creating and maintaining a climate for intimacy.

1. Never acknowledge disagreements or arguments. Doing so only upsets couple cooperation.

2. Avoid time together, except for TV watching or dinners with friends or relatives.

3. Whine, nag, and criticize daily.

4. Keep track of every slight or misdemeanor. This lets the partner know you are always watching for a mistake.

5. Never give the partner compliments or encouragement. This will only make him/her conceited.

6. Don't practice good hygiene, regular showers, or brushing teeth. Smell-sensitive people need to get over it.

7. Refuse to get into a conversation about your relationship. Your partner knows enough about you already.

The Seven Deadly Sins are only a partial exaggeration. This tongue-in-cheek list may make you smile, but it also shows why some relationships never make it to their first anniversary, much less to the level of intimacy.

DAILY COUPLE TALK:
(EACH PARTNER ANSWERS)
Which two of the Seven Deadly Sins would you most want to avoid? Why?

CREATING A CLIMATE
FOR INTIMACY

Intimacy is like a little silk ribbon gently binding a couple to-gether. The more they acknowledge that ribbon, the lighter their moods and attitudes as they go about their daily tasks in the world.

The ribbon does not inhibit performing those tasks nor does it prevent their frustration with daily difficulties and stresses. But buoyed up by an intimate relationship with a loved one, the frustrations seem more manageable. It's a reinterpreta-tion of the old adage about a good couple relationship: "It doubles the joy and halves the pain."

The couple has the same freedom as before, the same care-ful spacing of privacy and togetherness. The pressure of the silk ribbon is slight, and more than balanced by a heart full of gratitude for the joys of intimacy.

DAILY COUPLE TALK:
(EACH PARTNER ANSWERS)
What is something you are grateful for in your daily life that has recently happened? What is something you are grateful for that your partner has recently done?

CREATING A CLIMATE FOR INTIMACY

For a long time, Britton's understanding of the word intimacy was limited due to his upbringing. His was a wonderful family in many ways, but it was not a hugging family nor did anyone ever tell others "I love you." As a result when he met Bobbye, he had an uphill climb to be expressive with words. Britton was even talking about marriage before Bobbye reminded him that he had never told her he loved her.

In Britton's family of origin no one raised questions about feelings. His love language was (and is) acts of service, and his ideas of showing intimacy was kissing, hugging, and all things physical. Bobbye wanted (and still wants) to hear words of endearment and to discuss their feelings for each other. Recently she told him, "Bring me words!"

One of the great joys of their Marriage Enrichment training was to better learn to express feelings for each other, and that includes cards, flowers, Post-it notes, and sometimes poems. Both can now enjoy conversations about intimacy and the desire to be close. One beauty of a long marriage relationship is that each partner can learn through the years how to best express love and build a climate for intimacy that both enjoy.

DAILY COUPLE TALK:
(EACH PERSON SHARES)
Share with your partner how your upbringing has contributed to your ideas about intimacy. Share what you can do to create a climate of comfortable intimacy.

CREATING A CLIMATE FOR INTIMACY

Intervention is the term for outside involvement in a couple's issues when they are unable to cope. It describes counseling, Child Protective Services, law enforcement, or other social agencies who must step in to preserve safety and order. Intervention is like the ambulance supplying aid when the car has gone into a ravine at a dangerous curve in the road.

Prevention is the term describing education and enrichment for couples who are satisfied with their relationship but believe there are things both to do and to avoid that will help them achieve even more satisfaction. Prevention is the highway warning sign before the dangerous curve in the road.

Enrichment and education is what this book is providing. It assumes that interested couples know that much of their couple happiness lies within their own control. If greater intimacy is mutually desired, the motivation to achieve it is inherent in that desire and sends the interested parties seeking information that will be helpful. Try out various recommendations that make sense to you both. Do the Couple Talk exercises and listen to each other. Avoid the words and actions that do not lead to closeness and intimacy.

DAILY COUPLE TALK:
(EACH PARTNER PARTICIPATES)
If you were taking a course called Intimacy 101, what would you want to learn?

CREATING A CLIMATE FOR INTIMACY

Many couples count their steps every day and invest daily in brain-boosting supplements or vitamins, believing that attention to exercise and diet will make a difference in long-term health. Yet some of those same couples apparently consider relationship to be largely a matter of chance. They appear to believe that loving, trusting, close relationships either happen or they don't. Perhaps they have not heard that any couple can create a climate in which a long-term healthy intimacy is likely to flourish, as long as they both want it and are willing to make it a priority.

Begin by recognizing the intimacy you already have. Discuss it together, stating candidly the things you enjoy, and mutually reaffirm your desire to do the things that could make your times of intimacy grow even more enjoyable. Become partners in sharing feelings, revealing personal experiences, and making "I" statements. Listen to each other, occasionally repeating back what you hear so that your partner knows you heard and so that you can get clarification. Give priority to these times of intimate sharing of affection and conversation by scheduling time together as you would other important events.

Just as we work toward better health through diet and exercise, we can work together toward the maintenance of long-term intimacy, and it is just as important. Healthy hearts are achieved in a variety of ways.

DAILY COUPLE TALK:
(EACH ONE ANSWERS)
What are two things that could increase enjoyment of your already pleasurable times of intimacy? What is one thing you personally are willing to do to increase enjoyment?

CREATING A CLIMATE FOR INTIMACY

Playfulness and laughter bring needed refreshment to days of responsible and often tedious activity. In play with our partner we can be spontaneous, silly, and even surprising. Sharing playfulness can create a private world of intimacy. Playing together gives a strong sense of a shared life.

Playfulness and laughter reduce chronic pressure and stress. They allow us to be flexible and "in the moment." They let us relax. As we see our happy, laughing partner, we are suddenly more aware of his/her good qualities, traits that were part of the reason we wanted to marry that person in the first place. Playfulness and laughter increase our understanding of each other and of our need to really matter to one special person in this world.

Intimacy is made of many tiny, colorful strands, rather like a beautiful tapestry. Playfulness and laughter nurture the joy and satisfaction in our relationship, making our "us" laugh too. They also allow us to affirm each other at the heart's deepest level.

DAILY COUPLE TALK:
(EACH PARTNER SHARES)
When was a particular time that the two of you played together and it brought a sense of satisfaction? How can you get more playtime into your schedule?

CREATING A CLIMATE FOR INTIMACY

In an episode of TV's "Madame Secretary," Dr. McCord spoke at his father's funeral. He told the mourners that what his father hated most was a wedding. All that money spent for something that may not last, the father had explained. Why not wait ten years and have a celebration when you see what's working?

That father had a point. The great thing about true intimacy is that it takes a few decades for two lovers to hit their stride. The honeymoon is wonderful, but a "newly-wed" feeling can come again after many years together. Knowledgeable about each other's bodies and generous with praise and understanding, a couple can be overwhelmed by passion and joy, caught up in the wonder of two hearts celebrating a loving and growing relationship.

Intimacy is not all about romance, moonlight, and a beautiful princess in a white dress. Intimacy is also discovered by those who have spent years together and whisper in the dark, "I still do."

DAILY COUPLE TALK:
(EACH PARTNER PARTICIPATES)
Describe your wedding to each other, remembering especially how you felt as the ceremony was proceeding. Remember your wedding night and how you felt.

CREATING A CLIMATE FOR INTIMACY

Intimacy is the grease that keeps the marriage machine in top shape. All marriages can be stable with mutual commitment and good communication. They can feel prosperous when both partners work together through their conflicts and quarrels to some equitable resolution. When couples are able to develop a sense of "us-ness," they also develop a pride in what they have created between them, a real bond that stands firm in times of difficulty.

Intimacy gives the zest, the joy, the pizazz, the fun, the excitement, the tenderness, the creativity. Intimacy provides the entry level into an echelon of physical and emotional closeness. And the wonder of it is that it can happen at any age, at any length of marriage.

Kisses, gentle touches, goodbye and welcome-back hugs, back and shoulder rubs, hand and foot massages, terms of endearment, special jokes for two, tickles, and nicknames that sweetly draw partners together—these are the characteristics of intimacy. These are the daily words and behaviors that keep the marriage machine offering great service, a high performance rating, and a long-term contract of pleasure touring.

DAILY COUPLE TALK:
(EACH PERSON ANSWERS)
For your marriage machine, which is more important to you: regular check-ups, new spark plugs, a clean and clear windshield with adequate wipers for rainstorms, an inspection of wheel alignment, an approved safety record?

CREATING A CLIMATE FOR INTIMACY

Celebrations can be a big part of intimacy. When we are on the look-out for those things which please and satisfy us in our partner, we cannot at the same time be looking for the annoying habits that make us irritated. Finding the actions and accomplishments worth celebrating can keep our attention focused on the positive. Our attitudes will follow.

On the occasion of the 50th year of marriage, Britton and Bobbye decided to celebrate 50 Wonderful Things and make it last all year long. One of the 50 things was a cruise to Alaska (it was also the most expensive). Friends from Vancouver, Canada, took them to the ship and gave them a balloon saying, "Happy Fiftieth." There is much shared happiness in a close couple relationship, and keeping a focus on those happy moments and what caused them is one way to preserve the closeness and intimacy.

The celebrations do not have to be expensive. They can acknowledge job changes or insignificant accomplishments like finding a lost screw driver. The imagination that goes with them is as much fun as the reason for celebrating. A note on a pillow with a piece of someone's favorite chocolate accompanying it, a candlelight meal with a funny card for the partner, a shared jigsaw puzzle with kisses for finding a difficult piece—these are ways to keep intimacy fresh and sweet. Celebrations can happen often as both partners find new reasons and new ideas.

DAILY COUPLE TALK:
(EACH PARTNER ANSWERS)
What is one thing that we should celebrate today?
Tomorrow?

CREATING A CLIMATE FOR INTIMACY

Sharing feelings is a major part of creating a climate for intimacy. Sharing feelings can have surprising results, whether or not you grew up doing it or have done it regularly with your partner.

Many years ago Bobbye was teaching English to high school juniors and seniors. She had a student who consistently rolled her eyes at the friend she sat by in class. Bobbye thought she was being ridiculed and tried not to look at the girl, sometimes losing track of her place in her notes. Finally one day Bobbye asked the girl to stay after class after the bell rang. When everyone else was gone, the girl came up to Bobbye's desk and with good "I" talk Bobbye said, "Christie, when you roll your eyes at your friend, I think you are making fun of me. I am embarrassed and I want you to stop."

Christie didn't say anything and walked out of the classroom. Two weeks later this was the report from her friends who had been waiting in the hall. They had asked Christie, "What did she say?" Christie told them, "Dr. Wood really likes me." She then went on to explain to them that when adults really like you, they tell you what they think and feel. It was a surprising interpretation for a 17-year-old and one that is true for couples, as well.

Sharing feelings builds intimacy between a couple because it is not something you do with anyone but those whom you trust. It is special.

DAILY COUPLE TALK:
(EACH PERSON PARTICIPATES)
Tell your partner two things that are on your Bucket List. Tell your partner two things you want for the relationship.

CREATING A CLIMATE FOR INTIMACY

On a recent trip to Virginia, Bobbye and Britton made an informal survey about marriage. One of the questions was, "What advice would you give friends who were getting married?" The Woods got a big variety of answers from a big variety of ages. Melissa said that before the couple married, they should "Learn each other's Love Language." Callie said, "No secrets." Haley said, "Women need love; men need respect." Linda said, "Be a compatible team." Will said, "Run to be the first one to forgive." Actually, there were several suggestions about the importance of forgiveness.

Everyone carries around regrets about past words or actions that were said or done. They become like a beach ball which we are holding under the water, telling ourselves that it is not there just because it is not seen by others. Much effort and energy is required to keep the beach ball submerged and out of sight. Others can be playing in the sand, but we cannot join in the play because of the need to keep the beach ball under the water.

Forgiveness of ourselves and of others can be unexpectedly freeing. Coming to our partner without the exhausting effort of rehearsing our grievances in our minds and denying that they exist can amaze us with its simplicity. Releasing the beach ball frees us to interact with others. Forgiveness allows us to be intimate without judgment or preoccupation.

DAILY COUPLE TALK:
(EACH PARTNER RESPONDS)
What is something you need to forgive yourself for?
What is something you need to forgive your partner for?

CREATING A CLIMATE
FOR INTIMACY

Reducing stress in our daily lives has many benefits. Health-sapping stress robs us of sleep, energy, and motivation to do everyday things that keep closeness and intimacy strong.

The latest jaw-dropping statistics about returning veterans from various stressful military engagements in the world prove this to be true. Statistics show that as many as 80% of veterans divorce, a number far above the national average. Those veterans who do stay married often need years of intervening therapy, just to cope with everyday life. The body and mind seem to have a ceiling on how much stress they can handle, and the ceiling is different for every individual.

Feelings of stress can be the signal that something new is needed, according to Michelle Hernandez of the Family Wellness program. Perhaps those feelings call for more regular exercise, a different diet with more energy-boosting vitamins, a prolonged period of sleep at night, or a learned regimen of deep breathing.

New techniques in relationship-building can also combat stress and keep us in the Intimacy Zone. Practicing healthy techniques with each other actually arms our bodies to better deal with disease and aging, besides helping the relationship grow. Stress can be countered with the comfort and pleasure of two loving bodies mutually committed to make the most of their love.

DAILY COUPLE TALK:
(EACH PERSON ANSWERS)
What contributes most to your daily stress? What is one technique that could reduce your stress to keep your body and mind functioning well?

CREATING A CLIMATE FOR INTIMACY

Establishing a time every day to have a 15-minute candid conversation about couple issues and feelings keeps the marital air amazingly clear. That candor needs to include talks about sexual activity as well. Love songs and adolescent fantasies suggest that passion is a mystery, and in some ways that is true.

However, if the plethora of advertisements on sports talk radio are any indication, anyone over 35 today needs to get serious about some kind of synthetic aid for physical equipment. Couples who work at keeping the fire burning for each other sometimes have to do what a sign in an office promised: "We work around what does not work."

Intimacy calls for couple creativity, maximizing whatever feelings are there in order to get (and keep) the joy in a physical relationship. Add intimate couple talk, lighthearted laughter, sexual innuendoes, plenty of kisses, tender touches, and an innovative outlook. This is the recipe for a close relationship even if there are age and health issues. This recipe mixes the mystery of passion and desire, such as the song that refers to "that old black magic called love," with the candor of couple information identifying the pleasure areas for exploration.

DAILY COUPLE TALK:
(EACH PARTNER RESPONDS)
*What could you add to enhance
your intimate couple time?*

CREATING A CLIMATE FOR INTIMACY

The purpose of intimacy is drawing close to someone we love and are learning to trust. It includes sexual encounters, certainly, but intimacy is more than sex. It is giving ourselves in love and in that gift receiving a love gift in return. It is allowing ourselves to be cherished, stroked, praised, and enjoyed. It is relaxing into those wonderful words, "I love you."

Other people notice when there is real intimacy between a couple. They usually say things like "They are crazy in love" or "They are just wild about each other" but they are describing what two partners can achieve together when they are vulnerable with each other. Intimacy is transparent. It is living the truth of love before others so that the truth is visible and shows what power and joy lie within a close relationship.

Intimacy is at the heart of "us-ness," motivating our efforts to communicate well, to cooperate, to be a partner in the creation and implementation of a beautiful love song.

DAILY COUPLE TALK:
(EACH PARTNER PARTICIPATES)
Describe an intimate time you have enjoyed with your partner. Use lots of feeling words.

CREATING A CLIMATE FOR INTIMACY

To be successful in the long-term diets need to be a form of behavioral not caloric modification. The dieter has to be the one to make choices that affect his/her weight. Those choices matter more in the long run that which kind of diet he/she is on. The same is true for couples.

Most fad diets assure the dieter that he/she can hit the target weight. And that is true. Almost anyone can meet the goal of losing 10 pounds for the reunion or 20 pounds for the family wedding. But when the goal is met, and no further attention is being paid, it is astonishing how quickly the pounds return. The sensible thing to aim for in dieting, according to many experts, is a behavioral change that can last a lifetime. The dieter needs to make choices for better health, more energy, and higher amounts of self-confidence, and they need to be long-term choices.

Couples who take their intimacy needs seriously are the couples who are willing to make the daily behavioral changes that can insure a lifetime together of healthy connection. Those couples are aided immensely along the way during their intimacy times by generous amounts of brain chemicals called dopamine and oxytocin. Dopamine causes a spike in passion and pleasure. Oxytocin is secreted to form bonding (such as between mother and new-born) as well as a strong sense of well-being. Both are bonuses for working to maintain intimacy.

DAILY COUPLE TALK:
(EACH PARTNER RESPONDS)
Who is usually the initiator in your sexual activity?
How could that role be shared?

CREATING A CLIMATE
FOR INTIMACY

Marital intimacy is quick to heal wounds, help joy prosper, and keep daily life in a manageable perspective. However, misunderstandings between partners, as well as unstated hurts and doubts—these can affect the perceived presence of intimacy.

One key to enjoying and maintaining intimacy is trust. Partners need to be honest with each other about what they are thinking and feeling, so that each one knows the "world" of the other and its daily issues and concerns. These ideas, thoughts, and feelings, as well as attitudes and preferences, make up what Dr. John Gottman (of the Seattle Marital and Family Institute) calls a Love Map. Creating the Love Map helps each partner know how to support, how to pray for, and how to work with the other.

Partners can only make their Love Maps out of the information each one shares. Guesses, interpretations, and assumptions may or may not be correct, and cartography works best when its data is accurate. So a partner making a Love Map sometimes has to rely on trust—trust that the information given is correct. Trust allows us to be vulnerable and open before each other. Trust keeps us sharing our feelings and thoughts, so that misunderstandings can be aired and processed. Trust leads to intimacy.

DAILY COUPLE TALK:
(EACH ONE ANSWERS)
What is an issue concerning you in your immediate
future that your partner could put on his/her Love Map?

CREATING A CLIMATE
FOR INTIMACY

Teams seldom function well by focusing solely on correcting what's going wrong. These issues have to be addressed, of course, but a steady stream of criticism does not build the kind of rapport that keeps a team running smoothly. Couple discussions about improvement need to be balanced with couple discussions about dreams and values concerning the relationship. In this way intimacy and efforts toward improvement can walk hand-in-hand.

One way to start the process is by candid talks together about what each partner wants and is willing to do in order to change the climate of intimacy. Then one partner needs to accomplish something loving, something he/she knows the other partner will recognize as "soil amendment" for their couple rose bush. The gifted partner will then reciprocate with a love-gift as a statement of desired growth, understanding that this is the welcome beginning of a new period for both of them. Nothing so far needs to be of any monetary value, only symbolic of their desire for closeness. Next, share feelings so that both know some of the reasons intimacy is important to each partner. Some physical action together will also be helpful, such as a warm embrace or a kiss of over 15 seconds.

Every time there is a misunderstanding, a period of distance, or a troubling loss of some kind, this process can be repeated.

DAILY COUPLE TALK:
(EACH PERSON RESPONDS)
What is one way your partner has enriched your life since you have been together? What is one intimate thing you would like to do with your partner? When could you do it?

CREATING A CLIMATE FOR INTIMACY

Although an ancient epic poem, The Odyssey gives us very modern insights into intimacy. Odysseus, the hero of the poem, has spent ten years at the Greek/Trojan war, which he cleverly ends by designing the Trojan Horse. Then he spends ten more years getting home to his kingdom and to his wife Penelope, who has been raising their young son and outwitting the many suitors who wanted to marry her and claim Ithaca's throne.

Finally Odysseus returns and it looks like their commitment to each other will be rewarded, for the suitors are vanquished and the kingdom restored. But Odysseus and his Penelope do not immediately get a happily-ever-after experience.

First, they must work out a way to deal with their issues: jealousy, misunderstandings, desire to punish each other for difficult circumstances and for what they each supposed happened in their long separation. Only in working out their interpersonal issues were they able to restore and enjoy the physical harmony which each of them had expected and longed for. Homer wrote the poem centuries ago, but the relationship between intimacy and honest dealing with couple issues is still relevant.

DAILY COUPLE TALK:
(EACH PARTNER PARTICIPATES)
Why were Odysseus and Penelope unable to be intimate immediately? What do you learn from their difficulties?

MARЯIAGE FOR THE EVERDAY

COMMITMENT

"Winning is NOT the point.

Not giving up is the point."

PAT SUMMITT

COMMITMENT

David and Vera Mace, pioneers in the field of Marriage Enrichment, developed what they called the "coping system" for couples. The "coping system" advised:

1. A mutual commitment to the growth of the relationship

2. A communication style that works toward understanding

3. A creative use of conflict

Following this system, the Maces said, would allow any couple to cope with the issues of life and succeed at the same time with relationship-building.

Their idea concerning commitment is novel. The commitment is not just to stay married, no matter how noble a task that is. It is not a commitment to always love, as though a person could feel loving and angry at the same time. It is commitment to growth, the growth of their relationship.

Commitment to growth means that everything that happens to the couple is an opportunity to grow through it together. Growing closer, growing stronger,, growing adept at handling life's obstacles together—commitment to growth gives the couple a goal by letting them see even conflict as an opportunity to know each other better. The Maces' "coping system" regarding commitment is both practical and optimistic at the same time.

DAILY COUPLE TALK:
(EACH PARTNER RESPONDS)
Discuss the Maces' concept of commitment to the growth of the relationship. What are its major assets?

COMMITMENT

Communication was the top answer given in the informal poll taken by Britton and Bobbye where they asked many different people, "What makes a strong marriage?" The second most popular answer was commitment.

Bentley defined commitment as "perseverance." He said it was the one necessity in bringing about needed change. Chris said that without commitment "none of the other stuff works." Linda said, "We won't work through a problem unless we both have commitment." Stacy defined it as "connectedness" and expressed it as the ability to sense when you and your partner should not "freak out at the same time." Tony discussed it in the context of integrity, rather like keeping your word to do what you say you are going to do. All these variations of the idea of commitment are not only practical but offer insight into the importance of the word to a couple. Commitment is the glue that holds the couple together when there are misunderstandings and clashes of perspective. It is a promise, a pledge, a vow. It is meant to last.

DAILY COUPLE TALK:
(EACH PARTNER ANSWERS)
How would you define commitment? Why is your definition important to a relationship, to an "us?"

COMMITMENT

Mutual commitment to the growth of the relationship does not mean being "joined at the hip." In fact, for there to be real couple growth, there needs to be a separate and fully functioning "you" and "me," with separate interests and along with them separate friendships.

Keeping our commitments to causes and tasks we believe in enriches us as persons and helps us to value our together times as a couple more highly. As Kahlil Gibran wisely said, "the oak tree and the cypress grow/ not in each other's shadow." (The <u>Prophet</u>)

Commitment to couple growth means that whether we are together or apart, we are looking for ways to show each other our love and appreciation. Commitment to couple growth illustrates the importance of our actions because it so optimistically demonstrates that we believe whole-heartedly in our marital choice.

DAILY COUPLE TALK:
(EACH PARTNER PARTICIPATES)
Describe the kinds of commitments you believe are necessary in life. What would a mutual commitment to the growth of your relationship look like.

COMMITMENT

For every small commitment either of you keep, both to your partner or to the growth of your relationship itself, pretend you put $10 into a commitment bank account. For every large commitment, put in $50. No one deposit makes a big difference, but over time that account begins to add up. It is helpful just to know it's there in times of adversity or misunderstandings. It is a joint account, formed by both of you and available to both.

When the mythical account reaches a certain level, celebrate. Go to a concert, out to dinner, or to a sporting event. Make the celebration special in honor of conscious effort by both of you to keep commitments to each other and to your relationship.

Some people make assumptions that all couples who go through a marriage ceremony will automatically at that moment know how to relate to each other, make each other happy at all times, and settle every dispute. Finding the right person is all it takes, many people believe, and being the right person does not figure into the marriage equation. Fortunately more couples are realizing that more information than just their own experiences can be surprisingly helpful.

DAILY COUPLE TALK:
(EACH PERSON RESPONDS)
Name an action you did recently that showed a commitment to the relationship. Symbolically put $10 in the "commitment bank account." Watching it grow is one way of tabulating how your relationship is valued.

COMMITMENT

In a novel Bobbye was reading recently a husband was having severe difficulties with his extended family and withdrew into himself while he tried to work it out. His wife knew something was wrong, but in his pain he chose to shut her out. Finally he left town to return to his former home in an effort to resolve the troubling issues with his family.

His confused wife confided in a friend at work about her problem and asked his advice about what to do. He asked her to consider that if her husband were physically ill and bleeding from the mouth, she would not hesitate to hurry to his side. Your husband is bleeding from the heart, the friend said. The wife immediately took some personal days off from work and even though she was fearful of airplanes, flew to be with him. The wife's decision to honor her commitment "in sickness and in health" and to go stand by her husband's side unexpectedly pleased both of them. As soon as the husband saw her walking up to the family home, he felt his world steady and grow clear again. There was nothing they could do to help the family situation, other than be there together. That turned out to be enough. They eventually flew home and resumed their lives with a stronger commitment to share their problems with each other.

Commitment has a steadying effect in the midst of life's uncertainties. Keeping commitments builds trust, and trust is a major ingredient in building a strong "us."

DAILY COUPLE TALK:
(EACH PARTNER ANSWERS)
What commitments have you made to each other that keeps your "us" especially strong?

COMMITMENT

Commitment to the marital journey requires all our gifts and strengths. One partner may have lots of patience; one may be exceptionally creative; one may manage money well. Gifts and strengths are varied. Celebrating each other's strengths makes the marital trip easier.

❍❍DAILY COUPLE TALK:(EACH ONE RESPONDS)
What strengths did you bring to your marital journey? What strengths did your partner bring? What strengths do you rely on today?

Some things have to be left at home in order to lighten our luggage and make travel easier. Taking too much "stuff" is cumbersome and leaves no room to add souvenirs and gifts.

❍❍DAILY COUPLE TALK:(EACH ONE RESPONDS)
What is something you are willing to "leave behind" to make it easier on your marital journey?

Journeys can be instructive and good for our psyches. Many of us remember exciting family trips in growing up. Perhaps we have even saved souvenirs of one of those trips.

❍❍DAILY COUPLE TALK:(EACH ONE RESPONDS)
What is a "souvenir" of your marital journey that you remember with pleasure?

COMMITMENT

From small beginnings can come surprising, life-changing results. In 1519 Spanish galleons landed off the east coast of Mexico with 17 horses aboard. The Spanish sailors swam the horses ashore, tethered to the men in rowboats, and thus from that one simple action began a new adventure of travel, battle, exploration, transportation, hunting, and settlement in the western areas of North America. All the great horse herds of the American prairies came from this one event.

From the simple promises of commitment in the words "I do" come many surprising, life-changing results. Travels, deployments, and jobs have led families to adventures in far corners of the world. Babies have led many couples to today's adventurous blends of yours, mine, and ours.

The greatest adventures in life have been and still are "of the heart." Commitment to learning how to love someone and how to let ourselves be loved by that same person can lead to thrilling discoveries and awesome adventures. To participate in becoming an "us," growing a strong, enduring, life-changing connection between a "you" and a "me," is a commitment full of both self- and couple-discovery, an adventure not to be missed.

DAILY COUPLE TALK:
(EACH PARTNER ANSWERS)
What has been one of life's great adventures for you?
Why?

COMMITMENT

Commitment to growth implies that both partners are necessary. People have proclaimed the male as the "head" of the household, and pundits have agreed but added that the female is the "neck." The truth is that for there to be real growth in a relationship—a real building for the future—there needs to be an equality of power, privilege, and respect. One partner may have more education, more money, or even more fame, but to grow a relationship into a strong "us," it takes participation and effort from both partners.

In Larry McMurtry's Pulitzer Prize-winning novel, Lonesome Dove, a character named Clara falls in love with a handsome Texas Ranger named Captain Gus McCrae. Clara will not marry Gus, however, because she knows he is and always will be whole-heartedly committed to a life of adventure. There can be no equal relationship with Clara, and that is important to her.

When Gus dies, he wants to be buried where he and Clara used to picnic when they were young, but his is a romantic fantasy, a fine thing. Wise Clara knows that building something for the future with two committed partners is a finer thing. And she is right.

DAILY COUPLE TALK:
(EACH PERSON PARTICIPATES)
What is something in the future that you would like to plan for and "build" with your partner? What strengths does each one possess that could be helpful?

COMMITMENT

Loving behaviors are like making deposits in the Love Bank. One deposit will not pay for a cruise, but daily attention to the account will result in a surprisingly hefty balance. In lean or troubled times a couple can draw on that balance.

One facet of loving behaviors is that they need to be individually tailored. If one partner spends time preparing a special surprise for the other, but it wasn't a welcome surprise, it won't count as a loving behavior. If one partner plans a birthday party for the other with all extended family present, but that partner wanted an intimate evening at a new restaurant in town, that is not a loving behavior. Putting gas in the partner's car at times when he/she is rushed is a loving behavior. Taking time to listen during the partner's stressful moments is a loving behavior. Deposits in the Love Bank have to be thoughtful and mutually desired.

Another facet that counts as loving behaviors is trying to learn new skills that work with the partner. Learning together to say what you want and say it specifically, for example, can result in a clarity of communication that both appreciate. When one partner sees that the other is really working to accomplish what they have both agreed upon, that translates to loving behaviors. The point is that a commitment to keeping the Love Bank account full pays dividends to both partners.

DAILY COUPLE TALK:
(EACH PERSON ANSWERS)
What was a time when you put something in the joint Love Bank account? What was your partner's response?

COMMITMENT

Drs. Joe and Michelle Hernandez of the Family Wellness program lists the following as some of the characteristics of healthy families: they are good communicators, they share power, they show appreciation, they are committed to growth, they have problem-solving skills, and they have goals and values which they can clearly articulate to others. Since the couple is the lynch-pin of the home, let's assume that these characteristics start with the couple.

❤❤DAILY COUPLE TALK: (EACH PARTNER CHOOSES)
Pick the top TWO of the healthy characteristics and explain why you chose them.

When couples begin to prioritize the things they value in their relationship, they are making a cultural statement about who they are and how they want to be known in their community. They are saying that they plan to be the leaders in their home and that they want to transmit their values to their children.

Choosing values also implies a commitment to those values and a willingness to practice them with each other.

❤❤DAILY COUPLE TALK: (EACH PARTNER EXPLAINS)
Of the two characteristics you picked, which one is MOST important to you? How can you better use this characteristic every day?

COMMITMENT

Change and growth are part of life, as is decay. A mutual commitment to growth assures that the former will be the pattern, for unfortunately decay is what happens when there is little or no effort made by either partner to grow the relationship.

No one means for a relationship to wither. Sometimes we don't even know that it's happening until complete apathy gives the sign that something is very wrong. We are busy; we are stretched with job, children, and a packed schedule. Busy-ness can mask the fact that we never have a 15-minute conversation about our "us," we haven't shared feelings in months, and we cannot remember when we've spent an intimate moment together.

A mutual commitment to growth, however, challenges both partners to do the things that keep partners close, even in the midst of a busy life. Then because of attention to it, growth happens, and both partners become aware of it and of its benefits. Then comes a determination to nurture each other with gentleness and appreciation. It is a cycle of love: commitment leads to doing the loving behaviors that produce growth, growth leads to a new awareness of happiness and satisfaction in our lives, happiness and satisfaction keeps us committed to seek growth.

DAILY COUPLE TALK:
(EACH PARTNER RESPONDS)
On a scale of 1-10, with 10 being highest, where would you rate your relational growth today? Why?

COMMITMENT

Fidelity is a kind of commitment, and to some people it is the main commitment a couple must make to each other. In a relationship where both partners are making an effort to stay close emotionally and physically, fidelity is crucial.

Believing that we are the special one- and- only to one person is a major component of self-worth. Functioning confidently in the world is difficult at best, and helping the partner achieve a healthy self-confidence (and getting reciprocal help) is not just a courtesy but a life-affirming action.

Close relationships sadly do not happen for all couples. But for those for whom it is a viable possibility, those who want to risk taking the great adventure of loving and being loved, close relationships contribute not only to couple growth but to personal growth as well. Close and committed relationships are the fast-track to feeling secure in the world and able to cope with life's demands.

In a world that treats sex as a disposable action hardly more meaningful than a handshake, fidelity makes a strong statement, both to the couple and to society as a whole.

DAILY COUPLE TALK:
(EACH PARTNER ANSWERS)
What actions or words help you know that your partner considers you special?

COMMITMENT

Commitment to our values keeps us centered in the world. It allows us to make an impression on others and an imprint on life. Commitment to our values keeps us in the game, hoping for the best in the times when little appears to be going right.

Some of our commitments we decided on early, guided by our parents or guardians. Some of our commitments may be faith-based, allowing us to follow ancient guidelines for our life-script. Some commitments we make to a job, a career, a cause we believe in. Commitment to growing the marriage relationship gives life one beautiful form of loving, as two people become better together than they could be on their own, and others see that commitment lived out before them.

As the relationship grows over time, curiously the couple's fiercely-protected personal independence comes together freely in interdependence. Learning about each other deepens, along with tenderness, respect, and compassion. Then in special moments of introspection and repose, the couple is able to see how commitment to their values have shaped their lives and the lives of those they love.

DAILY COUPLE TALK:
(EACH PARTNER RESPONDS)
What are two values you are committed to and consider important to your daily well-being?

COMMITMENT

"I'm only one call away, I'll be there to save the day," says the song. That's just the blend of optimism and loyalty that commitment calls for. The loving, purposeful, and sometimes sacrificial actions couples make on behalf of each other can regularly inspire a grateful family.

But important as this kind of commitment is to the self-confidence of both partners, so is a commitment NOT to do and say things that cripple and diminish the other. The closer the couple, the more vulnerable each becomes, with revelation of private information that could be damaging if it is brought up in public or in ridicule. Keeping couple secrets becomes imperative, and undermining confidences is also undermining trust.

Even common admonitions such as "Get over yourself" or "Grow up" can hurt when they come from someone close and valued. Claiming to be "only teasing" does little to mitigate the damage of a rude statement made over time. If couples want to be emotionally close, repeated critical statements do not accomplish that goal.

Looking at life through the prism of couple commitment is looking at life through the prism of love. Both the deeds we do and the deeds we choose not to do are important.

DAILY COUPLE TALK:
(EACH PERSON ANSWERS)
You are Superman or Superwoman. What is one action you have done for your partner that "saved the day"? What is one action your partner has done for you?

COMMITMENT

The map of the heart shows commitments, the ideals we believe in that keep us moving through the world with some degree of confidence and optimism.

The lowest level of commitment to the partner is the "as-long-as" style. One partner promises to stay "as-long-as" the other is faithful, does not argue too much, gives sex on demand, or generally pleases. This level is conditional and one partner (or both) have one foot in and one foot out of the marriage. There is the constant threat of "If you do (do not do) _____, I will leave." There is little warmth or joy.

A higher level of commitment is the keeping of the marriage ceremony promises "as long as we both shall live." This does not include staying in a marriage with an addiction (drugs, alcohol, gaming, pornography, abuse). But if both partners are willing to do the things that make the marriage work, divorce is a dim option. With this kind of commitment they begin to find enough happiness with each other to make it worthwhile.

The highest level of commitment is the commitment to the growth of the relationship. On this level partners not only take their vows seriously but aim for using every opportunity to develop a strong and sturdy "us." This level has the greatest benefit, a deep intimacy that only grows through time. At this level the heart's map is large, expanded in wonder at what two devoted lovers can create together.

DAILY COUPLE TALK:
(EACH PARTNER ANSWERS)
Assuming your level of commitment is to growth, what choices have you regularly made that please both of you?

COMMITMENT

The first word in Israel's most important prayer is "Hear." Listen. The prayer of course is talking about listening to God's commandments, but it also suggests the importance of listening to those we love. When we do, we often find them eager to tell us more than they had intended.

Commitment to better listening with each other is a novel and overlooked goal. It allows us to discover the many ways our partner is our helper and advocate in our dangerously divided world. It reveals to us what consistently makes the partner laugh and what will quickly provoke a response of frustration or irritation. It makes us aware of the funny, often quirky, points of view our partner holds. Commitment to better listening gives us the information to put on the Love Map, that goldmine of facts, attitudes, preferences, worries, anxieties, and beliefs that make up much of the data we have about our partner.

In the relationships of couples committed to growth, commitment to better listening provides far more than the usual announcements about schedules and finances.

DAILY COUPLE TALK:
(EACH ONE PARTICIPATES)
Tell your partner about an exciting thing that has happened to you in the last two weeks. Keep it fairly brief. Ask your partner to say back in his/her own words what he/she heard. Analyze what happened.

COMMITMENT

You are a citizen of the democratic nation of Marriage. There are citizens all around the world, and many of them are eager to see their nation prosper. But how to do it?

First of all, VOTE. Make your wishes and needs known. Say what you want with your vote. Say it with good "I" statements and no criticism or blaming. You do not always get what you prefer in elections, and neither will you in the nation of Marriage. But the chances improve when you vote your convictions, especially when you are also willing to listen to another citizen. Voting is a right and an obligation of citizenship in a democratic nation. It should be used responsibly.

Second, KEEP THE NATION'S RULES AND LAWS and support those who also follow the rules. Rules need to be developed together and stated clearly, designed for the good of its unique constituents. No one entity makes all the rules in an egalitarian nation. Make rules that are important to a growing relationship.

Keep those rules whether you feel like it or not. Many psychologists speak of the fact that feelings will follow behavior. Behave your way into feeling law-abiding and warmly proud of your nation.

DAILY COUPLE TALK:
(EACH PARTNER ANSWERS)
In your marriage nation what is a rule already established? What is a new rule that you two citizens might need to develop?

COMMITMENT

Bobbye and Britton sat in a restaurant booth one evening with two of their grandchildren. Four-year-old Hannah had just learned her left hand from her right and was very impressed. "Everybody raise your right hand," she said. We did, and Hannah looked carefully at each hand. Then she told her grandfather, who was sitting just opposite to her, "That is not correct, Papa B." Everyone at the table including her brother David jumped in to explain to Hannah about opposites. But she did not listen. She only knew her right hand and that her grandfather had not raised the right one. Hannah did not have the Big Picture.

Looking at the Big Picture in marriage is committing to a broad view. It is realizing that this relationship's history together as a couple is broader and higher than some short-term view of personal frustration and struggle. It is refusing to focus on the partner's defects without also acknowledging his/her strengths. Looking at the Big Picture also commits us to work on our own habits and to take responsibility for change in order to make things better. Change can be an arduous, inch-by-inch struggle, but in the context of the Big Picture of marriage, it is decidedly worth it. Commitment to the Big Picture—and to those affected by it—is a commitment to doing the things that will make the marriage last.

DAILY COUPLE TALK:
(EACH ONE RESPONDS)
In the Big Picture of your marriage, what is one thing that really pleases you? One thing that could be improved? One thing you can do to help?

COMMITMENT

Growth in marriage is possible whether you are newlyweds or ready for retirement. Three bones are needed.

A BACKBONE is the first. This bone is strong and complex. It is able to carry heavy burdens. This bone keeps a couple centered in what they want to accomplish together. It houses the nerve center of the relationship and provides the fortitude to follow through with commitments.

The second is a WISHBONE. Made of two sections, this one carries the hopes, wishes, dreams, and desires of the couple. For fulfillment these ideals need to be expressed to each other so that each can help the other. Goals give direction, yes, but setting the goals mutually also provides the encouragement to reach them.

The FUNNYBONE is a useful and flexible joint. It gives mobility to everyday actions and in a close relationship keeps us aware of all that is amusing, witty, quirky, hilarious, and silly. It lightens up the atmosphere and lets us laugh at ourselves and sometimes at our mistakes.

DAILY COUPLE TALK:
(EACH PARTNER RESPONDS)
Which of the three needed bones do you find most important and why?

COMMITMENT

Simple commitment to a couple's vows and promises gives them power. The demand of difficult circumstances sometimes LOOKS like it is in charge of what a couple does. But that is like the view of a tugboat chugging through a harbor apparently pulling by a hawser an enormous cruise ship. As an audience watches, it sees that the lines connecting the tugboat to the cruise ship are slack, revealing whose motor is really working hardest and who at any time could demonstrate exactly who has the most power.

Couples need to believe that their "cruise ship" can get them through life's challenges. Together, committed to each other and to the future, couples can safely sail into and out of most harbors.

What makes the couple-power is different for each couple. But what can squelch the power of the "cruise ship" is when either of them chooses to concentrate steadily on the defects of the other. Then the confidence that comes from affirmation and encouragement gets lost. The peace that comes from resolving conflicts dies. Intimacy, once fueled by affection and inventive sex, gets harder to maintain. Talking together about their relationship gives way to conversation exclusively dedicated to the mundane. Then the little tugboat of life's difficulties can easily push around the powerless cruise ship.

DAILY COUPLE TALK:
(EACH PERSON ANSWERS)
Your marital "cruise ship" is sailing into some exotic port. What are three things in your relationship that give it its power?

COMMITMENT

One summer in Alaska Bobbye became intrigued with the sea otter. She learned that at one time in the past, the Russians, who owned the land, had hunted the sea otters almost to extinction. The Cossacks loved the dense pelts for hats and boot liners, and when the sea otters were almost gone, Russia sold Alaska to the United States for a song. And the sea otters over time made a strong return.

That kind of historical short-sightedness is still around today. Many couples decide after the waning of the first wildly romantic months together that they perhaps made a mistake. Some separate before their first anniversary. Others stay together, disillusioned about the disappearance of their early feelings, giving little effort to building a new relationship.

The sea otters made a return because their environment suddenly began to provide them with what they needed to survive and thrive. Their comeback included a habitat safe from the daily threat of invasion and danger; it gave them the peace to hunt, fish, mate, and raise their young.

Couple health is similar. Dormant feelings can revive with the right nourishment of a new energy bent on creatively re-establishing a once-valued relationship. The return of the sea otters is nothing compared to the joyful comeback of couples determined to love each other with a new commitment.

DAILY COUPLE TALK:
(EACH PARTNER RESPONDS)
To which animal would you compare your partner?
What are some characteristics shared by both?

COMMITMENT

All relationship-building proceeds at an uneven pace. One partner at any time does more sharing of feelings, or gives more attention to making schedule space for a daily 15-minute conversation, or works harder at the steps to resolve conflict. Relationship-building will not be 50/50. Divorce is 50/50.

But commitment to trust-building needs to be 100% for each partner. The business model of "Trust but Verify" will not work in trust-building. In trust-building the best motivation possible is assigned to the partner's words and actions. In trust-building we risk ourselves to our partner.

COMMITMENT TO TRUST-BUILDING:

❦ Allows us to have a balance between separateness and connectedness. It is producing a growing couple relationship while helping us as individuals to do the things that contribute to a strong "'me" and "you."

❦ Keeps us sharing our thoughts and feelings with each other, confident that they will not be repeated to others.

❦ Frees us to believe that for couple growth practicing "I" talk in the midst of disagreements is more valuable than "you" talk.

❦ Relieves us from the habit of inspecting for the partner's defects, imperfections, and ways needs are not being met.

DAILY COUPLE TALK:
(EACH PERSON PARTICIPATES)
Which of the four stated outcomes of trust-building is the most important to you? Why?

COMMITMENT
PART 1

Here are some of the things to keep "in the front of the mind," as an NFL football player said about what he needed to concentrate on most. A COMMITMENT TO GROWTH makes us look for opportunities to make that happen. It's like a good investment opportunity or a bargain. We need to jump on them when they are available.

PAYING ATTENTION TO THE WAY WE TALK TO EACH OTHER changes the dynamic of our relationship. First to be listed on every kind of couple success measuring tool, good communication is the quickest way to bring about change. Communicate to achieve understanding, not just to be understood. Listen to make sure that happened. Simple but effective.

GETTING A HANDLE ON THE WAY WE DISAGREE brings so much satisfaction that we wonder why we tried to avoid this for so long. Sharing feelings about a disputed subject and really listening to our partner's point of view both lowers the emotional level of the argument and places us more quickly at the point of discussing ideas about solution. The more we practice our agreed-upon technique, the less stressful are our conflicts.

DAILY COUPLE TALK:
(EACH PARTNER RESPONDS)
You have a friend who is thinking of getting married.
What advice would you give him/her?

COMMITMENT
PART 2

The NFL football player beginning his August training camp also said that he had some things "in the back of the mind" that he intended to accomplish.

Having a 15-minute conversation every day is a way to stay close and current with each other. Keep the talk about what is happening to you. If there are children, help them respect this time and leave you alone. Short of an emergency or a hungry baby, this time can be a teaching opportunity for children: that the couple is important and its time together is valuable.

Keeping couple successes "in the back of the mind" is a way to stay in touch with the positive changes that make couple life easier. Remembered successes form a reservoir of wellness that can be drawn from in droughts. Rather than thinking "He will never get it" or "She will always act like that," remember past successes. They keep us clear on our mutual goals.

Belittling the partner in any form produces the same feeling a bereaved person has who hears one of the many hurtful phrases such as "It was for the best" or "You'll get over this" or even "You'll have other children." Instead of the kind of teasing that diminishes, try words of affirmation and appreciation that build up and encourage love and trust.

Keeping these ideas "in the back of the mind" is a way to keep moving forward in the commitment to growth.

DAILY COUPLE TALK:
(EACH ONE PARTICIPATES)
Describe a couple success that you have enjoyed. Who benefits from that success other than the two of you?

133

COMMITMENT

At a couple time recently Britton and Bobbye asked each other which of the three parts of the Coping System had been most important to them (a mutual commitment to growth, an effective communication style, a creative use of conflict). Both picked the same one—the commitment to growth--but for very different reasons.

Britton said it put every subject, every experience, inside the couple circle. There was nothing off-limits to discuss. It gave scope and perspective to every day and elevated the couple by assuming they would be capable of dealing with any issue. It meant growth was unlimited and progress certain. It made marriage a grand adventure, enriching both partners and making them better than they would have been on their own.

Bobbye was astonished. She defined the principle as setting a goal and concentrating on the tiny steps that would move them toward that goal. It was like setting out to lose 20 pounds, she said. The goal was important, but more important were the daily choices of what to eat (and what not to eat) that would help lose the weight. Even a fraction of a pound per week was a worthy achievement to celebrate. The little steps were what enhanced the broader principle.

Perhaps this difference is true of many couples. Perhaps it is also the genius of coupleness: astounding each other with our differences and still working together toward accomplishing the same goals. Hmm.

DAILY COUPLE TALK:
(EACH PERSON ANSWERS)
*Do you think you learn more when you
win or when you lose?*

COMMITMENT

In Larry McMurtry's novel <u>Lonesome Dove</u> a character named Jake Spoon drifts from one violent episode to another until he finally joins a gang of cattle thieves. The gang murders a rancher and steals his herd, kills a prairie farmer and burns his body, and exacts "tolls" from those trying to cross rivers.

The main characters, former Texas Rangers named Captain Gus McCrae and Captain Woodrow Call, find the cruel evidence as they drive their herds northward toward Montana and know they must take action, even though they learn that their old friend Jake Spoon is now riding with the gang. When they find the outlaws, Gus and Call surround them, subdue them, and plan to hang them all. Jake argues that he didn't intend to stay with that gang and that his participation was just a "mistake." Gus tells Jake that he should not have stepped "over the line." Jake says he didn't see "the line." Having few personal commitments Jake had assumed that none were needed. Jake was hanged along with the rest of the outlaws.

It is a powerful scene and suggests that in everyone's life there may be a "line" that defines our commitments (or lack of them) and thus our future. It may be true for marriage as well. Our commitments may change over time as we mature as individuals and as a couple, but they are important for keeping us steady in the world.

DAILY COUPLE TALK:
(EACH PARTNER RESPONDS)
What are some commitments that are so important to you that you would want to pass them along to your children? What is one commitment that you find important in your relationship?

COMMITMENT

In landscape photography, only one picture in 1,000 will be magic, but when it happens, everyone is impressed. Who has not marveled at a photo of the precise moment when the salmon jumps up a waterfall and the bear cub at the top opens his mouth at exactly the right time? That one photo is worth his time.

Sometimes during the plateaus of every marriage remembering the rush of a "magic moment" gets us through. If we are working together toward preserving and enriching our "us," there will be more and more of these special moments. But keeping the ones in mind that have already happened is also useful—with or without a corroborating photograph.

A commitment to knowledge is one of them. The photographer needs education in his/her craft, knowledge about light, cameras, perspective, and development. Similarly, couples profit from knowledge about each other. The more they can learn about each other's rhythms, preferences, personal habits, and past experiences, the easier the understanding of the special person who shares our life.

A second commitment is to patience. A landscape photographer has to spend time observing nature's phenomena, everything from the flight of birds to the emergence of a tiny flower. Couples must have patience with each other. "Magic moments" are worth waiting for, but they don't come every day.

DAILY COUPLE TALK:
(EACH PARTNER RESPONDS)
Picture a "magic moment" the two of you have shared.
When you recall it, what is one thing that stands out

COMMITMENT
PART 1

Occasionally money-managers have to send out letters and e-mails to anxious stock market investors assuring them that the market has regular "peaks and valleys" and that a recovery will be sure to come sooner or later. "Peaks and valleys" in the marriage experience are also well documented (Drs. John Van Epp, Wayne Sotile, and David Olson, to name only a few counselors who have studied in this field).

One of the "valleys" all of the counselors speak of is the dramatic drop in marital satisfaction that occurs after the birth of the first child. Overworked and underappreciated new parents are often dismayed to find themselves too tired for any activity unrelated to caring for a baby. In Daniel Silva's novel called <u>Black Widow</u> there is a revealing scene where a new father comes home one evening to find his wife dozing in a rocking chair with one of their weeks-old twins at her breast. Without even opening her eyes she says to him, "If you wake him, I'll kill you." It is a telling scene regarding the stress new babies put on new parents and their relationship. Marital satisfaction eventually returns but not without the concerns of those who feared the loss of an important connection and not for many years to its original level.

Commitment is what keeps many couples together during the "valleys," or as son-in-law Dale defines it "keeping your promises." Commitment makes the "valleys" habitable when life's circumstances cause couple-stress.

DAILY COUPLE TALK:
(EACH PERSON ANSWERS)
What have been some of your couple "peaks"?
Couple "valleys"?

COMMITMENT
PART 2

"Valley"-tools are simple and basic. They are what couples use when they are experiencing stressors that cannot be changed (job, kids, deployment, health issues). They are for couples who remain hopeful that the "peaks" of couple satisfaction can once again be theirs.

Commitment is a basic "Valley"-tool. Commitment keeps couples believing in their values even through tough times. Commitment is like the Jewish teen-ager hiding in an attic during the awful years just as WWII began. After he was arrested, the poignant story goes, these words were found sketched on the attic wall:

"I believe in the sun, even when it's not shining. I believe in love, even when I don't feel it. I believe in God, even when he is silent."

Another basic "Valley"-tool is to keep talking to each other. If even a 15-minute conversation cannot be managed, supplement with telephone calls, texts, e-mails, or Facebook entries. Staying connected verbally keeps the priority of the relationship on each other's mind. It helps us remember the pleasure we have known together and keeps hold of our couple identity.

A final "Valley"-tool is to squeeze out moments to relax and have fun together. Dealing with our divisive issues can provide a stability of sorts, but simply being good friends who can play reminds us why we need to be together.

DAILY COUPLE TALK:
(EACH PARTNER RESPONDS)
What "Valley"-tools do we use effectively and which ones might we need?

COMMITMENT

Support from other couples who also want success for their marriages is extremely helpful. Committing to other couples in a Marriage Enrichment Group (MEG) helps to keep our focus on getting the most out of our marital relationship.

Couples with multiple responsibilities and full schedules (two jobs, children, parents, volunteer causes, congregational or political involvement) are exactly the couples who most need their energy enriched by taking time once a month to work on their marriage with other like-minded couples. Showing that you value your relationship by attending a monthly MEG meeting elevates the status of your marriage to children, parents, congregation, or friends.

The informal MEG program is simple: a short time for catch-up conversation among friends regarding concerns and celebrations; a time for private couple dialogue on a common issue for couples; a time to gather again to talk about the impact of the couple time in a shared setting.

All MEGs are meant to aid couples by providing a place and time to talk about issues such as money, play time, communication, growth, FOOIE, goals, in-laws, or household tasks. The website of better marriages.org is a good place to learn more about MEGs and whether one might be available near you.

DAILY COUPLE TALK:
(EACH PERSON PARTICIPATES)
Discuss your interest in finding some couple friends who might want to meet together regarding some of the Couple Talk issues in this book.

MARЯIAGE FOR THE EVERDAY

CREATIVE USE OF CONFLICT

"Living in a family group generates more anger than any other social situation."

DAVID R. MACE

CREATIVE USE OF CONFLICT

The couple is the foundation of any home, and children born into that home know it, even if they sometimes behave as if it were not so. The home is the foundation of any country, stronger than schools, government, or the military. This makes the couple special and its relationship important in the world. But the couple is only as strong as its ability to deal with the divisive issues that come to everyone and threaten the longevity of many relationships. Britton has often observed that we train our children to divorce. When they reach their teen-age years and begin to date, they often break up as soon as they have their first conflict and look for someone else. That relationship then lasts until they have a serious conflict and they too break up. Etc.

Marriage is just a more formal arrangement and costs to dissolve it have escalated, but it is always an option for those who cannot or will not meet each other fairly over arguments and conflicts.

Finding a mutually agreeable way to handle disputes is often the difference between gaining closeness and growing apart. No couple can stay intimate if one partner will not cooperate and must always "win." No couple can grow a strong "us" if only one can be engaged in discussing whatever troubling issue is at hand. Couples who discover and practice a fair way to handle their conflicts are as important to their country as those who vote and pay taxes.

DAILY COUPLE TALK:
(EACH PARTNER RESPONDS)
What would be a fair way to handle your arguments and disagreements?

CREATIVE USE OF CONFLICT

Dr. David Mace, who with his wife Vera founded the Association for Couples in Marriage Enrichment (now called Better Marriages), once said, "Never waste a good conflict!"

For Dr. Mace a conflict was important because behind every conflict lie deep feelings. If the feelings were not strong, the person would not care enough to be involved in the quarrel. Wasting identifying and stating the feelings is wasting an opportunity for growth, both for self and for the couple.

Feelings are often a part of the conflict itself and sticking only with the intellectual analysis of what needs to be done leaves out a vital part. Also, leaving out revealing the feelings probably means that the subject will only come up again in another form.

Feelings and emotions are a part of the human psyche. They are too valuable to be blurred and ignored by the overriding power of mere anger.

DAILY COUPLE TALK:
(EACH PARTNER ANSWERS)
Practice sharing feelings by answering the following:
1. How do you feel when your partner
points out that you made a mistake?
2. How do you feel when you are
buying a gift for your partner?
3. How do you feel when others notice
the closeness between the two of you?

CREATIVE USE OF CONFLICT

PART 1

Anger behavior is largely learned from our past experiences plus years of observation. Most people have variations of only two ways to handle anger. They suppress or they vent.

Those who suppress dodge quarrels whenever they can and spend energy trying to convince themselves and others that nothing is bothering them. Venters express their anger like a blast of steam, blaming others with whatever comes to mind.

Neither of these two styles work well in a close relationship. Suppressors can manage only a superficial relationship because they have so many unexpressed resentments. Suppressing not only shuts the partner out but does not deal with whatever issue is between them. Venters hurt others, leave scars, make others defensive, and still do not constructively deal with the disputed issue.

Making a decision together about handling anger when neither of you is angry is often the most practical step toward resolving issues.

DAILY COUPLE TALK:
(EACH PARTNER RESPONDS)
Discuss what you do when you are angry. What does your partner do? What did your parents do?

CREATIVE USE OF CONFLICT

PART 2

The first step in trying a different style of handling anger and conflict is to agree not to attack or blame the other person. Attacks usually lead to counter-attacks of one kind or another and to the escalation of emotions beyond the issue at hand.

The second step is to acknowledge the anger and to avoid making the partner guess what is happening and why. One person begins (usually the one who is angriest). He/she needs to make "I" statements to share feelings and to clarify ideas of the issue. The partner listens, paraphrasing the words and affirming the emotions heard. Then switch roles. The other side of the conflict emerges as the partner's feelings and ideas are stated, listened to without editing or rebuttal, and paraphrased back.

This back-and-forth sharing of feelings goes on until both are sure that every feeling about the disputed issue has been revealed and heard. There is no need to move on to discuss solutions until emotions have cooled and both are able to participate intellectually.

Trying a new behavior to replace an old habit will take time and feel awkward at first. But as couples begin to understand each other better AND resolve some of their issues, both suppressors and venters encounter a more healthful way to get and stay close.

DAILY COUPLE TALK:
(EACH PERSON PARTICIPATES)
Are there any parts of this anger management style that seem usable? Which ones? Why?

CREATIVE USE OF CONFLICT

Managing conflict is like an airplane trying to take off from the runway. One of its wings is named Problem Solution and one wing Problem Discussion. It takes both wings for the plane to get in the air. One wing is no more important than the other. Using only one wing will cause the plane to circle around, unable to lift off.

Each partner comes to the marriage with a set of skills for handling conflict issues, but they often are not the same skills. It gets further complicated if one partner uses his/her skills in a job and is paid for that successful use (such as the military, the police, or trial attorneys). What the couple needs is to use together one partner's skill-set or to DEVELOP a new set of skills that works for them. Otherwise their couple plane will have a hard time getting off the ground.

Britton came to the marriage with a skill-set saying: confront all disputed issues immediately and work them out on the spot. Unfortunately, Bobbye came with a determination not to engage in disputes and to face them with a polite smile and a change of subject. Very soon it was clear that Britton's skill-set was more usable. Together they added and developed the skill of sharing feelings about the disputed issue. They have proved over the years that this plane can fly.

DAILY COUPLE TALK:
(EACH PARTNER RESPONDS)
If you could amend your current Problem Discussion style, what suggestions would you offer?

CREATIVE USE OF CONFLICT

Sociologists such as Dr. David Mace believe that finding a constructive way to deal with anger and conflict between a couple is a valuable contribution to their health and happiness.

Dr. Mace reports three styles of marriages built around this issue. A *one-vote system* of marriage seeks to eliminate conflicts by having one spouse in charge and making all major decisions. In the past, this has been the spouse who made the most money, but sometimes a culture simply assigns this role to the male. The partner who is not in charge does not argue in exchange for being taken care of. There is only one vote and one decision-maker, and this style can work at eliminating conflict if both partners agree to it.

A second style developed in the 20th century, as more women went to work outside the home and made money. This style was more democratic, a *two-vote system*, in which conflicts were reduced by assigning roles to each partner. Each had responsibilities and duties; conflicts only developed when one failed to accomplish their assigned talk.

The third style, a *three-vote system*, is modern. The person best equipped to perform the task (or has the time) is the one who does it. There will be conflicts, but the relationship itself, the "us," casts the third vote and keeps the couple seeking ways to handle their disagreements fairly.

∞

DAILY COUPLE TALK:
(EACH PERSON ANSWERS)
Couples use each style today. Which style do you think
the two of you use most?

CREATIVE USE OF CONFLICT

The behavior affects children they see in their families of origin. If they see parents who are honestly trying to find ways to relate to each other, even while dealing with disagreements, those same children will want that kind of creative, open process when they get married. More to the point, they will see how to get it.

The home is the child's earliest education on how partners can achieve a stable, affirming relationship. It equips them for an independent future or limits their abilities to form healthy relationships of their own.

No subject is more important to helping children feel secure and confident in the world than the issue of conflict. When parents can show their children how to face realistically life's stressful issues, they are teaching them an invaluable lesson. When the stressful issues are between the couple, and the couple still faces those issues realistically and with purpose, the children learn to deal with their own issues with friends, at school, with bullies, and in life. Parents are the front-line educators, the child's first picture of a healthy marriage relationship.

DAILY COUPLE TALK:
(EACH PERSON RESPONDS)
What major lessons did you learn from your parents?
How have those lessons been helpful to you today?

CREATIVE USE OF CONFLICT

Gardening and marriage counseling are often alike. Experienced gardeners can look at a flower bed after the plants have been established for just a short while and with few exceptions tell which plants will survive. Marriage counselors say that they can watch couples talking together on a disputed subject and with few exceptions tell which couples will merely survive, which ones will be happy, and which ones will split up. Skills in managing disputes and disagreements are the key to couple health.

Intimacy is important to the life of a couple, bringing spice and keeping each one aware of the power of affectionate touch. Good communication, both verbal and non-verbal, is necessary to a clear understanding of each other. Commitment to growth gives any couple a plan and a goal, as well as confidence in each other. A sense of "us-ness" showcases our uniqueness as a couple.

All of these subjects are important, but getting a handle on dealing with conflict is essential to a happy, long-term relationship, according to all marriage counselors. View anger and conflict as normal, and agree as a couple that you will work together. Do not attack each other when you are angry; instead acknowledge the anger and make "I" statements to get in touch with its source. Focus on only one issue. Share feelings about that issue and only that issue.

DAILY COUPLE TALK:
(EACH PARTNER PARTICIPATES)
Discuss this statement:
Conflict need not be the enemy of a relationship—
it can be an ally in gaining more understanding.

CREATIVE USE OF CONFLICT

A friend recently went to work as a realtor in a resort area. She said that there was a lot to learn, but one of the hardest things to learn was working with couples whose decision-making skills often led them to conflict. Neither would say what he/she wanted at the outset of condo looking, but both would be upset with each other when the realtor showed them something they did NOT want.

Saying specifically what we want is helpful in interaction with others. Most people have no trouble saying it to clerks, waiters, hairdressers, or lawn-care workers. But for several reasons they hesitate when it comes to conversation with the partner.

Perhaps we fear that it will sound too much like a demand. Perhaps we didn't grow up in a family that stated things directly, and we prefer the hint or the suggestion, hoping the other person will know what we mean and maybe even think it's their idea.

Saying what we want is our best chance to get it. It forces us to be clear ourselves about what we want. Communicating it specifically allows the partner to know exactly where we are. "We never go out any more for fun" could sound accusatory to the partner and could lead to an argument refuting the statement. "I'd like to go out with you for Mexican food Friday night after work" sounds specific and clear. Whether you go out or not, there is a better chance with saying what you want.

OO DAILY COUPLE TALK:(EACH PARTNER RESPONDS)
What is your response to "saying what you want?"
How could it be used to cut down on conflicts?

CREATIVE USE OF CONFLICT

Picture a typical couple going through a conflict. Their struggles are like pulling on a disputed piece of rope between them, each intent on pulling the other off balance to win the struggle. Facing each other, not aware of anyone else observing them.

Now picture another couple dealing with a conflict. They are standing side by side as a team, facing the disputed rope on a table. They have planned and are using their skills to work though the plan. They want to resolve the rope-issue in such a way that it becomes a win/win/WIN (a win for "you," a win for "me," and the "us.)"

What are the differences between the two couples and how they are handling the conflict?

1. One couple has a plan for dealing with conflicts. They agreed on the plan when they were not angry. They believe that being a team is more important than one partner being "right."
2. One couple lets the rope-issue come in between them as they struggle for a solution.
3. One couple even LOOKS like they value their relationship, standing side by side.
4. One couple pulls each other forcefully, an action that leaves resentment.

Seldom can two honest adults see eye-to-eye on everything. But when there is a way for a couple to grow through them, everyone benefits.

⚙️⚙️**DAILY COUPLE TALK:**(EACH PERSON PARTICIPATES)
What other differences did you notice about the two hypothetical couples dealing with their rope-issue? How can the two of you use any of those differences?

CREATIVE USE OF CONFLICT

Differences between partners often lead to disagreements. If they are heated up with anger, they can become conflicts. Conflicts are disruptive and if they cannot be resolved quickly, lead to long-term resentments and to what Henry Thoreau once called "quiet desperation."

The very practical approach to differences is to learn to appreciate those you can and learn to accept those you can't change. Then the rest need to be discussed and negotiated, as both partners aim for change. The odds are in your favor if you will be specific. If the issue is one partner's habit of belching at the dinner table and the issue can neither be appreciated nor accepted, stay with only that issue until some resulting change can be negotiated. Avoid wandering off to discussing bad habits in general and speculating about which partner has the most.

As unacceptable differences are addressed and change can be negotiated, celebrate. Make it clear that the "us" is in the celebration. That way both partners know that change is not merely a one-sided demand but a joint decision made in cooperation.

DAILY COUPLE TALK:
(EACH PERSON ANSWERS)
What is a difference between you that could bring more harmony into your daily living if a change could be made? How could that change be negotiated?

CREATIVE USE OF CONFLICT

Many times, issues are hard for couples to clean up because the focus gets blurred. When too many issues are discussed at the same time, it is difficult to resolve any one of them. It's like trying to clean every room in the house at the same time. Very little visible progress gets made.

Staying with one issue in an argument makes it easier to "clean" up. Write that issue down, if necessary, so that both can see it and know exactly what the argument is about. Both need to take turns sharing their feelings about the one issue; both then offer ideas as a possible solution. Choose one, compromise if one solution is not agreeable to both, and set a time to review the solution for analysis, to see if it's still working satisfactorily.

Resolving an issue efficiently is no small accomplishment. Keeping the relationship free of the annoying clutter of unresolved issues is another accomplishment. The household runs more smoothly, feelings are not so easily bruised, children (if they are present) get a very instructive lesson in handling conflicted issues, and the "us" takes a giant step forward.

DAILY COUPLE TALK:
(EACH PARTNER RESPONDS)
What is one issue between you that you are pleased to have resolved? What is one issue you would like to "clean" up soon?

CREATIVE USE OF CONFLICT

Compromise is what healthy couples do after a conflict. During the dispute, there were no attacks and counter-attacks, the feelings on both sides got shared and listened to, and ideas for a solution got proposed and discussed.

Compromise is the next step. In some disputes after hearing the feelings, one partner may be so surprised and touched by the other's feelings that he/she "gives in" and agrees to the partner's point of view, but this won't happen very often. If someone cares enough about the issue to argue about it, it is unlikely that the point of view will be changed. Nor will it work if it is the same partner who "gives in" every time. Compromise needs to be 50/50 and manipulation won't work more than once.

Compromise happens when both partners want a successful relationship, a strong "us," more than they want to win the argument and get their way. Compromise happens when partners do not run from an argument or deny it is a reality but need a way to handle it. As compromise happens again and again, the couple grows more confident that a big disagreement does not have to mean a loss of intimacy. It is a technique for couples who value fairness. Follow a compromise agreement with loving behaviors and the relationship purrs on.

DAILY COUPLE TALK:
(EACH PARTNER RESPONDS)
What is one compromise that has brought peace in your relationship? How was it worked out?

CREATIVE USE OF CONFLICT

The issue in working through a conflict situation with your partner is not to control either the situation or your partner but to grow as a couple. If we can learn to use our misunderstandings as opportunities to discover new facets of personality and ideas in each other, we are far down the road to re-establishing closeness once again.

Conflicts, like sex, can be messy. Emotions get jumbled in with facts and ideas. Tears and harsh words can tumble out. Having a plan to go by when you are angry and hurt is immensely helpful. A plan, written down and agreed to by both of you at a time when you are not angry, can restore calm just knowing that it is there. Following a plan can insert needed logic and order into a situation where voices get raised and words can be said that cannot be taken back. Verbal sparring and insults are counter-productive, and a plan gives a method both to process anger and get toward some kind of reasonable resolution.

Traveling in the west one summer, Britton and Bobbye heard someone say that the state of Wyoming only had two seasons, winter and road repair. That was supposed to be funny, but unfortunately it describes many couples who feel stuck in a cold cycle of conflict where words like hope, playfulness, and contentment do not fit their everyday experience. Creating a plan to address conflict makes a "road repair" that allows our travels together to be a pleasure.

DAILY COUPLE TALK:
(EACH ONE PARTICIPATES)
Design an Anger Agreement that you can use in times of disagreement. Make it simple. At first, just say what steps you will use, but eventually write it down and agree to it.

CREATIVE USE OF CONFLICT

Some aids to memory can be helpful for a lifetime. Bobbye still remembers spelling aids such as "I before e except after c" and the word separate has "a rat" in it. Aids for handling a conflict can also be useful.

This aid involves the words STOP, LOOK, and LISTEN. STOP means do not attack the partner with words. This only causes anger to increase and makes it nearly impossible to get at the issue in dispute. Using phrases such as "you always" or "you never" may be familiar, but it slightly shifts the argument to provoke defense, rather than addressing the issue. Stopping attacks is a useful strategy.

LOOK means that anger is often a superficial response to an issue. The real feelings lie deeper and need to be looked for. If you can't share this immediately, take time alone to discover what your feelings really are. Is it hurt? Overloaded with pressure? Fear? Look below the surface to see what emotions led to the anger.

Finally LISTEN to what your partner is saying. If you cannot repeat most of the words you hear, you are not listening carefully enough. Listening instead and paraphrasing what you are hearing give information about the partner's point of view and about feelings. Both are important, just like your feelings and point of view.

Agreeing on a resolution to the conflict comes next, but using this simple aid should make getting there easier.

DAILY COUPLE TALK:
(EACH PARTNER ANSWERS)
Which is a harder step for you, STOP, LOOK, or LISTEN?
Which might be most useful?

CREATIVE USE OF CONFLICT

As the deadline for adding new players approached in major league baseball, local fans began to ask their team's manager, "If not now, when?" "Let's try to win this season."

Couples also ask that question. In fact, setting up an appointment to deal with couple issues is a practical technique when the couple cannot deal with that issue on-the-spot. Setting an appointment time is done easily with doctors, plumbers, and hairdressers

In the first place, setting an appointment time lets each part-ner know that the issue IS going to be dealt with. One partner is not going to avoid or withdraw just because the timing is not right to deal with it immediately. This especially helps the one who brought it up or who cares the most about it.

Some people do not get their ideas or find their feelings quickly. Letting a bit of time go by gives opportunity to sort through ideas and feelings and get to the ones most rele-vant to the issue. If the conversation is rushed, one partner may be like the cat who turns on its back with his stomach up. This looks as though the cat is in a peaceful mode, but actually it is giving a sign to the enemy that limbs, claws, and teeth are all ready for use.

Asking "if not now, when?" lets both partners participate at their best level AND makes sure that the issue is dealt with.

DAILY COUPLE TALK:
(EACH PERSON PARTICIPATES)
What is one issue that needs to be discussed when we can find the time? If now is not the time, when could we do it?

CREATIVE USE OF CONFLICT

In spite of the daunting statistics regarding divorce today, dating sites on the internet flourish. People driven by their hopes for a happy relationship are willing to pay money and spend time filling out forms just on the off chance that they might find the man or woman of their dreams. The fact that some do it successfully keeps the dating sites in business.

Clarifying one's goals and preferences is extremely helpful before entering into marriage. The dating sites also provide an opportunity to meet, talk face to face (cyber talk can still mislead), and evaluate physical attraction.

There is no way, however, to know how each one behaves when there is a conflict. In the relationship's early stages both are eager to make a good impression and put the best foot forward. Conflict management styles are only fully discovered when a couple has been together for a while.

Repeated conflicts, unaddressed and unmanaged, can sabotage even the most hopeful of relationships. Most of the closeness and happiness people understandably long for can drain away under the relentless pressure of unresolved anger and strife. If the "us" is made mainly of a truce—with no work to get at the dividing issues—chances for success are minimal.

DAILY COUPLE TALK:
(EACH ONE ANSWERS)
Of the various methods for managing conflict, which one of the following is currently of the most use to you: avoiding attacks on each other, avoiding denying anger, using a Time Out, setting an appointment, sharing feelings, listening and paraphrasing, dialogue on possible solutions? Why?

CREATIVE USE OF CONFLICT

Drs. David and Vera Mace, founders of the organization today called Better Marriages, designed a communication tool they called "Acting on the Pinch." By this they meant that each partner should inform the other when there is a word or action that feels annoying or hurtful. It would be a small thing, like a pinch, easily overlooked or explained to oneself, but many times conflict erupts when small things stack up unaddressed.

Sometimes one partner does not want to seem to nag about dirty clothes on the floor that the other partner left. But the clothes are noticed and the earlier requests to pick them up are perceived as being ignored. It is a "pinch." Saying something about it is better for both partners than silence and resentment.

Sometimes our reluctance to speak up about such a small "pinch" is due to the fact that the standards in the world of business, where we spend much of our day, are different from marriage standards. Business is RESULTS-oriented, results in sales, in cases tried or settled, in projects completed on time. Marriage should not be competitive. Marriage is PROCESS-oriented and that is a big difference.

Taking care of the everyday petty annoyances and hurts with the "pinch" technique involves us directly in the process of growth and "us"-building.

DAILY COUPLE TALK:
(EACH PARTNER RESPONDS)
What part of the "process" of marriage-building do you enjoy most? Why? What part is confusing to you?

CREATIVE USE OF CONFLICT

So far the words about a creative use of conflict have been a bold attack on the corrosive effects of unresolved anger. They have warned couples about how growth, happiness, and intimacy can be stifled simply by failing to address the issues that divide. They have delineated the ways society as a whole benefits from families who have and use practical skills to resolve conflict. They have touched on some tragic and very public results of children who grew up in families which did not prepare them to deal with this issue.

According to the late Dr. David Mace, differences are always going to be a part of any couple experience. When differences collide, the couple will have disagreements. When disagreements get heated up with anger, there will be conflict.

So it seems to make sense that couples acknowledge, discuss, and deal with as many differences as possible. That is the easiest and safest level to begin, because so many of those differences are merely expressions of personal preferences, rather like a choice from a restaurant menu. In the early days of courtship some of the differences might even have been regarded as appealing and endearing.

When the differences have already led to disagreements, they need to be discussed and even analyzed. If there are changes that could be made, this is the level to choose what they might be.

DAILY COUPLE TALK:
(EACH PARTNER RESPONDS)
What is your definition of success? What is one way you can successfully approach differences?

CREATIVE USE OF CONFLICT

An Ethiopian folk tale describes a young wife who comes to the village shaman to get a magic potion to end the conflict that is ruining her marriage. The shaman agrees to make the potion, but he tells her that to do it, she must bring him a hair from the tail of the lion who lives down by the river and terrorizes the villagers.

The young wife is fearful but agrees to get the hair, driven by her fears that conflict will end their marriage. She bravely begins to throw food to the lion every day, until one day he comes close enough to her that she can pluck out a hair. Then she runs to the shaman and demands the magic potion. He tells her there is no such thing, but she has the two qualities necessary to end the conflict: determination and courage. If she really loves her husband, the wise shaman says, she will go home and use what she has.

Determination and courage. Bravely facing anger and hostility to see what emotions could lie behind them. Pushing oneself to find rational ways to connect and cooperate even during a disagreement. These are qualities and actions that can lead to healing and peace.

The folk tale says nothing about the fact that this must be a mutual effort for any long-term progress. It does not mention physical violence, a deal-breaker from its first use. But it does suggest that many couples contemplate the end of their relationship before they ever use the very skills they may already have.

DAILY COUPLE TALK:
(EACH PERSON PARTICIPATES)
Describe a difficult task you faced in growing up (or in your marriage). What happened?
What was the outcome?

CREATIVE USE OF CONFLICT

Everyone knows that the IQ (intelligence quotient) is measurable. It has been around for centuries and is used to place children in certain learning environments and to assess entry level for certain organizations.

The EQ (emotional quotient) is a later addition. Used mainly by businesses, it is a tool that measures one's ability to cooperate, to follow directions, to work on projects with others, and delay gratification. The story of the marshmallow illustrates the point. A pre-school teacher gave each of her children a marshmallow. She told them they could eat the marshmallow but if they waited for her to run a brief errand, they could have two marshmallows. The test was to measure who could delay gratification to double the benefits.

There is currently no commonly used instrument to measure the MQ (marriage quotient), although various researchers have designed tests. If there were a MQ, it should measure one's ability to participate constructively in an argument. If one partner must "win," if one partner must avoid conflict, if one partner turns to intimidation and refuses to listen to another point of view—these are red flags that suggest, there will also be frustration and distance.

Resolving conflict is the key that unlocks the important areas of couple growth. Like the IQ and the EQ, the MQ could help couples bring constructive change to an important subject.

DAILY COUPLE TALK:
(each partner responds) What would the MQ reveal about your strategies for resolving arguments?

CREATIVE USE OF CONFLICT

Several years ago, in an effort to have a more egalitarian relationship Britton and Bobbye divided up many duties, including driving. In town, Bobbye would drive one way to their destination, and Britton would drive back. On trips out of town, they shared the duties.

The problem was that Britton considered himself the one in charge of the car. This meant that even when Bobbye was driving, he felt obliged to tell her when to change lanes, when a light was green, and where to park on arrival. Bobbye objected. They discussed the issue and negotiated a truce. Still the advice continued.

Next, feelings were explored. Bobbye said that under the stream of directions she felt like a student driver, inexperienced and unable to make wise judgments about driving safety, she felt like a little girl being parented. Britton said he was a symphony conductor, and Bobbye was the first chair of the flute section. That information was interesting but the advice continued.

Finally, they found that the real issue to Britton was coming to a complete stop at a stop sign. Bobbye agreed to work on this action, and Britton agreed not to comment unless there was an emergency.

Working through issues is difficult. Having a plan helps, working the plan helps, but the biggest help is sticking with the plan until something fits for BOTH partners.

DAILY COUPLE TALK:
(EACH PERSON ANSWERS)
If you were choosing a gift today for your partner to celebrate some issue you have worked through together, what kind of gift would you choose and why?

CREATIVE USE OF CONFLICT

The bricks that form walls of hostility or indifference are often made of resentment nurtured in secret. Resentment is what you feel when you think an injustice has been done to you but you choose not to say anything about it. It allows you to feel wronged while avoiding having to stand up for yourself. It can cause you to make statements like "whatever" or "Have it your way, as usual," delivered in a tone of bitterness.

The only cure for resentment is to confront the person with whom you are upset and openly share your feelings. Unfortunately, this "cure" is hard to practice for people who feel chronically resentful and inferior.

To communicate resentment, simply say to your partner what you are feeling and why. If the partner can listen and perhaps paraphrase your words, you know you have been heard. If there is an apology it is up to your partner, but verbalizing the resentment in this way frees you and helps you grow as a person by taking care of yourself.

Few relationships can prosper when one or both partners hold grudges or reveal their unhappiness only to third parties, never to the partner. An open policy of honest communication and practical, joint strategies of conflict resolution is the doorway through which healing and hope can come in.

DAILY COUPLE TALK:
(EACH PARTNER ANSWERS)
"You can't stop the waves, but you can learn to surf,"
someone has said. Regarding couple growth, what does
this statement mean?

CREATIVE USE OF CONFLICT

For years Dr. David Mace wrote a column for a monthly magazine no longer in publication. It was called "Can This Marriage Be Saved?" Couples wrote in to the magazine to ask about their relationship. Invariably Dr. Mace gave practical and optimistic advice.

One of Dr. Mace's recommendations was getting out of marital ruts by means of a technique he called Couple Dialogue. Facing each other in two chairs, and turned knee-to-knee, couples were to begin to talk to each other. Turn back the clock, he suggested, to view a time when things were fun together. Remember what you did and how you brought out the best in each other. Take turns talking about it. Then talk about something fun you would like to do together now. Take turns sharing ideas. The warm atmosphere this produces is ideal for discussing the ideas and even for devising plans to implement them. Soon you both are laughing and relaxed. Couple Dialogue is a good way to get (and keep) the relationship going when there is distance or a feeling of the "same old thing."

Besides Couple Dialogue, another recommendation was to deal with anger. Dr. Mace's most important book was <u>Love and Anger in Marriage.</u> His work emphasized the importance of not withdrawing nor venting in anger. He suggested to resolve conflicts by sharing and discussing the feelings each partner has about the issue. Discussing the feelings should precede any discussion of ideas for resolution. Offering new ways to process disagreements helped many couples find a way past difficult issues.

DAILY COUPLE TALK:(EACH PERSON PARTICIPATES)
Why do you think conflict and argument is such an important issue for couples?

CREATIVE USE OF CONFLICT

J. K. Rowling, the British author of the popular Harry Potter series, was interviewed regarding her philosophy of life, reflected in her books and a recent play. She pits the "forces of light" against the "forces of darkness" and designs her plots to show the realistic clashes of these forces underneath the whimsical and imaginary worlds of her characters.

Rowling identifies the "forces of light" as kindness, empathy, acceptance and inclusion. Growing couples work every day to make these qualities survive both outside threats and harsh circumstances that arise within the home.

Trying to understand our partner, for example, and to empathetically communicate that understanding is not only building relationship but is bringing "light" to a sometimes-shadowed environment. The daily efforts to share our feelings are "forces" that illuminate and serve to bring about inclusion.

The "forces of darkness" are fear, rage, and an authoritarian will to power, Rowling says. Finding ways to keep these forces subdued in and out of the home help to ensure that the "you" and the "me" live in peace and equity and are free to grow as individuals and partners. Occasionally couples may have to battle, but the methods for doing so will reveal that the "forces of light" are more than equal to the struggle.

DAILY COUPLE TALK:
(EACH PARTNER RESPONDS)
Which of Rowling's "forces of light" can you best use to show your love to your partner? How would you demonstrate its effectiveness?

CREATIVE USE OF CONFLICT

In earlier years, the South African gold mine workers were thrilled when they saw the wattle tree in bloom. Although they had no calendars, watches, or mobile phones, the workers knew the yellow December blooms meant that Christmas was coming, and they would soon have their one-week Christmas holiday vacation to spend with their families. The yellow wattle tree was a "marker."

"Markers" can be evidence of our accomplishments and in revealing what we are proud of. Trophies, medals, plaques, and special photographs often serve this purpose. "Markers" can also symbolize what we as couples have done well, such as find a way to handle our differences.

Every time Bobbye looks at a small lazy-Susan by the left side of the bathroom basin, she sees it as a "marker." Left-handed Britton had long objected to her placement of her contact lens solution bottles just where he would knock them over when he washed his face. Bobbye did not think it was important, and there was no room on the right side. After months of discussion, Britton bought the little lazy-Susan, and Bobbye agreed to put her bottles there still within easy reach. It was a compromise but an important "marker."

DAILY COUPLE TALK:
(EACH PERSON ANSWERS)
*What is a "marker" in your residence that celebrates
something you are proud of?*

CREATIVE USE OF CONFLICT

Failing to deal with conflict often sets couples on a downward spiral. They stop doing the loving behaviors that once pleased them both. They stop having honest, intimate conversations with plenty of self-disclosure. Whether the downward spiral leads to indifference, outright hostility, or looking for "greener pastures," the result is the same.

Either partner needs to step in at any point in the spiral and ask for conversation. If the other partner is willing, talk about goals and the kind of relationship you would like for the future. Keep the atmosphere light and celebrate what you still have in common. Make an appointment to discuss ONE of your issues.

Preceding the appointment ask each partner to write down all his/her feelings about that issue—just the feelings, not what each partner should or shouldn't do. When you meet, share the feelings, either verbally or by sharing each list. Then discuss the feelings. If a resolution to that one issue can be reached, discuss it. If not yet, tell three things you like about the other person and end on a positive note. Do this again and aim for compromise and resolution.

Trust, commitment, and being a team player are all qualities that take time to develop but can be quickly lost when conflicts stack up unaddressed. As you begin to face your conflicts and demonstrate a willingness to do so, it's amazing how quickly these qualities can return.

DAILY COUPLE TALK:
(EACH PARTNER ANSWERS)
On a scale from one to 10 (with 10 being highest), where would you put your personal ABILITY to handle conflict successfully? Your WILLINGNESS? Explain.

CREATIVE USE OF CONFLICT

A newspaper article about mental training for athletic competition has some curious comparisons to re-training ourselves to be more responsible arguers with those we love. All couples have to deal with the subject of disagreements, and training to improve our techniques for reaching a clear resolution may be one of our most important decisions.

Shane Murphy, former sports psychologist to the U.S. Olympic team, recommends starting with a mental rehearsal of what we want to happen. Just as skiers imagine perfect executions to "train" their bodies to perform on the slopes, partners can brainstorm about what they do in an argument and within each one's mind create a better procedure. If you tend to withdraw when an argument begins, picture yourself staying in the room and decide what you could say. If you are more likely to attack, soften the beginning words in your mind and imagine the effect that might have.

Put in lots of details, recommends Murphy to the athletes. Get a handle on what you do during the argument and picture what you want to do instead. Practice sharing your feelings; practice offering several ideas for resolution. In doing this you are replacing habits that may not be working with this partner. You are envisioning possible words and actions that might work. As Louis Pasteur once said, "Chance favors the prepared mind."

DAILY COUPLE TALK:
(EACH PERSON RESPONDS)
*What is one technique for resolving conflict
that would benefit you?*

CREATIVE USE OF CONFLICT

Working through conflicts not only strengthens the relationship, the "us," but it also increases the capacity for intimacy and closeness. It's like clearing out the storage shed of bitterness and resentment to make room for positive and friendly feelings. Also, working together draws on team skills, and this leads to increased confidence in the couple-team's abilities. It's a win/win/WIN situation.

Providing satisfaction for both partners is very different from the usual approach to a disagreement. When you are free to listen, and understand your partner's ideas about the disputed subject, you are already in a different place, physically and emotionally, from the typical desire to prove the other person wrong. Since the goal is different, so are the procedures. If you are seeking to improve the relationship as your goal, you simply have different options for what you choose to say and do.

Give the issue a specific name (to be sure you are both on the same page) and aim the whole conversation at exploring only that topic. Name and aim. No blame. Be honest about your feelings. No games or guessing. You are a team and couple growth is the goal. As a team decide how to resolve the issue.

DAILY COUPLE TALK:
(EACH PARTNER RESPONDS)
What to you is the most useful idea in this whole recommended process? Why?

CREATIVE USE OF CONFLICT

Fighting FOR Your Marriage describes itself as a "divorce prevention book." In the Introduction, it says, "Today marriages require more skill in negotiation between partners than ever before, because there is less that is automatically accepted and more that needs to be decided." That is certainly true, making all the more important a couple's problem-solving skills.

How you begin a conflict or a disagreement often determines the outcome. If one of the partners is yelling, swearing, or red-faced, it is already harder to move the confrontation to a level ground where reasonable ideas can be discussed. If one of the partners is determined to withdraw by turning his/her partner's concerns into a joke, that strategy only leads to defensiveness and anger. Negotiation is impossible. You might as well make an appointment for another time.

Outcomes matter also. Keep in mind that settling this issue needs to be handled fairly by both partners. Be aware not only of saying specifically what you want and think but of listening carefully to what the partner is saying. At the outcome of the argument both need to feel that they were heard and understood. Without this feeling, the issue is sure to come up again, just in a different form.

DAILY COUPLE TALK:
(BOTH PARTNERS PARTICIPATE)
Which is more important in a conflict? Personality?
Understanding? Structure? Winning? Explain.

MARRIAGE FOR THE EVERDAY

FOOIE

"Marriage is our last great hope

of growing up."

ERMA BOMBECK

FOOIE

FOOIE is an acrostic for Families of Origin Impact Everything. It means that sometimes we unexpectedly find ourselves adamantly defending some point of view that makes little sense in the present context.

For example, Bobbye, hearing a CD in her head with words that say "a good little girl eats everything on her plate," continues to eat past the time that she is full. It makes little sense, but the words on the CD come from far in the past and reach across the decades to influence present actions.

That is the power of our families of origin. It might be our attitudes toward money, or vacations, or holidays, or conflict, but the homes we grew up in can still pack a wallop when it comes to some of our ideas and actions.

One way to free ourselves from this hold is to acknowledge it. As long as we hear it play in our heads but do not recognize that it is there or that we are listening to it, we will be unable to make an appropriate choice in the present. Then we can tell our partner about it. Saying it out loud objectifies it and gives us a better chance to decide if that old action or attitude is needed in our present relationship.

DAILY COUPLE TALK:
(EACH PARTNER RESPONDS)
What is one value you brought from your family of origin? What is one value you would not want to bring to your present relationship?

FOOIE

The old story is told of a young husband who watched his partner prepare a ham for dinner. She cut one end off the ham and placed the rest in the oven. "Why did you cut the end off that ham?" he asked his partner. "I don't know," she said. "That's how my mother prepared a ham, and hers always tasted good."

The young husband later asked his mother-in-law why she cut the end off her ham, and she said, "That's how you cook a ham. It's the way my mother always did it. Don't you like my ham?" He did not let it rest. The next time he was with his wife's grandmother he asked her about it. She said, "When we were first married, my oven was very small, so I had to cut one end off the ham to make it fit." There was the logical reason for the action, but two generations had been doing it without knowing why.

Bobbye and Britton told this story at a Marriage Enrichment conference in Australia. The audience there had a similar story, only the meat was leg-of-lamb. Apparently, the story points out a common episode. We cook, argue, imitate, use mannerisms, choose products, or speak to children very much in the style used in the homes where we grew up.

If we are doing something annoying or disappointing with our partner, it may need a small adjustment to replace it with an action more in keeping with the new home, the new relationship, a different setting.

DAILY COUPLE TALK:
(EACH PARTNER PARTICIPATES)
What is one of your partner's mannerisms or habits
that reminds you of someone in his/her family-of-origin?

FOOIE

Often the conflict management skills we witnessed in our families of origin are the skills we try to apply long after we are out of that home. We were not taught these skills but we "caught" them as we saw them being used. Even if some of these skills worked, there are now two different adults working from two different sets of FOOIE. Those two adults need their own methods and techniques.

In reaction to watching his father storm out of the house when there was a disagreement with his mother, Britton early decided to confront issues head-on and work them out on the spot. The problem was that Bobbye had witnessed a different conflict style in growing up and had decided not to be involved in a disagreement. Until they developed a style that was right for them both, they were bound by past decisions that left them both frustrated and the issues unresolved.

A good time to discuss how disagreements might be handled is when neither partner is angry and when both know and can identify the conflict management styles each grew up with and adopted. Working together on this one issue lessens the impact of the past while it charts a new direction for the future.

DAILY COUPLE TALK:
(EACH PARTNER ANSWERS)
What did your mother do when she was angry?
What did your father do? What do you do?

FOOIE

Families of origin provided us with a sense of belonging. They defined our nationality and gave us our name and birthday. They endowed us with shape, eye color, hair color, height, talents, skills, and tendencies toward certain allergies and diseases. Genetics is so amazing that a baby can inherit his/her grandfather's ears and his/her great-uncle's curly red hair and freckles. Families of origin help us define our place in the world.

When a couple come together in marriage, they become a new family. Two heritages meld together and new bonds with new priorities are formed. A new sense of "belonging" needs to be established so that the individuals involved can feel centered in the world and secure about their joint plans for the future.

DAILY COUPLE TALK:

The following statements may help in the transition that all couples must make and re-make as they grow together.

1. We are a family who _____.

2. We are proud that we _____.

3. We believe in _____ and therefore plan to _____.

4. I came from a family who valued _____.

5. We want to _____ as we face our future together.

FOOIE

At a Mother's Day lunch of our big family, we were discussing important things that we learned from our mothers. Terry said his mother had once asked him, "Don't you want to be anything?" It was a particularly unmotivated time in Terry's life and the question forced him to examine his future. When he went back to college, he made A's in the very courses he had failed. It was a turning-point question for Terry, a question he never forgot. Today he is an engineer, a designer of rockets and missiles, and his mother's question set him on the course.

Many people remember a point when life took a new and better direction because of a situation or event that stirred self-examination and new choices. Couples do the same thing. Life flows along in the same old routines, sometimes even the same ruts, and the couples begin to accept patterns and habits just because they are there. Some of these patterns and habits are helpful; some could—and probably should—be discarded or amended.

Raising each other's awareness of what COULD BE is a simple step but a profound one. As long as one partner wants change in the relationship, there is the possibility. When both begin to participate in a new and innovative design, sparks begin to fly.

DAILY COUPLE TALK:
(EACH PARTNER ANSWERS)
What was an important decision you made as an adolescent? As a young adult? What couple decision would be helpful to you at this point in your life?

FOOIE

Eleanor Roosevelt once said, "Every day is a gift. That's why they call it the present." Families can "gift" their children with helpful skills and positive attitudes toward life, and if they do, those children often grow up to do the same thing for their children. The future grows more secure.

As the foundation of the home, couples need to set a standard both practical for daily commerce and far-reaching in social application. Each couple gets the chance to deal with the family-of-origin issues that did not go well for them in the past and to develop new ones for a happier future. If those issues are not dealt with, they tend to be a drag on our energies and attitudes, whether we acknowledge them or not. We are all products of the past, certainly, but we don't have to be prisoners of the past. Becoming aware of the claims of the past on our present actions and attitudes is often what it takes to help us see that we do have a choice. We do have an option.

Couples can help each other in this regard. But the great thing is to see that every day is a new opportunity to perfect our "us," our relationship, our "gift" to the future. When we can feel that we are truly collaborating with each other, as free as possible from past restraints and pain, we are contributing to making the "present" a better place.

DAILY COUPLE TALK:
(EACH PERSON RESPONDS)
*When you were growing up, what family
issues did you encounter about commitment?
About communication? About conflict?
Any changes you want to make for the two of you?*

FOOIE

One September in their monthly Marriage Enrichment Group (MEG) the Woods learned that Christmas was to be the subject for the evening. The exercise included questions such as "When does the Christmas spirit start for you?" and "How do you like to spend Christmas Eve?"

In discussing the subject Britton and Bobbye discovered a great deal of frustration in how they celebrated the Christmas holidays. Bobbye put the tree up the day after Thanksgiving. She baked, decorated, and shopped for presents. That's what her mother had done. Britton did nothing to help until Christmas Eve day, when he bought a few presents and visited someone in the hospital. That is what his parents had done. Bobbye resented doing all the work in getting ready for Christmas; Britton thought she wanted to do it all herself, if he thought about it at all.

In less than 30 minutes of sharing their feelings about it, they discovered that they had allowed FOOIE to create the script they had been following. They divided up the tasks that HAD to be done; they left off the ones that neither really cared about; and they planned to shop and put up the Christmas tree together. It not only made the next Christmas season more enjoyable but it gave their "us" a needed boost when they made the present more important than the past.

DAILY COUPLE TALK:
(EACH PARTNER RESPONDS)
What is one thing you would like to change about your current holiday celebrations?

FOOIE

To get in touch with some of your attitudes and preferences about food preparation, tenderness, doing laundry, holiday traditions, conflict, or hobbies, do the following exercise and share it with your partner.

Pick a house in which you partially grew up (most families move at least once while their children are growing up). Picture yourself there at a specific age, and answer the following questions:

1. What was your neighborhood like?

2. Which room in your house felt especially warm and welcoming to you and why?

3. Where did the family eat and who did the cooking?

4. How were chores handled in that house?

5. How was affection expressed in that house?

6. How was conflict handled in that house?

7. Which holidays had celebrations and what did the family do? Did you have a favorite? Why?

When you have answered these questions, choose one answer that is very different from your partner's answer and discuss it further.

DAILY COUPLE TALK:
(EACH ONE PARTICIPATES)
What did you learn from this exercise?

FOOIE

At a Marriage Enrichment Group Date Night, a couple announced that after a conversation together about FOOIE they had had an "aha" moment. The husband reported a discovery that as the youngest of four boys he grew up with brothers always looking out for him, siblings who did the major part of domestic chores, and a family who catered to him because he was the youngest. Now as an adult he was finally seeing that replicating those attitudes with his partner was not especially appropriate. The partner was very excited about his discovery.

Oldest and only children can grow up to be self-reliant and even bossy, very confident that their way is "right." They are basically rule-keepers, but also can be adventurous. The same can be true for the first boy in the family, if girls were born first.

Middle children often grow skillful at negotiation and bargaining. They can be adept at understanding other people's motivations and make good committee members. Some middle children blame their problems on their birth order and having to share everything—hand-me-down clothes, for example—in growing up. Youngest children can be charming and good performers, adept at creating plans for entertainment of others. They tend to be confident and able to tackle difficult projects. Some, like the young husband, prefer to "just let things happen" rather than make plans.

DAILY COUPLE TALK:
(EACH PARTNER RESPONDS)
What was your birth order in your family-of-origin? Has that mattered in any way in your adult life?

FOOIE

The statement made by many teen-agers that is supposed to end an argument with their friends is "I was just raised that way." Family-of-origin is the trump card that will settle the dispute. It cannot be argued with because it claims that the person involved is being loyal to a much higher power and has no need for another point of view.

How we were "raised" is a rather subjective experience. Often siblings cannot even agree on the same experience, viewing it from memory of a particular time and set of feelings on that day. Yet many people claim that the family we grew up in has programmed us to look at life in a certain way and that is that.

As the late Erma Bombeck said, "Marriage is our last great hope of growing up." Marriage offers us new opportunities to change some of our habits, some of our biases, and some of our views about various subjects. As we are daily confronted with a partner who grew up a different way, we are challenged to review and perhaps revise some of our ideas. Some of those ideas and beliefs are essential to our sense of self; we will decide we should not abandon them no matter what someone else thinks. Some grow amusing as we try to defend or explain them to someone else.

As in marriage we move toward shared power, cooperation, and attention to feelings, we are also moving toward a new maturity.

DAILY COUPLE TALK:
(EACH ONE PARTICIPATES)
Do you agree or disagree with Erma Bombeck's statement? Why?

FOOIE

Looking through the eyes of the media, we see a world torn by violence, terrorism, and war. For too many families this also can be the interior picture of their home life, seldom reported unless it is so severe that there must be an intervention by police or an overworked social service agency. Often society does not know until some egregious crime is committed, and an investigation of the perpetrator reveals the family he/she grew up in or the damaged relationships he/she has had.

Looking through the eyes of love, couples can avoid the behavior that so endangers our families, and by extension our neighbors, schools, and even churches. Learning to fight fairly and responsibly is a skill that must start with the couple.

Wanting to win an argument, NO MATTER HOW, dooms the outcome from the start. There can be no compromise or give-and-take if one intimidates or frightens the other. Fighting by rules the couple has decided on together gives some guidelines during high emotions.

The good news is that no matter what kind of families couples came from, learning to fight fairly equips the new family with skills that directly influence the future.

DAILY COUPLE TALK:
(EACH PARTNER PARTICIPATES)
The couple is the epicenter of the family. What physical health habits do you believe need to be passed on? What relational habits?

FOOIE

Comparison, they say, is the thief of joy. Whatever kind of family you came from and whatever worked well for the couple in that family, it is a new relationship now with two different adults. Trying to force-feed the habits and procedures remembered or a private determination NOT to repeat those habits and procedures—either one will not work.

If one family-of-origin system worked well and replicating it seems important to the partner from that home, remember that the current partner knew nothing about that system and furthermore came from a different system. Techniques that seemed dependable and easy will now have to be explained and discussed as to their current viability. Everything else is fantasy. If the family-of-origin system was dysfunctional, the same is still true. One partner must not assume that the other will be doing the hurtful things of the past. Both partners have to know what happened in the original family and help each other be on guard. Frank discussions are critical. Both must be in the loop.

Both partners must take stock of where THEY are, inventory THEIR strengths, define THEIR goals, and figure out how to work TOGETHER to defeat the "thief of joy."

DAILY COUPLE TALK:
(EACH PARTNER ANSWERS)
When you were growing up, who was your favorite relative and why? Who was your least favorite relative and why?

FOOIE

Dr. David Olson, formerly of the University of Minnesota, is the designer of the helpful pre-marital inventory called Prepare and Enrich. Thousands of couples have used this on-line tool over the years, as they move through engagement and toward marriage. Dr. Olson sets the couple's answers into two basic categories: Strengths (for the areas in which they have a high agreement) and Growth Areas (for the answers that reveal limited agreement). For example, if the inventory reveals one person is not sure that he/she wants children and one is looking forward to a big family, frank discussion is needed.

One piece of advice Dr. Olson gives to couples is to separate from the family-of origin as early as possible. This differentiation, as it is called, can be a tricky separation, and one that needs more discussion. The family-of-origin for both partners can become an important resource, especially if there are children or financial arrangements involved. However, clear boundaries need to be established, and to keep families-of-origin from becoming a source of conflict, couples have to declare in many ways that the new top priority and commitment is to the marital partner. This is the Boot Camp for future behavior.

DAILY COUPLE TALK:
(EACH PARTNER RESPONDS)
In what way(s) have each of your families-of-origin been a help to you? In what way(s) have you felt an unexpected intrusion?

FOOIE

Jane was raised as the only child. Her parents were older when she was born, and they wanted her to have every advantage they could give. A fund was established for her college tuition by the time she was three. Her parents came to all her sporting events as she grew up and never missed her piano recitals, church youth choir performances, or school honors programs. Jane had many friends and all her relatives praised her accomplishments.

Jonah grew up with two younger brothers raised by a single-mom. He did not know his father, because he lived in another state and had a new family. As a boy, it was clear that Jonah was a talented athlete; by high school he was a basketball star. He wished that his mother and his brothers could see some of his games, but she had to work at night and they did not like sports. Jonah eventually won a scholarship to a Division II school. He was disappointed to learn that he was not good enough for the NBA but by then he had met Jane.

Jane and Jonah met at the end of their junior year in college. Sparks flew immediately. They also discovered that they liked the same music, shared the same faith, and had many of the same ambitions. They married two days after graduation. They both went to work in Jane's uncle's business. They moved into a house in Jane's old neighborhood that her parents bought for them while they were on their honeymoon.

DAILY COUPLE TALK:
(EACH PERSON ANSWERS)
If you were good friends of this couple, what family-of-origin issues would you suggest they address? What advice would you offer for their relationship?

FOOIE

Shakespeare's <u>Hamlet</u> is the tragic story of family-of-origin issues on steroids. In the story Hamlet and Ophelia are in love, but before they can get married, like many young men today, Hamlet must complete his university training. On his return to the court in Denmark for his Christmas break, Hamlet learns from a ghostly appearance that his father the king had really been murdered by Hamlet's uncle, now king. Hamlet's mother Gertrude is now married to the new king, after a whirlwind romance.

Ophelia's father, a court official, tries to help, but he is accidentally killed by Hamlet. This brings Ophelia's brother home from his university breathing fire against his former buddy Hamlet. The family intrigues and pressures become so complicated for the lovers that Ophelia goes mad and kills herself. Deceptions and misunderstandings eventually lead to the deaths of all family members, including Hamlet.

Not many families involve each other in quite such dramatic circumstances, but it does point out the need for a couple to be very clear very early about their priorities. Forming a new family means forming new loyalties. Being drawn into former family feuds, grudges, and past mistakes is never helpful to a couple trying to establish a healthy relationship for themselves. The play would have been much less tragic (and much shorter) if Hamlet had recognized that FOOIE was at work and discussed it with Ophelia.

DAILY COUPLE TALK:
(EACH PARTNER RESPONDS)
How have you as a couple dealt with FOOIE issues?

FOOIE

Ernie Pyle was a famous WWII American war correspondent who gave front-line reports to an anxious country. He once said, "I love the Infantry because they are the underdogs. They are the mud—rain—frost—and wind boys. They have no comforts, and they even learn to live without the necessities. And in the end they're the guys that wars cannot be won without."

Occasionally Britton and Bobbye get asked how they have made it for 60 years of marriage. But one evening they responded to a serious question about what was the "secret" to a long-term relationship.

Bobbye said: I think I have finally learned to say straight-out what I feel and want. It has been an education for me. I did not grow up in a family that valued straight talk. Those family-of-origin issues had to be un-learned before I could re-learn some more effective styles of speaking for myself. It has taken many years to break old habits, but in the end it was what, as Ernie Pyle said, "won" the war against the many enemies of couple closeness. Britton said: I think the "secret" is listening. I need to hear what the most important person to me is saying. I need to be able to respond in a quality manner. I need to give evidence that I am emotionally present. Listening is saying to your partner that he/she is valued.

These two qualities are probably "underdogs" in the world of marriage education. But for the Woods they have made a big difference.

DAILY COUPLE TALK:
EACH PARTNER ANSWERS)
*What might be other "secrets" to a
long-term marriage relationship?*

FOOIE

The 2016 Rio Olympics were a high moment in athletic competition. They opened amid concerns about security, water, the Zika virus, terrorism, and cost overruns. They closed with an impressive and colorful ceremony, after more than two weeks of great performances and Golden Moments.

Marriage also has its Golden Moments that have nothing to do with anniversaries or Valentine's Day. One such Golden Moment happened to Britton. The Woods had dealt together with their different "training programs" regarding conflict that happened in their families-of-origin. They both knew that one of Britton's models was to watch his father stomp out of the house when he was angry. One of his sisters developed a brain tumor, and her siblings were all gathered in her Albuquerque apartment to plan how to help her. When one sister disagreed with something Britton was proposing, he got up and stomped to the door. Halfway there he recognized that he was following an old model, turned around with the confidence that he now had a different option, and sat back down. The discussion continued.

That episode for Britton was a Golden Moment. He saw how easily one could fall into an old pattern and short circuit any profitable outcome. His analysis and earlier discussion with Bobbye helped him choose a new option.

DAILY COUPLE TALK:
(EACH PARTNER RESPONDS)
*What is a Golden Moment you have
shared with your partner?*

FOOIE

Several years ago on a cruise Bobbye and Britton heard a speaker recounting the power of FOOIE (Families-of-Origin Impact Everything). The speaker told about playing football in junior high and high school because that was what his father wanted him to do.

In college he majored in business, as his father directed, and specialized in an Oil and Gas degree because his father convinced him that was the fastest way to make money. Not until he was an adult, twice married, and a father himself that he finally made his own choices.

The speaker ended his talk by telling that at one critical point in his decision-making, he wrote a letter to his dead father and dropped it into the sea from a ship. The action was designed to symbolically limit the father's expectations and free him to feel good about his own choices. He then went on to say that we all in one way or another have felt the influences of the past. Sometimes those influences are so heavy that we feel weighed down as though we are letting someone down whom we have loved. The speaker closed by suggesting to his audience that if there is something or someone from our past who has power over us, we write about it on a piece of paper and drop it overboard. In this way we are taking charge of ourselves and choosing to be released.

DAILY COUPLE TALK:
(EACH PERSON ANSWERS)
What is one thing from your past that you would like to be released from? How can you help each other to bring this about?

FOOIE

At a teacher in-service meeting, Bobbye once heard a speaker list the top 15 things people say they are afraid of. Five of the top six are all things couples deal with in marriage. No wonder so many couples struggle to find and feel happiness and success. Many people brought the fears with them to marriage; many still struggle daily to deal with them

Fear of public speaking is number one. Next in order are making mistakes, failure, disapproval, rejection, and angry people. Fears can be inhibiting in a close relationship. They can keep us from risking failure or rejection, for example, so that we lack spontaneity or creativity.

No Single Thread was the name of a book about the results of a research project studying happy families and what made them that way. The researchers discovered that there was no one quality that every family had to possess in order to be happy, thus the book's title. The closest they came was to identify praise as the quality many of the researched families used. The families loved each other, said so often, and gave praise freely both directly and indirectly when speaking to others.

Praise is a simple antidote to fear. Whatever happened to us before we met our partner, whatever kind of home environment we grew up in, finding amiable and appreciative words and actions given to us by someone we love makes the world a friendlier and less fearful place.

DAILY COUPLE TALK:
(EACH PARTNER RESPONDS)
Give your partner some amiable and appreciative words. Even if he/she is not troubled by the list of most common fears, the words will be welcome.

FOOIE

One spring morning Bobbye was working in a backyard flower bed when to her astonishment, a grey fox walked by. He did not see her because his focus was on a rock ledge on which sat a big green metal lizard, a thoughtful gift from daughter Carol and son-in-law Dale. The fox leaped upon the lizard, then sat down on the ledge. Bobbye imagined that he might be telling himself, "I knew it wasn't real all the time."

The whole scene was astonishing: a grey fox in the city walking in a fenced back yard and stalking a metal lizard.

Astonishing marital dramas can also stir feelings. Bobbye's parents were married during the period now called by historians The Great Depression. Their wedding rings were plain and inexpensive. But on one anniversary after many years of marriage, Bobbye's mother gave her father a new wedding ring, one with diamonds making a strong and visible statement. She gave it to him in the bedroom of his parent's farmhouse, and he fell back onto the bed in utter astonishment. A hard-working man all his life, he could not believe such a thoughtful and commemorative surprise.

Like the sudden appearance of the grey fox and the new wedding ring, surprises in families can occur at unexpected moments. Our task is to keep an open mind to be appreciative when they happen.

DAILY COUPLE TALK:
(EACH PARTNER ANSWERS)
What was an "astonishing surprise"
experienced in your family-of-origin?

FOOIE

Which of the following is the most important quality in a person: good looks, a sense of humor, loyalty, a desire for adventure, or talent? Why?

The discussion today merely expresses opinions of the mind and of the heart. There are no right or wrong answers, no competition, no minefields of the past, just two friends exchanging ideas and feelings that reveal personality.

How great holidays could be that we spend with our families-of-origin if all conversations could proceed in exactly this relaxed manner of acceptance and understanding. Unfortunately there seems to be some relative who is in competition with someone else and tries to enlist others to take sides. Someone wants to tell secrets and to extract vows of secrecy from others. Old stories designed to embarrass someone may be told and retold. In other words, the typical family gathering for a holiday meal or visit can bring out old issues never satisfactorily resolved.

Families-of-origin can be wonderful. They can give solid support when we need it, offer wise counsel, and share wholeheartedly in our celebrations. That they can sometimes be complicated and perplexing can also be true. But when we can reduce our own holiday expectations and enlist our partner in helping to keep conversations on a relaxed and friendly level, we are moving toward acceptance and understanding.

DAILY COUPLE TALK:
(EACH PERSON PARTICIPATES)
Who is the most eccentric person you have met in your partner's family-of-origin? The most original? The funniest? The sweetest?

FOOIE

At a marriage education meeting Bobbye and Britton once met a young wife struggling with life's typical energy-drainers—work, worry, multiple demands on time, and little perceived support from her partner. But her biggest concern was that she had no models for maintaining a long-term marriage relationship. Her parents had divorced at her birth; no relatives she had ever lived with and none of her friends had witnessed a long-term relationship.

She remembered that she had once visited her great-grandparents and had been very touched by the fact that they had held hands with each other in her presence. As a girl she had mentally registered this scene as one she could aspire to someday, but she had few ideas and no models for achieving this ideal. This young woman was a sad commentary on too many modern marriages. Too few are equipped to handle the very thing they most need.

How do couples reach this goal of a long-term relationship such as marriage? One answer is surprisingly simple: take a careful look at what you do individually to make this happen. Give your actions as thorough an inspection as you would give your checkbook for a record of monthly expenditures before making a budget. Listen to how you talk to your partner and listen to how he/she talks to you. If there are needed changes, start making them. Then discuss together the goal of achieving longevity. You might just be on the brink of some exciting discoveries.

DAILY COUPLE TALK:
(EACH PARTNER RESPONDS)
*What does this young woman need
to know about marriage?*

FOOIE

After Bobbye graduated from college, she noticed that her parents had a new car and both were wearing new clothes and shoes. That's all; she just noticed. As the Talmud observes, "We do not see things as they are. We see them as we are." Much later (and thankfully with more maturity) she was astonished to realize that her school-teacher parents had sacrificed for her education. And they had never said a word about it.

Maturity can bring insights into our past, often enabling us to view it with generosity and gratitude, and the same can be true of marriage, when we can let go of past resentments. But just as important is becoming capable of noticing new skills and abilities in ourselves—both personally and as a couple— that can bring pride and satisfaction. For those couples committed to growth, some of those abilities might be:

1. A broader perspective on beauty in life

2. A stronger will to be fair and to avoid getting even

3. A relieving effort to give up the need to "win" all disputes

4. A renewed interest in giving and receiving affection

5. A growing desire to be an encourager for each other's goals and desires

DAILY COUPLE TALK:
(EACH PARTNER RESPONDS)
Of the list above, explain two items
that are important to you.

FOOIE

For many years Britton was a single adult minister in a large church. He was often surprised to hear single women, both never-married and formerly married say things like "when I get married, I am going to let my husband be in charge." Britton found this ironic in that it was the wife-to-be who was going to "let" the husband-yet-to-be-named be in charge. This unrealistic view of how marriage is going to be often is carried into the marriage itself, brought from other experiences or from the family-of-origin.

In reality, neither spouse needs to be "in charge" of the other. From a faith perspective, both need to be submissive to God and on equal ground with each other. It seems impractical that one human being can assume responsibility for another in every decision.

What often takes place in a relationship is the attempt to live an idealized fantasy from earlier in our lives about how a marriage "should be." It is so much smarter to learn together from situation to situation about what feels right for THIS relationship. David Mace once said that trying to resolve all issues before marriage was like learning to swim on a piano bench. You just have to be in the water and in the relationship before some skills and tasks can be accomplished or before you even realize that you need them. Many long-term relationships see quite a few things differently than when they first married.

DAILY COUPLE TALK:
(EACH PERSON PARTICIPATES)
What are some expectations you had earlier as to how your marriage would look? As you share, see what can realistically be valid for your relationship now.

FOOIE

Former President Harry Truman supposedly had a plaque on his desk saying, "The Buck Stops Here." It was to remind him of the power (and the responsibility) of the Oval Office. That reminder of power and responsibility can be true of families as well.

Our morning newspaper had a long picture article about local dancers performing with sports' teams; along with their pictures were the answers to a set of questions such as "Who is one of your heroes?" More than half answered "my parents." They spoke with glowing compliments of things like courage, patience, a work ethic, and support of children's involvement with sports and dance. Those qualities demonstrated daily in the family were "heroic," according to the children.

All of us, even those long out of the households where we grew up, act (and react) every day according to what we experienced in those formative homes. We can mimic, hold opinions, repeat ideals, celebrate, demonstrate habits, join faith-based organizations, and use certain products according to behavior witnessed and choices made from long ago. Families-of-origin are important influences and hold much power.

DAILY COUPLE TALK:
(EACH PERSON ANSWERS)
Share an admirable belief or action that one of your parents has passed on to you.

FOOIE

The Sandwich Generation is a term some people use to describe the situation when a couple has aging parents that require care, but their children are not yet raised and out of the house. The couple feels "eaten on" from both sides, more than likely just when careers are also demanding.

Bobbye had a conversation about this with a fifty-something friend very concerned about her mother's worsening Alzheimer's. The stepfather is currently the caretaker but at 86 his is a difficult position, and neither of them want to consider Assisted Living arrangements. One of the friend's two daughters is a senior in a private high school and the other is in college. The friend feels nibbled on from both sides of the generations, but it's "what you do," she says.

Couple strengths are needed during specialized stressful family periods such as the Sandwich Generation. There are of course no one-size-fits-all strengths for couples, but there is one help that gets needy couples through. That is the healing power of touch. When one partner's hand reaches for the other partner's, when one partner's head rests comfortably on the other's shoulder, when warm embraces are freely exchanged, when both snuggle up together drowsy at the end of a long day—those tender touches have the power to restore flagging energy and will. They keep couples connected at an emotional level that defies stress.

DAILY COUPLE TALK:
(EACH PARTNER RESPONDS)
Name three of your couple strengths that you rely on.

FOOIE

At a family gathering during the Christmas holidays one year, daughter Leigh Ann asked Bobbye and Britton to share some of their personal history. They complied. Then Bobbye asked the grandchildren and their guests to describe in one word their impressions of THIS family. The answers were interesting—connected, quirky, accepting, to name a few but no more interesting than any other family. All families make impressions on the generations that grow up with them, and all families can profit from knowing what some of those impressions are.

Siblings that are separated or estranged from each other or the families that raised them often have strong feelings about what happened in the family-of-origin. Those feelings often impact their current relationships, carrying forward some of the same interactions that produced the bitterness or estrangement. As long as those persons choose not to think about the impact of the family-of-origin, they are likely to repeat some of those same objectionable interactions.

It can be liberating to face and review some of the family events of our growing-up years. In this way we can also learn to recognize our own less-than-ideal actions and make any changes that might be helpful to the over-all health of our current family.

❍❍

DAILY COUPLE TALK:
(EACH PERSON PARTICIPATES
What is one remembered family-of-origin event that was significant to you?

FOOIE

We do not get to choose the families we were born into. Whatever the circumstances of our family-of-origin backgrounds, an ancient Middle Eastern statement suggests two ways to deal with those circumstances:

- 🐛 Life is full of froth and bubble,

- 🐛 Two things stand like stone:

- 🐛 Kindness in another's trouble,

- 🐛 Courage in our own.

Whatever troubling legacies came with us from the past, facing them with kindness and courage can be a liberation by shining a different light on the legacy. Bobbye was once surprised to learn that her father had been only 30 years old and a veteran of WWII when he was very free to correct her with a belt. It allowed her to see the situation in a different light and to understand that youth can be prone to hasty actions it may later regret. Facing the situation with courage enabled her to avoid imposing that past situation on present circumstances. Looking at it with kindness added new and more charitable tones to a remembered terrifying childhood time. Kindness and courage and the support from an understanding partner can set the future on a steadier course.

DAILY COUPLE TALK:
(EACH PARTNER RESPONDS)
What is an act of either kindness or courage that you have appreciated in your partner?

FOOIE

At the monthly MEG Date Night one Friday Bobbye and Britton were emphasizing the power of FOOIE. Couples doing an exercise together on the subject were to draw one of the houses they grew up in and answer some questions about them, such as, "what room in that house felt especially welcoming to remember" and "what room in that house felt distant, even unpleasant."

One couple was not participating and appeared distressed, so Bobbye tried to help. The young husband said that he could not face the memories from the house of his youth. He did not even want to hear his partner's memories, so painful were his.

Children who grow up hearing fairy stories and folk tales learn a powerful fact early: for every glass slipper, awakening kiss, and pot of gold, there are also trolls, malevolent giants, and wicked stepmothers. Learning to face the scary forces within and without is part of growing up. If we can do it in the safety and warmth of an early supportive environment, great. If we can't, the task is still ours. And when we accomplish it, it frees us to participate more fully in our current relationships and to give ourselves more trustingly to our partner. Families-of-origin have a powerful effect on emotions, but an understanding partner does as well, and relying on the partner to help us face past difficulties sets the future on a steadier course.

DAILY COUPLE TALK:
(EACH PARTNER RESPONDS)
In a house you grew up in, what was a warm and welcoming room you remember? Why was that so?

FOOIE

We are all products of our past. How could it be otherwise? But we do not have to be prisoners of the past, unless we choose to. Getting free from the limitations of the past, in fact, is a worthwhile task and one that can take many years to accomplish. Whether it is a family-of-origin issue or a painful legacy of a past relationship, getting free from the insidious intrusions that mysteriously hamper our daily interactions needs to be attempted in order to allow us to give our best efforts to our most important relationships.

One way to get free from the claims of the past is to FACE them steadfastly. In fact unless we do admit that they are likely to have an influence on us, we cannot get a handle on what to do about them because the awareness of their claims is avoided. A second way to get free is to DECIDE that a change needs to be made for maximum health. When that decision is made, the energy to begin—and to continue--often comes with it. Finally, consistently and intentionally MAKE EFFORTS toward change.

As Richard Rohr has said, let go of what you don't need and who you don't want to be. Only then will you find that the place where you are is more than enough.

DAILY COUPLE TALK:
(EACH PERSON PARTICIPATES)
Who is someone your partner admires?
Why do you think this is true?

MARRIAGE FOR THE EVERDAY

BOBBYE AND BRITTON WOOD

FRIENDS AND LOVERS

"Love is a many-splendored thing"

FRIENDS AND LOVERS

When you got married, you thought of your love as full and complete, rather like the circle of your wedding rings. Inside the circle were all the things you liked about each other and were attracted to. At the edge of the circle were all the necessary intersections with the world (extended family, job, church, friends, etc.). Those intersections let in more knowledge and information about your partner, and the joyful little circle was complete.

At time passes, the circle of love should expand and grow bigger, as more and more knowledge about your partner confirms the reasons you fell in love in the first place. How can more couples enlarge their circle and claim more rewards?

A TV commercial for a ring might offer some advice. The ring is made of two hearts that stand for Best Friends and Lovers. Best friends talk to each other candidly, tell each other secrets and keep confidences, play and have fun together, and support each other's interests. Lovers continue to find ways to give pleasure and affection to each other. They snuggle together in the physical and emotional intimacy that marks life's greatest human relationship. Continuing over time to be both Best Friends and Lovers automatically enlarges the circle and makes you wonder after several years together how you ever thought the little circle of love felt at your wedding was enough.

DAILY COUPLE TALK:
(EACH PARTNER RESPONDS)
What is one thing you value in a friendship? What is one thing you want to give as a lover?

FRIENDS AND LOVERS

A friend is a safe haven, a companion in life, a strong and dependable support. A friend is someone we can count on. Many best friends are married.

Some couples start out as friends but walls of conflict, un-addressed and unresolved, drive them apart. Other couples become indifferent over time as neglected opportunities for intimate conversation rob them of the friendship they once had. Some couples spend so little time together that they become like assigned roommates in a college dorm, polite to each other but preferring the company of others.

Making time to maintain friendship, to talk, play, and plan together as a couple, is paramount to a growing relationship. Tell stories to each other, laugh, share feelings, and relax. Talk about books you have read, movies you like, concerts you went to, and board games you like to play. Discuss current events or what you have seen on Facebook. In short, the conversation with your partner should be very much like conversations with other good friends. The difference is that you do it more often and with a tenacious determination. Lose this special quality of being good friends and you begin to lose the easy intimacy that defines happy couples.

DAILY COUPLE TALK:
(EACH PERSON PARTICIPATES)
Quality time together is important to every close relationship, including friendship.
What could be one helpful way to get more quality time together into your schedule?

FRIENDS AND LOVERS

Part of the inspiring Soldier's Creed says "I will always place the mission first. I will never accept defeat. I will never quit. I will never leave a fallen comrade." That's the kind of "I've got your back" dedication that couples have who are best friends.

Friendship for couples helps define their "mission"— growth:

❦ In understanding each other

❦ In building a unique concept of "us-ness" that shows the quality and the boundaries of the relationship

❦ In learning and practicing the skills of communication and conflict resolution that keep the relationship balanced and free from stress

Friendship for couples causes them to log enough time together to build trust. Trust keeps the fires of intimacy burning by forging confidence that the partner is firmly on your side and won't give up in difficult times. Trust maintains the pleasure and joy that are the hallmarks of every healthy couple. Mutual trust and growth cannot be defeated.

DAILY COUPLE TALK:
(EACH PARTNER ANSWERS)
Who were your good friends in growing up? What did you learn from them? Where are they today?

FRIENDS AND LOVERS

Friends and lovers both prosper under words of encouragement and kindness. Harsh or sarcastic words will NOT promote growth or a strong "us." They are much like Performance Enhancing Drugs (PEDs) that may seem to athletes a quick solution for strength and success. They are not, as many athletes can testify who have experienced suspensions, loss of reputation, loss of money ranging up to the millions, and even loss of Hall of Fame possibilities in their sport.

Marital PEDs (that sound like they might work but don't):

1. "Just do what I say." Unless you are a drill sergeant speaking to new recruits, this one is a high-risk statement. It is sometimes accompanied by a push or a grab. It announces control.

2. "I'd hate to be (so sloppy, so stupid, so stingy, such a loser, so much like your mother)." This one not only puts the partner down but implies that the speaker is one-up in importance.

3. "If you love me, you will _____." This conditional statement not only puts getting one's way above anything else, but unfairly asks the partner to endorse it as a test of affection.

Just as using PEDs is a risk for athletes, so is it in marriage. If growth and closeness are couple goals, the risk is not worth it.

DAILY COUPLE TALK:
(EACH PARTNER RESPONDS)
What are some other PEDs that hinder progress as friends and lovers?

FRIENDS AND LOVERS

PART 1

Like Yoda of "Star Wars," Dr. David Mace was a mentor to many Luke Skywalkers. His early work, along with his wife Vera, established many marital principles designed to enrich the average couple. For their efforts the United Nations recognized them with a special award during its Year of the Family. The Maces' work targeted those couples who felt that they already had a good relationship but were looking for ways to make it better.

The Maces often said they believed there would be no peace in the world until there was peace in the home. Toward this end they organized their work around three major ideas.

The first idea had to do with commitment. They recommended a goal of becoming what they called "CLOSE COMPANIONS," good friends who have logged time together but want the intimacy and connectedness that so easily slips away under the pressures and routines of life. "Close Companions" use practical skills of relating to grow personally and as a couple. "Close Companions" never consider themselves too old, too tired, too busy, or too stressed to work at keeping the values of friendship alive and well.

DAILY COUPLE TALK:
(EACH PERSON PARTICIPATES)
What values should "Close Companions" hold that could lead them to peace?

FRIENDS AND LOVERS

PART 2

The second idea introduced and promoted by the Maces was the necessity of effective couple talking and listening skills which they called COUPLE DIALOGUE. It is a simple verbal exchange, recommended to be practiced every day. Several generations of Luke Skywalkers credit Couple Dialogue with keeping their relationship growing and their home peaceful no matter what is happening around them. There is no way to stay "Close Companions," many couples testify, without staying current by means of conversation and a healthy exchange of ideas. Although the Maces never considered themselves counselors, sometimes at meetings and retreats they became coaches for couples whose publicly demonstrated talking and listening skills were leading toward damage to the relationship. The ideals of "Close Companions" were too important not to use every opportunity to build understanding.

The Maces' third idea was the novel use of SHARING FEELINGS in a couple argument. Often emotions are a part of the subject under dispute, and not including them only shuts out a way to reach real understanding. Sharing feelings unexpectedly produces a different and calmer atmosphere during a quarrel, even when there is not agreement. Sharing feelings moves the whole process of argument to a speedier and more peaceful resolution.

DAILY COUPLE TALK:
(EACH PARTNER RESPONDS)
If you were writing a book about peace in the world, what are some ideas you would include?

FRIENDS AND LOVERS

It was Benjamin Franklin who observed that "an ounce of prevention is worth a pound of cure." Franklin never heard of a delete button, but most modern partners devoutly wish they could erase some of the things said or done to each other in a not-so-loving moment. "Pounds of cure" do work, but how much less trouble (and sometimes expense) for couples to judiciously value the "ounce of prevention."

One preventive "ounce" is the Couple Dialogue. Just a 15-minute-a-day conversation can keep partners current with each other's events, schedule, and feelings. If there are relational issues that can't be dealt with at this time, setting an appointment to deal with them can free both partners from worrying about them. The simple Couple Dialogue is a relational-fitness "ounce."

Another "ounce of prevention" is steadfastly clinging to roles of Friend and Lover. If either of these roles has slipped a bit under pressures of job demands and/or raising a family, returning to the pleasurable tasks of Good Friend and Affectionate Lover can set the relationship on what feels like a new and exciting course. Don't wait to take action when either partner feels stressed or unhappy. Decide together what you want and if possible help each other achieve those desires. Quite simply, in relationships "ounces" are more valuable than "pounds."

DAILY COUPLE TALK:
(EACH PARTNER RESPONDS)
What is one "ounce of prevention" that you would choose to explore?

FRIENDS AND LOVERS

Growing relationships to be sturdy, productive, and self-sustaining is full of wonderful surprises. Just when a partner feels that he/she knows the other really well and education is nearly complete, the partner can cause astonishment with something—an unheard story, a gentle and unexpected caress, a revelation of depths of passion. The world of a thriving relationship challenges us with its energy and endless supply of new information.

The sequoia tree in the western part of the United States manufactures propagating seeds that are so protected by an impenetrable shell that new trees are unlikely to happen. The shell simply cannot be opened. But living in the forest with the sequoias is one species of squirrel that has exceptionally sharp front teeth. That squirrel loves those sequoia seeds. When it opens the shell, out comes enough seeds both to feed the squirrel and to insure the continuation of new sequoias. It is a wonderful and funny fact of nature, but no more wonderful than the surprising facts that friends and lovers enjoy when they stay committed to each other over time.

That friends can stay close over the years is not surprising. The surprising thing is staying lovers, with as much or more interest in physical contact as when the relationship was young. Not time's ravages, not health issues, not tiring schedules, not children's demands can permanently change the need to give and to receive physical affection.

DAILY COUPLE TALK:
(EACH PERSON ANSWERS)
What is a surprise about your relationship that you discovered recently?

FRIENDS AND LOVERS

Valuing romance and passion in your relationship throughout marriage not only is a pleasure to both partners but is a benefit to the extended family.

Gathered for a beach vacation, the Wood family one evening had dinner at a restaurant advertising that it was the "best place to watch the sunset." Later in the sun's dying rays some of the family stood on a dock to take commemorative pictures. Granddaughter Hannah had some photography plans in mind and arranged the family accordingly. When it was Bobbye and Britton's turn, she wanted them to stand with their arms around each other silhouetted in the red sky. "Now, kiss!" she ordered, as though it was the most natural position she could imagine.

Staying enthusiastic lovers who value romance is comparable in some ways to Cooking 101 for busy partners. Part of mealtime success is BEING PREPARED and having the right ingredients on hand. With a well-stocked pantry, you have the makings of a healthy meal even if your day left no time for baking or concocting a fancy dessert. So with romance. With plenty of conversation-for-two, courtesy, shared duties, and laughter stocking your relational pantry, you can have a delicious and nutrient-rich meal ready quickly.

DAILY COUPLE TALK:
(EACH PERSON PARTICIPATES)
On a scale of 1-10 (with 10 being highest),
how much do you value romance in your relationship?
How much do you value passion? Explain.

FRIENDS AND LOVERS

Couples play many roles with each other throughout the years but none more important than friends and lovers. As Dr. Georgia Wilkin once said about couples in long-term relationships who had over time become each other's best friend: "They feel accepted with their faults and have come to accept their mates as a package deal."

This is an easy level to maintain. Support each other's interests and spend quality time communicating, and you will never have to use the familiar excuse for a mid-life separation: "We just grew apart" or "We didn't have anything in common anymore."

The role of lovers is harder to maintain on a steady course. In fact, after the first exhilarating months, many couples experience a decline both in frequency of sexual intercourse and desire in general. Somebody observed years ago that if during their first year together a couple put a bean in a jar every time they made love and took out a bean for every love-making time thereafter, they would never empty the jar the rest of their lives. That prediction may be a bit over-the-top, but many marriage educators suggest that the child-bearing and child–rearing years do take the focus off the couple. Fortunately as empty-nesting approaches, most couples find the embers of desire bursting into flames again and many of those beans disappearing.

DAILY COUPLE TALK:
(EACH PARTNER RESPONDS)
What is something that you really
count on in your partner?

FRIENDS AND LOVERS

Ralph Waldo Emerson once observed that "to have a friend you have to BE one." That general observation applies to couples as well. BEING friend and lover is so much more important than measuring what the partner is doing wrong. It is so much more important than just getting through the day with its tasks, problems, and difficulties. It gives us a focus and a definition. BEING friend and lover is committing to pleasing the partner, finding interesting resources within ourselves, and emptying the heavy baggage of regrets, jealousies, grudges, and vendettas.

BEING friend and lover frees the imagination to get to work on possibilities for mutual joy and broadens the vision of opportunities for growth. With concentration on how we can demonstrate both our friendship and physical attraction, we can step out of our comfort zones and open up new kinds of loving behaviors. This then changes the way we look at ourselves, the way our partner sees us, and finally the dynamics of the relationship itself. BEING friend and lover adds new roles, new playfulness, new perspectives, and new insights.

Dr. Keith and Ruth Wills were a couple who married in later years. Keith had been a widower and Ruth was divorced. They demonstrated the roles of friend and lover so vividly that others noticed and often commented on their happiness and enthusiasm for life. Every time this happened, Keith would say, "Yes, she's added years to my life and life to my years."

DAILY COUPLE TALK:
(EACH PARTNER RESPONDS)
In what ways does your partner add pleasure to your life?

FRIENDS AND LOVERS

"Healthy relationships," says Dr. Michelle Wiener-Davis, "are based on mutual caretaking." That also includes sex. As a TED speaker on "The Sex-Starved Marriage," Dr. Wiener-Davis addressed the person in the relationship who has the "lower sex-drive" and who, according to this speaker "controls the marriage."

The lover with the "lower sex-drive," she says, asks a lot. This lover expects the partner to accept the situation, not to complain, not to feel lonely, rejected, or unloved, and to stay faithful. This lover needs to know that being connected in love is a basic human desire. We are all "hard-wired" for connection, Dr. Wiener-Davis says. Being connected to someone we care about makes us feel attractive and interesting. Touching, embracing, kissing, and cuddling increases our sense of well-being and according to some marriage experts even boosts our immune systems, helps us ward off illnesses, and provides a faster recovery from the illnesses we do have. This lover needs to be a better "care-taker."

Being a good "care-taker" means having sex, talking about it, seeking ways to make it pleasing and exciting to each partner, listening to the partner's opinions and feelings, and regarding it as a fundamental way to keep connection, affection, and health in the relationship. Being a good "care-taker" means the "us" is regarded as too important to abandon or leave to chance. Being a good "care-taker" is being both friend and lover.

DAILY COUPLE TALK:
(EACH PERSON ANSWERS)
Besides being a full participant in sexual activity, what is a way you show your partner "care-taking"?

FRIENDS AND LOVERS

Maintaining the positions of being each other's friend and lover has a surprising influence on physical health in general. Those who have kept in place these two positions of social interaction with each other do not need the abundant corroborating research which exists to know that they feel better, work better, and deal with life's difficulties more effectively.

Several years ago the pastor of our church lost his wife to cancer after a long and arduous struggle. Although many church members befriended him and tried to keep him involved socially, he began to visibly age in the way he walked and talked. He even developed a tremor in his hands and a hacking cough.

After a while he met a pretty, friendly, outgoing woman and eventually married her. She told him jokes, sat close to him in the car, complimented his clothes, listened to his stories, held his hand whenever possible, and dressed fashionably. She was a good, supportive friend as well as an affectionate partner. The pastor immediately began to look better physically and to stand up straighter. He lost the tremor and the cough and laughed often. He was a visible testimony to the therapy of having both friend and lover in the same person.

Kindness, cooperative support, loyalty, touch, embraces, physical closeness—these qualities are invaluable to healthy couples.

DAILY COUPLE TALK:
(EACH PERSON ANSWERS)
What one quality in a friend do you value most? Why?

FRIENDS AND LOVERS

In Victor Hugo's famous novel <u>Les Miserables</u> Jean Valjean dies in a rented room in a poor Paris neighborhood, even though he had amassed a great fortune. On the fireplace mantel in the shabby room stood two expensive silver candlesticks and some priceless silver plates. He had kept them all through his life to remind him of an early scene in his life when an elderly bishop had called him "brother," saved him from arrest for stealing the candlesticks, and given him the priceless plates to insure a fresh start in life. They were to remind him of the kind of encouragement he had never before received and of its importance.

Marriage is at its best when it frees and encourages each partner to reach his/her best potential. Whether it's a job or career change, developing a new skill, returning to school for a new degree, or just changing to a new hair style, small or large, when partners feel encouraging support, they are grateful both for the gift and the giver.

Like Valjean's encounter with the grace-giving bishop, partners profit from being given ample opportunity to do their best. Often the impetus to follow dreams or succeed in a particular task comes from a partner who as both friend and lover gives empathy, space, and encouragement. No one would have believed that the brutal prisoner at the beginning of Hugo's story would turn out to enrich the lives of so many others.

DAILY COUPLE TALK:
(EACH PARTNER RESPONDS)
What is one interest of your partner that you could encourage and support? How would that encouragement best be shown?

FRIENDS AND LOVERS

With a blend of amity and intimacy, friends and lovers have many awesome opportunities to touch each other's hearts and lives. Nowhere is this opportunity more evident than in the power to affect each other's self-esteem.

Friends and lovers know each other's strengths and weaknesses. They have the ability to increase the partner's strengths by regular expressions of appreciation. They both have the ability to diminish each other's weaknesses by addressing them with tact and gentleness and by making visible efforts to change what is reasonable.

Friends and lovers can take responsibility for themselves without blaming or excusing. They can readily admit when they make mistakes. They can apologize without keeping score. They can communicate their own wants and needs in the safety of a close relationship.

Thus in this encouraging environment, self-esteem flourishes and can even spill over into professional life. Touching each other's lives with honesty seasoned with gratitude enriches everyone.

DAILY COUPLE TALK:
(EACH PARTNER RESPONDS)
As your friend I enjoy the way you _____.
As your lover I am grateful for the way you _____.

FRIENDS AND LOVERS

The wolves of worry tend to hunt us in packs, and some days they seem more savage then others. One way to outwit or avoid the wolves is to think about the loving behaviors we have experienced or the ones we are going to give. Either way changes our frame of mind and makes us less vulnerable to worry and anxiety.

We all agree that it makes us happy when our partner affirms us and acts affectionately. If touch is our Love Language, we immediately feel the impact. Doctors of various kinds tell us that these actions can lower our blood pressure and release helpful brain chemicals. Affirmation and affectionate actions appear to be physically and emotionally needed at all ages.

Physical actions of touch are one example of loving behaviors, things such as holding hands, patting, kissing, massage, and hugs. Verbal behaviors include calling each other by endearing names, thanking each other for doing something needed, saying what you appreciate about the other. Other behaviors are being patient when one has made a mistake, cheering each other up during bad times, or leaving sweet Post-it notes. All these behaviors are the delightful business of loving and being loved, and no wolves of worry are equal to their effect.

DAILY COUPLE TALK:
(EACH PERSON PARTICIPATES)
Read through the last paragraph again and pick the loving behavior you value most.

FRIENDS AND LOVERS

Friends are companions in life that you like to spend time with. Friends accept you as you are, help you when you need it, raise your spirits, and forgive your mistakes. Being married to your best friend makes a positive difference in your life because of encouragement, understanding, and good advice. To be loved just for yourself contributes to individual growth and self-acceptance. To be supported in the pursuits you find important, to be joined in sadness and in laughter, to be soothed in times of doubt and fear—all these and more make close friendship one of the greatest benefits of marriage.

Lovers add a different dimension, a different layer of awareness. Although lovers feel all the things friends do, the physical pleasure experienced by being close to the loved one has the ability to draw hearts together in an ancient dance of desire and exhilaration. Friends dance the two-step, the polka, the jitterbug; lovers dance the tango and the waltz. Breathing can be affected in the presence of the lover, as is heart-rate and pulse.

Marriage offers both friendship and the physical pleasure of lovers. Both roles are meant to last a lifetime. Both are blessings that give life a special vibrancy and texture. Both are gifts. Both are needed. And when they come together in one glowing relationship, hearts can truly celebrate.

DAILY COUPLE TALK:
(EACH PARTNER RESPONDS)
If you were planning a romantic evening for the two of you, what would you want to include?

FRIENDS AND LOVERS

Being intimate with our partner includes our emotions, our values, our problem-solving skills, and according to psychotherapist Eric Fromm, our human need for union. Intimacy obviously includes the physical, but intimacy is more powerful than merely satisfying a sexual urge. Being life-long lovers is connected to all other areas of our lives and is a growing, positive, and life-enhancing experience.

A couple can do real harm to their intimacy feelings by criticizing, blaming, ridiculing, or giving each other the silent treatment. Instead, behave with respect and support, including daily courtesies. Take time to do relaxing and enjoyable things together. Keep couple skills fully exercised and be candid with each other about medical issues such as prostate problems or psychological issues such as depression. Create a companionable environment of mutual care and mutual concern.

The way to increase intimacy enjoyment over time then is simple and achievable: to want it, and to want it enough to do the things that produce it. Intimacy enjoyment over time is achieved by (1) continuing to express appreciation to each other, (2) being mutually considerate and affectionate, (3) sharing a commitment to a talking time every day where intimate and personal couple-talk is a viable part, (4) being emotionally available for support, and (5) expressing love through physical touch.

DAILY COUPLE TALK:
(EACH PERSON PARTICIPATES)
To increase your intimacy enjoyment level, which of the last five actions would be most beneficial to you?

FRIENDS AND LOVERS

PART 1

The reason some partners live with such divided hearts and unfulfilled emotions is that they have failed to sink their roots into the fertile soil of trust and love. Too busy to be fully present anywhere, not much relational nourishment reaches their needy leaves and branches. Nothing valuable can be harvested for later enjoyment because they take no time for it; if anything blooms, it is short-lived and largely unnoticed in the daily rush to get things done. The human gifts of Time and Life, gifts that blossom in the joy of a happy marriage relationship, are regarded on the same level as accomplishment.

The resources for dealing with this too-common situation cannot be overlooked: friendship and love. There are few substitutes for the simple pleasures of friendship. When the spouse is best friend, trusted and appreciated, the heart is open to the ways joy can touch the heart and make it sing. Friends support us; friends remember what we like and value; friends share themselves and their humor with us and accept our preferences and quirkiness. If we let them, friends have the capacity to cheer us up. They share in the honors of our achievements and give us thoughtful commemorative presents. They also share in the sadness of our disappointments. They rejoice in the blossoming of those gifts of Time and Life, and as Shakespeare says in a sonnet to a friend:

❦ "For thy sweet love such wealth brings
❦ That then I scorn to change my state with kings."

DAILY COUPLE TALK:
(EACH PARTNER RESPONDS)
As your friendship deepens, what is one quality you highly value in your partner?

FRIENDS AND LOVERS

PART 2

Loving behaviors given freely and generously to the marriage partner can influence our own emotions and allow us to notice and accept loving behaviors in return. It is an equation that leads to growth. Rushing through our duties and appointments, we are sometimes not fully present anywhere and thus miss the sweet actions that are the evidence of the partner's esteem. Taking the time to sink our roots into the fertile soil of love and trust, we are able then able to let those qualities reshape our days and fill our hearts with needed nourishment.

Loving and being loved by the same person is the second resource. Often the key to maintaining a thriving love experience is giving loving behaviors. Remaining on the edge of relationship, watching to see what the partner is going to do, telling ourselves that we are too busy or that we don't "feel like" being affectionate or admiring—these actions retard the free-flowing nourishment that should be ours. Psychologists say that the reason some people fail to experience personal and relational growth is quite literally that they prevent themselves from doing the loving behaviors. It is the behavior that causes our feelings, not the other way around. Rushing through life without awareness of this love equation is a tragedy. Love and loving in marriage is available to all, one of the few things in life where money, education, status, gifted personality, intelligence, or knowledgeable skill-sets do not matter. And its benefits, if we let ourselves choose them, are growth and health.

DAILY COUPLE TALK:
(EACH PARTNER ANSWERS)
*What is a loving behavior that you enjoy
giving to your partner?*

FRIENDS AND LOVERS

Fireflies are heralds of summer, captivating children and adults alike with a single flash. Called lightning bugs in some regions, the fireflies use their flashes as a signal for mating. After one inquisitive flash, for example, the females emit a double flash. Males answer with six flashes and the deed is done. The whole complicated process has only a two-week window of time, but the successful continuation of the firefly population depends on what scientists call synchronization. In other words, coupling partners need to read each other's signals and make the correct response.

The same is true in marriage. Like the firefly's continuation, the future of the couple often hinges on accurate signals and responses. Enough missed, and one or both assume they married the "wrong" person with the "wrong" chemistry.

Both partners are constantly sending signals of a need to be affirmed and a need for affection. On the surface it does not seem this signal could be as meaningful as the lowly firefly's flashes, but myriads of couples credit this one signal/response as the way to breathe vigor into a crumbling relationship.

For those who tend to confuse gestures of affection as nothing more than invitations to sex, Willard F. Harley, Jr. explains that "affection is the ENVIRONMENT of the marriage and sex is an EVENT."

DAILY COUPLE TALK:
(EACH PARTNER RESPONDS)
What is one way you show affection and affirmation to your partner?

FRIENDS AND LOVERS

Friends tell each other the truth, including being straight about opinions and ideas; it is almost as important as giving accurate and specific information to 911.

Suppose you are involved in an accident on the Interstate and need help. Giving your exact location to the 911 Dispatcher is important, including which direction your car was headed. This is crucial to a speedy use of the information. The more specific, the quicker the response. The same is true in expressing ideas and opinions to friends and partners. Neither should have to guess or interpret what help is needed. Being specific satisfies both speaker and responder.

The language of friendship is not only words of honesty and directness but also of meanings. Being present in times of trouble is an example of meaning. Bobbye once went to the house of a friend whose husband had committed suicide and at the front door told the friend, "I don't know what to say." The friend responded, "You don't have to say anything; you are here." Presence had a deeper significance than mere words—a meaning shared by the emotions of both.

Speaking specifically and knowing when to let a kind action be the needed communication—both of these require a level of intelligence that engages our minds and hearts. And as friendship in marriage deepens, we often find that the value we place on it deepens as well.

DAILY COUPLE TALK:
(EACH PERSON ANSWERS)
What did you learn about friendship in growing up?

FRIENDS AND LOVERS

Even partners who consider themselves happily married still get depressed, fight, lose jobs, struggle with infants and teenagers, worry about money, and have sexual problems. No one snapshot of marriage covers it all; there is no such thing as "ten easy steps" to success in marriage; no vaccination against marital strife exists.

Yet marriage as an institution goes on, ever changing its rules and expectations but still desirable for a vast majority of the population. One reason is stated by researchers Judith Wallerstein and Sandra Blakeslee in their ground-breaking book The Good Marriage:

> *"The home is the one place where we have the potential to create a world that is to our liking; it is the last place we should feel despair. As never before in history men and women today are free to design the kind of marriage they want."*

Yet far too often the couples who are experiencing this love in a happy, fulfilling relationship do not share their game-plan with others (sometimes not even with their own children). They believe that marriage is the best place for love, and they believe that marriage offers the freedom for each couple to create an intelligent and balanced design of what they want in a relationship. But they keep quiet about their successes, often achieved in the midst of oceans of troubles and losses.

DAILY COUPLE TALK:
(EACH PARTNER RESPONDS)
If you were making a design for how your marriage relationship would work best (and that design is going to be published), what are two things it should definitely include?

FRIENDS AND LOVERS

One goal of marriage is the creation and maintenance of a loving sexual relationship. However a couple chooses to define it, it lies at the heart of a good marriage and remains the antidote to the many stresses of living.

Science supports couple health benefits as well. An AARP article states: "Recent studies show that married couples are more likely to survive cancer and less likely to develop dementia or be hospitalized with pneumonia." Christine Proulx, associate professor of human development and family science at the University of Missouri, explains the health benefits of a happy marriage by saying that "having someone you love and want to keep around encourages healthy behavior." In other words, friends and lovers want to use good health habits in order to prolong their marriage for as long as possible.

Other studies reported at the Gerontological Society of America targeted couples married more than 40 years. They found that couples who had an optimistic outlook on life and relationship (sometimes even just one partner) experienced fewer chronic illnesses such as diabetes and arthritis. Apparently our bodies react to the loving behaviors of a friend and the physical satisfaction of a lover. Being friends and having a committed sexual relationship may be the key to becoming a healthy centenarian. At least it provides a happy journey as we move toward that possibility.

DAILY COUPLE TALK:
(EACH PERSON PARTICIPATES)
What are your major concerns for your physical health?
For your partner's health?

FRIENDS AND LOVERS

One of our modern tragedies is that many married couples are wasting the best human resources we have. In their unhappiness and confusion they overlook the love, trust, tenderness, comradeship, and capacity for mutual support that lie within each person. Albert Einstein is reported to have said that the average person only uses about 10% of his mental powers, wasting the rest through lack of development. Something like that happens too often in marriage.

Partially what creates the tragedy is that partners who are friends and lovers fail to recognize that they have everything on their side. Stereotyped patterns of relationship are rapidly disappearing and the roles can be shaped and reshaped to suit the partners. Marriage today offers individual fulfillment, personality development, emotional security, and a strong sense of unity. An aura of romance can frame every day, if that is what you want. Closeness and intimacy, those longed-for goals, can be achieved. Differences and disagreements can be handled. Sexual enjoyment can be discussed. As Dr. David Mace said, "sex is the supreme expression of married love, and loving couples are bound by no rules except their own sense of what brings them mutual happiness."

DAILY COUPLE TALK:
(EACH PARTNER PARTICIPATES)
Tell your partner one thing you really want in your relationship. How can you work together to get it?

FRIENDS AND LOVERS

Marriage partners who are also best friends forever (BFF's) support each other's interests. Marathon runners can expect to have the partner cheering on the sidelines. Partners of duplicate bridge players go to competitions in other cities just as a visible form of "way to go!" It is an example of "turning toward" (Dr. John Gottman's term) which designates both pride in another valued individual's accomplishments and a willingness to show that individual that we know how much those accomplishments mean to them.

Pam and Tom Stoker, partners and BFF's, are a good example. Tom contracted cancer and fought over a long period of time. Before cancer, music had been Tom's great interest and also his profession, both as business manager for a men's barbershop chorus and as minister of music in many churches. At Tom's funeral one of the speakers told the audience that on the evening that he lay dying, Pam got in bed with him, held him in her arms, and sang his favorite hymns in his ear. This sweet action shows a best friend supporting her partner with something he valued and loved.

Marriage is a partnership in many ways. It is a gift to encourage the partner to pursue interests; it is also a gift to be involved in the support of those interests. It is an invaluable "turning toward" affirmation.

DAILY COUPLE TALK:
(EACH PERSON ANSWERS)
What is one illustration of when you have "turned toward" your partner in a supportive way?

FRIENDS AND LOVERS

WIN/win or win/WIN is different from win/win/WIN. The first or second version of this interaction can make one partner feel smart and powerful, but it will never build a strong relationship or bring intimacy to lovers. Neither will blaming, nagging, angry attacks, sarcasm, silence, or judgmental "shoulds"—all ways of exerting intimidation that can be effective if all you want to do is WIN.

For lovers to be fully engaged in a reciprocal exchange of hearts and bodies, there needs to be a sense of respect and a shared sense of power. A rewarding, loving, and fulfilling sex life is not just relegated to what happens in the bedroom. Its foreplay can be done anywhere and includes trust, encouraging healthy self-esteem, fair negotiation of issues, and using good people-skills such as courtesy and kindness. These qualities are far from intimidation, and although a relationship can rock along without using all of them, it cannot grow when one partner must WIN.

Both lovers need to value a warm and tender relationship, a sweet and exciting "us." When they do (and can sense the difference when it is damaged), it gives new motivation to change interactions that leave one partner hostile or tearful. It comes down to the same thing within the bedroom or without—turning all conversations, disagreements, encounters, or love-making into a win/win/WIN.

DAILY COUPLE TALK:
(EACH PARTNER RESPONDS)
"How do I love thee? Let me count the ways," says poet Elizabeth Barrett Browning in a sonnet. Tell your partner some ways that you express your love.

FRIENDS AND LOVERS

Seated in the lobby writing and waiting for a ladies' luncheon to begin, Bobbye said hello to a friend named Liz. When Liz learned what Bobbye was doing, she said that she wished everyone had a husband like hers. "He is a man of absolute dedication," Liz said, "and I could not make it through a day without him. He is my best friend." Liz has had several surgeries, and Ray's tender care during her long convalescence has captured her attention and gratitude.

It is one outcome of a long marriage. Eventually both partners reach a point where some physical condition necessitates care. Those who have remained friends receive kind attention with grateful hearts, humbled by their own inability to perform simple tasks. Bobbye once fractured her right wrist on a neighborhood walk and could not believe the number of things that needed a strong right hand to do. One of the benefits of friendship was the care Britton provided during this time.

Liz continued the conversation at the luncheon, and others joined in. Angela said she would second Liz's ideas about dedication, but she preferred to call it commitment. "It is the cement that holds a marriage together," Angela said, adding that it is a quality that many young couples lack today. At the first sign of trouble, she said, one or both partners assume they have made a mistake. Thus they never reach the point of a deep friendship that can face adversity and still lovingly serve.

DAILY COUPLE TALK:
(EACH PERSON ANSWERS)
What is the "cement" that helps your relationship?

FRIENDS AND LOVERS

Ann was discussing friendship as an essential part of a successful marriage. She said one key to enduring friendship is "flexibility." She went on to state regretfully that she did not have it but fortunately her partner did. Angela immediately jumped into the conversation to reframe her friend's claim by calling Ann "disciplined" and "organized," not just inflexible. Ann was someone who could get things done. Angela admitted that it WAS humorous to make a written list of jobs to be performed every 10 minutes while in the kitchen. She told about the time Ann's husband secretly inserted a task into the every-10-minutes list. It said, "Go pee."

Flexibility with friends can become an asset. When we are willing to hear and consider someone else's opinion, we often learn things we didn't know. When we can avoid self-preoccupation, the world is enlarged and much more interesting. Sometimes there is a gold mine of new and exciting information just waiting to be discovered.

At one point as friendship deepened and the couple relationship seemed to prosper with the addition of what Britton and Bobbye called "our time," they had to decide what was important to them. Their days were already full and had been for some time. Could their schedule now include a flexible new arrangement of time? Did the activities of "our time" matter as much as the current schedule? Flexibility won. Friendship and Romance won.

DAILY COUPLE TALK:
(EACH PARTNER RESPONDS)
What could be a reasonable schedule-change to include more couple time?

FRIENDS AND LOVERS

Some days it seems all our praise for coupling goes only to the young or the very old. Young love on the verge of the great adventure of marriage often get parties, gifts, white dresses, best wishes, flowers, champagne toasts, and family celebrations. Fifty+ years' anniversaries get a scaled-down version of the same praise, usually with a question to the couple about how they did it.

Shakespeare's young lovers, Romeo and Juliet, had many people on their side. The bawdy and down-to-earth nurse arranges for the lovers to meet and cheerfully lies to protect them. Their priest tries to save them from a chauvinistic culture. The city administrator makes a beautiful speech at their tragic deaths and vows to wipe out prejudice. He even puts up a statue in their honor.

The strong and stalwart couples in the trenches lie In between the celebration of young love and the respect for the achievements of the elderly. These couples often work two jobs, raise and educate their children, pay their bills, and try to be responsible citizens. These are the couples who deserve real praise and attention as they seek to stay close and loving in the midst of the busy-ness of life. Theirs is the devotion that should inspire song lyrics, even if it is not as glamorous a status as young ideals or the perseverance of the old. Their determination and dedication to stay friends and lovers calls for a special kind of recognition. Hip, Hip, Hurrah!

DAILY COUPLE TALK:
(EACH PERSON ANSWERS)
What are some things that keep couples together even in times of trouble?

FRIENDS AND LOVERS

"Friends don't let friends drive drunk." "Love makes the world go round." "Friendship—just a perfect blendship." "Love is nature's way of giving a reason to be living." "Stand by me when you're not strong." "I'll be loving you always." "He/she speaks in the language of friendship." "I love you. You love me. We're a happy family." These songs and sayings celebrate an ideal that the world cherishes. The world values both friendship and love, but it goes one step farther to hope that the close bonds of friendship and the intimate connections of lovers can meet in the same relationship called marriage. The honesty and loyalty of friends goes so far as to tell each other if something gross is stuck between teeth. The warmth and beauty of marriage can be seen when lovers work side by side during the day and snuggle in each other's arms at night.

The combination of these two ideals—friends and lovers—is a combination of Realism and Romance that fuels couples when they have run out of energy. It is a driving force for marital progress. It gives direction and hope to a somewhat jaded society. It may seem foolish and impractical in the light of divorce statistics and the many marriages stuck in the swamps of hostility, but it is still what children rely on to be a steadying and dependable influence in their lives.

DAILY COUPLE TALK:
(EACH PARTNER RESPONDS)
*What other ideals are important
that can keep society strong?*

COLLABORATION

"*The Constitution only gives people the right to pursue happiness. You have to catch it yourself.*"

BENJAMIN FRANKLIN

237

COLLABORATION

When your dialogue feels safe, loving, and interesting, your relationship feels secure. When talking together becomes tense, rude, or dominating, the relationship feels insecure and unappealing. Connecting by conversation, like sexual connection, both expresses and consolidates your relationship.

The way you talk to each other is often the result of the family-of-origin. If there were demands, accusations, and complaints in the home you grew up in, that may be the way you convey concerns. If there were hints, ambiguity, and underlying efforts of control, you may still be echoing these styles. Learning to break old unpleasant and ineffective styles of talking is difficult but rewarding.

The new goal in conversation will be collaboration. It will feature shared understanding rather than trying to prove who is "right." It aims for consensus building. It does not avoid sensitive areas of difference, since collaboration, not criticism, will be the method used. Neither partner becomes irritable or defensive because each is busy looking for the useful and productive in what the other says.

The main way couples enjoy or disrupt the business of living together is through the exchange of words. If couples can move toward communication habits that lead to productive conversations, every day feels more loving, respectful, and healthy.

DAILY COUPLE TALK:
(EACH PARTNER RESPONDS)
Discuss the next-to-last paragraph. What might be helpful to conversations between you?

COLLABORATION

Gardening and marital relationship-building have things in common. Some of them jumped out of a newspaper column today with the words, "Making Gardening Fit Our Needs."

One of the first recommendations made for a practical approach to gardening was to "Use a smaller scale." T h i s also makes sense for couples working to grow a strong "us." Start collaborating to identify little ways you can make each other happier. Listen and make some plans about putting this information into action. You can move on to bigger challenges later, but it takes much less energy to start on "a smaller scale."

Another gardening recommendation was to "Keep plants watered and fertilized." Healthy plants are a lot less work. Give plants what they need and they will take care of resisting insects and disease. Relationships that keep in touch with each other, stay current with at least a 15-minute conversation every day, and practice loving behaviors often are meeting basic needs that provide a healthier environment. Being pro-active about the basics saves a lot of work later.

A final gardening recommendation for both having a garden and enjoying it is to "Choose plants that are adapted to your area." Trying to grow a tropical oleander in a Minnesota yard will be a futile endeavor. Grow your relationship to be what you both want. See what fits your needs and collaborate on what might work.

DAILY COUPLE TALK:
(EACH PARTNER DISCUSSES)
What "marital plants" would you want to cultivate?
Collaborate on what would work for you both.

COLLABORATION

Self-talk is a kind of collaboration, one that goes on within our minds. Self-talk often precedes some action we are about to perform, rather like an athlete telling himself/herself how well the next sports performance will go. For example, swimmers at the Olympics are often photographed in deep concentration before they ever get in the water.

Self-talk can help bring about change for couples. The Serenity Prayer used by Alcoholics Anonymous speaks of the need to change what we can and accept what we cannot. The last part of the prayer asks for "the wisdom to know the difference."

Of course, we cannot change the past. That bell has rung. That ship has sailed. Whatever mistakes we made are made. Also, we cannot change another person, not even one we love. That change must be his/her decision. So, we have to change what we can, and that's ourselves.

That's where positive self-talk comes in. Suppose you and your partner have just had a disagreement. Instead of telling yourself that you are the victim as usual, stand up for yourself. Tell yourself that you can hear the partner's point of view and clearly express your own. Tell yourself that you can be a part of an understanding, if not a resolution. Tell yourself how strong you are. Then plan to collaborate.

DAILY COUPLE TALK:
(EACH PERSON ANSWERS)
How does practicing positive self-talk prepare you to say what you want to convey?

COLLABORATION

Few acts of love are as beneficial as simple encouragement because it can change a person's resolve to succeed even in the face of adversity. Encouragement can be verbal or non-verbal (a hug, a card, a small gift), but it effectively says, "I am on your side and I am proud of you." Encouragement is collaboration of the highest kind.

Marital encouragement implies commitment to the relationship, communication of good wishes for the partner's welfare, and a desire to be a good team member. Used often, it does wonders for morale. It implies that one partner has been attentive and caring, because he/she can see just how the other partner needs support.

If you are on the receiving end of encouragement, accept it. Don't worry about feeling inadequate or unworthy. Accepting encouragement in a good spirit will help the partner find enjoyment and will create the kind of interdependence that builds trust in each other.

If this high form of collaboration has not been a regular part of your relationship, put a higher premium on growth. Think of encouragement as a kind of nurturing exercise that helps build a stronger sense of "us-ness."

DAILY COUPLE TALK:
(EACH PARTNER RESPONDS)
What are some challenges you are facing in which you could use some encouragement?

COLLABORATION

Triangulation is a kind of collaboration we should avoid. It happens when rather than confronting the partner about a particular issue, we draw in a third party (sometimes even a child). Then we ask him/her not to share some information, keeping it a secret from the partner. "Don't tell your father that I spent all this money on my hair," one might say, or "Don't tell your mother that I played golf." Triangulation means that one partner is not being forthright with the other, and even worse, that partner is enlisting a third party to be on his/her side.

Triangulation usually means that the person using it feels powerless and not an equal partner in decision-making. It can be a form of conflict-avoidance, but a sneaky form. It leads to secrets and lies. It confuses children who are drawn in. It does not look to them that the parents are the strong, secure unit that children need. It leads to divided loyalties. It sets a bad example. It sabotages trust.

The cure for triangulation is to speak directly to the partner. Even if it leads to an argument, the family is better served when its leaders show that they can handle disagreements and poor choices. A partner collaboration trumps triangulation every time.

DAILY COUPLE TALK:
(EACH PERSON PARTICIPATES)
Discuss triangulation.
What steps can you take to avoid it?

COLLABORATION

No one word or action completely defines us. But they are a part of the whole picture. This was illustrated one day as the NFL Draft approached, and a radio sports-talk commentator was counseling against a high draft for a certain college player who had incidents of shoplifting, cheating, and allegations of sexual assault. "It's not that any one of these incidents is so important by itself and cannot be explained," he said. "It's just that the drip, drip, drip draws a picture that suggests a warning."

When the drip, drip, drip of a certain worrisome or annoying habit is brought to our attention by a concerned partner, we do have a choice of what action we will take. Some habits are deeply ingrained and hard to change, but the wonderful part about relational growth is that we CAN adjust. When we do, and when the partner sees us trying, the encouragement he/ she can give provides us with even more motivation.

Telling ourselves "That's just who I am, take it or leave it" will not work, since the partner knows (as we do also) that we are all BECOMING and no one person at any time can consider himself/herself FINISHED, as good as he/she is ever going to be.

Collaboration with someone on our side can make a big difference both in our desire to bring about the change and in making the change. The drip, drip, drip can be fixed so that its effect on the relationship is negligible.

OO

DAILY COUPLE TALK:
(EACH PARTNER RESPONDS)
When you were growing up and first learning to drive, what was one change you had to make? What did you learn from the change?

COLLABORATION

PART 1

The goal of collaboration is the growth of the relationship, the unique "us" that every couple has. In collaboration both the "me" and the "you" intentionally work together. Collaboration will not work if either partner enters into it with an attitude of "We could be happy if only YOU would change.""

Britton has done much counseling with those in grief over the years. He often speaks about the need to establish a "new normal" for the one who has experienced the loss of a close relationship.

Collaboration can be a "new normal" for couples. It happens as an outcome when partners:

1. honestly express their feelings and ideas to each other, sometimes about a subject they do not agree upon
2. listen to each other's feelings and ideas without judgment or editing
3. seek common ground on which to proceed that honors BOTH partners' opinions.

Gaining confidence in working together as a couple is more important for the long-term than merely arriving at a reasonable and beneficial decision. Couples who find a "new normal" of honesty and cooperation also find a new closeness in their everyday interactions.

DAILY COUPLE TALK:
(EACH PARTNER PARTICIPATES)

Suppose as a couple you are going to move for a year to a different country, with good jobs for both of you. Which country would you choose? Collaborate on this completely hypothetical choice.

COLLABORATION

PART 2

Collaboration requires trust between partners. If experience has led to arguments about WHY one feels a certain way or WHETHER one should have a certain idea, there will understandably be reluctance to collaborate. Sharing ideas and feelings, an important step in collaboration, is hard to do when there is little trust in this process.

Trust-building takes time. Old unprofitable habits and styles of talking take time to overcome (and willingness, of course). The demonstration of respect for another person's ideas goes slowly if we are used to looking only for the flaws. But repeated efforts to cooperate (and to be perceived as cooperating) eventually leads to the kind of trust that enables both partners to safely disclose themselves and their ideas. When this mutual disclosure is welcomed, trust in the process begins to thrive.

Making joint decisions, tackling difficult issues, or creating a reasonable schedule of shared household duties together may never be a pleasure, but they can be accomplished and with a minimum of hard feelings. The whole process moves toward a "new normal" when there is trust.

DAILY COUPLE TALK:
(EACH PARTNER ANSWERS)
What is the hardest part for you about collaboration?

COLLABORATION

Collaboration is a form of teamwork. Its goal is working together to accomplish a desired result. It tries to capitalize on EACH partner's strengths and skills by acknowledging and celebrating them. It features cooperation, unselfishness, compliments, honesty, and creativity. For hard-working couples used to making unilateral decisions on-the-spot, collaboration can be unexpectedly multi-faceted and productive when it is done in an atmosphere of camaraderie and sharing. Collaboration is needed on big couple issues, when both person's ideas and opinions need to be included.

Collaboration has a more inclusive goal than merely getting a job done efficiently. Either partner could do that alone. Collaboration seeks to accomplish a big task or jointly to examine an idea for a decision—all the while concentrating on building the "us." It is a high form of teamwork.

DAILY COUPLE TALK:
(EACH PERSON PARTICIPATES)
What is your favorite room in your current residence? If you could make one substantive change in that room, what would it be? Collaborate on how this change could be accomplished and use the recommended techniques. When you have finished, analyze the process you used. What felt comfortable? Encouraging? Productive? Whatever decision you explored, remember that the real goal is feeling good about the "us."

COLLABORATION

Marriage Enrichment is not counseling and not therapy. It is, as the words suggest, directed toward the growth of the couple. It addresses the subjects of parenting, in-laws, sex, or money (to name some common couple issues) only as they impact the partners, the center of the family.

It is important that the couple stays "centered." Each might have come to marriage for very different reasons; each may stay in the marriage for different reasons. But for the relationship to progress, there must be some core of principles that both believe in and both agree to follow. Those principles are defined by the couple and give stability and balance to their unique relationship.

The principles also need to be verbalized often, as dynamic relationships constantly change. It is a simple way to stay "centered," even though the activities of every day swirl around you. It makes the couple very much like the gymnast on the balance beam. That gymnast must keep the core centered on a four-inch wide beam or the balance is easily lost.

Core principles need to be stated and discussed. They should be realistic, and achievable by both. Then the core principles on which the couple has agreed can guide any willing couple toward their mutual goal: growth.

DAILY COUPLE TALK:
(TOGETHER, EACH PARTNER PARTICIPATES)
Decide together on at least one Core Principle.

COLLABORATION

A girls' volleyball team coach was recently interviewed about her different approach to winning. Instead of more practices on shots and strategy, the coach scheduled a week-end retreat for the team. The purpose was to draw the players closer together. In this way, the coach said, they will learn how to rely on each other and how to use each other's strengths and skills.

When the players were interviewed, it sounded like they understand the coach's plan. When we understand others, one player is reported to have said, we know "why they are the way they are and why they do the things they do." This helps us "get closer as a team and fight for each other." By increasing the unity that the players begin to feel, the team hopes to have a winning season.

It is a concept very similar to couple team-building or collaboration. And it is accomplished in a very similar way—getting to know each other and thus to know how to work with, play with, and understand each other. Feeling connected as a couple-team is important. But for the best results it has to happen in the present tense. Like the volleyball coach's theory, it is a plan to use each other's strengths and skills.

DAILY COUPLE TALK:
(EACH PERSON SHARES)
If you could invite two people to dinner tonight (one living and one dead), who would you choose and why? What one thing would you say about your partner when you introduce him/her?

COLLABORATION

The "Lonesome Dove" mini-series ends with an enterprising reporter trying to interview the legendary Captain Woodrow Call. After being repeatedly ignored, the reporter blurts out, "They say you are a man of vision." Then Captain Call says, "Hell of a vision."

For many years Bobbye interpreted his statement to mean that Captain Call was denigrating his accomplishments by sneering at the reporter's statement. A very complex man, he feared he could never accomplish enough and only truly relaxed with his friend Gus.

Recently Bobbye saw the statement in a new light. Perhaps Captain Call was admitting that he had done some outstanding things in his time. "Hell of a vision" might be a tiny recognition that he could congratulate himself, even if he would allow no one else to do it.

Marriage partners do not always catch the right meaning of words. Personal filters sometimes keep them hearing what they expect to hear. How important on these occasions to use the paraphrasing technique to make sure that the interpretation is correct. Simply asking, "Are you saying....?" can clear up many misunderstandings. No one knows what author Larry McMurtry meant by Call's statement, but the couple has a chance to stay on the same page with each other by using this simple technique.

DAILY COUPLE TALK:
(EACH PARTNER RESPONDS)
*Filters can cause us to hear a message
with only our own personal interpretation.
What could some of those filters be?*

COLLABORATION

Self-talk steeped in self-pity is a kind of one-way collaboration that can lead to misunderstandings between partners. Instead of instantly asking for clarification regarding an ambiguous statement (Are you saying….?), one partner takes a message and makes a private interpretation.

In this scenario, there is no need for another person. In fact, self-talk arising from the habit of self-pity is a collaboration that the partner does not know is happening. It is far, far from the definition of collaboration as seeking together for understanding.

One of Britton's favorite comic strips shows a husband holding a roll of masking tape and asking, "Is this all there is?" This led to the wife's interior self-talk where she decided that the subject was his dissatisfaction with their life together and that he was observing that there was very little pleasure left for them to experience. He is probably about to tell her that the relationship is over. Hurt and anxious, she makes a pre-emptive strike and tells him that she too has been worried about the quality of their relationship and wondering what to do about their future. Puzzled, the husband asks, "Are we talking about masking tape?"

DAILY COUPLE TALK:
(EACH PERSON PARTICIPATES)
Communication can sometimes be difficult. What are some reasons (besides self-talk) that this might be true?`

COLLABORATION

Many marriage educators have observed that it is hard to change someone else, but some people get married with the expectations that they can change the partner to fit their estimation of his/her potential. "He drinks too much," "She keeps her credit card maxed out," "He can't keep a job," "She is very bossy," are some common recognitions accompanied by the private assessment and expectation that a change will be made in the other person after the wedding.

Occasionally changes DO happen, but in most situations, it is because the person himself/herself decides to make the change. No amount of pushing or lobbying can bring about someone else's expectations. Bobbye and Britton held a conversation with two couples who have twenty+ years of marital experience each. They revealed some common ideas about expectations.

Leigh Ann said, "Expectations can be tyrants. If you are ruled by your expectations, you do not even listen to what the partner wants." Bill added that each partner needs time to mature and "let go of expectations." Kim observed that "what you see is what you get." Frazier thought you should accept the partner "as they are." Freeing your partner from a check-list of your expectations is a love-gift of infinite proportions.

DAILY COUPLE TALK:
(EACH PARTNER RESPONDS)
What were some expectations you had before marriage? What is one surprise you have had about those expectations?

COLLABORATION

People get married for many different reasons—getting away from the family-of-origin, needing safe sex, simplifying taxes, clarifying the visa status, finding a parent for a child, escalating to a better financial status, to name only a few. No matter the reasons for getting married, nearly everyone finds the beginning months of marriage interesting and intriguing enough to hang in for a while. Getting launched is not the challenging part, nor does it last very long.

Let's assume you have been married nine months, a critical point according to many counselors and therapists. You have discovered many differences between you, and some of them are not pleasant. You are wondering if this relationship has a chance to last. If the differences are addictions, domestic violence in any form, or severe personality disorders, it's questionable. Almost every other difference can be dealt with.

Get acquainted with your strengths and those of your partner. Make a list of the strengths for both to see. Pretend those strengths (or tools for living well) are in a tool box and both of you are examining them carefully to see which ones you really need. Talk about what you most need to accomplish to get through the next few months, and plan how to use the tools you already have.

DAILY COUPLE TALK:
(EACH PARTNER RESPONDS)
Make a list of what each partner does well (such as, listening, making a budget, working hard, fixing things, nurturing, sense of humor, for example). Which of the listed strengths do you value most? Why?

COLLABORATION

Collaboration on reshaping, reworking, and reforming the marriage relationship goes on every day for couples who invest in their relationship and are allowing it to grow. Individuals spend much of their lives on education and its benefits, changing and growing in job skills and career advancements. Marriages also change with the individuals in them, allowing flexibility and growth as time passes. The fact that the following traditional myths about marriage are still around and still unchallenged is worthy of a Sherlock Holmes investigation as to why.

<u>Marriages are made in heaven</u>. Divine help may be available, but the daily making of a marriage is a job that must be done on earth.

<u>A wedding is a marriage</u>. Weddings are no more than the beautiful starting point of a life-long endeavor in which a couple must build a marriage out of the raw materials each brings.

<u>You have to accept your partner "for better or for worse."</u> Whether the relationship turns out to be better or worse depends almost entirely on how effectively you work together to make it what you want it to be.

<u>Happily married couples never disagree</u>. No two people can live a closely shared life without frequent disagreement. What enlightened couples do is to resolve each disagreement as it arises.

DAILY COUPLE TALK:
(EACH PERSON PARTICIPATES)
*Which of these traditional "myths about marriage"
would you especially want to challenge? Why?*

COLLABORATION

The collaborative model of conversation has at its heart the desire to make talking lead to understanding for both persons involved. It works in business, with friends, with salespersons, and especially in marriage. It is predicated on listening, listening carefully enough that you could paraphrase what you've heard, if necessary.

At first listening this intently is hard because it runs counter to our habitual style, where we listen just enough to pick up a few key words and extend the conversation if we so choose. Or we listen while we plan in our minds what we will say next.

In this model, we are proactive with our listening. For example, if the other person talks so long that we cannot possibly remember everything, we have to interrupt and say something like "Let me see if I've got it so far. Are you saying. . .?" The listener can also check to see if the speaker understands his/her paraphrase: "Did I get that right?" "Is there more?" And the feelings can be validated with statements such as "That makes sense to me because..." or "This is causing a problem because..."

Of course, this style of talking and listening is not a technique for every conversation, maybe not even many of them. But for giving directions, discussing emotional subjects, making business transactions, or resolving conflicts, it leads to better understanding by both parties.

DAILY COUPLE TALK:
(EACH PERSON PARTICIPATES)
Tell your partner about a dream vacation you would enjoy taking. Pause often enough to allow for paraphrase as practice.

COLLABORATION

Many couples find team-building to be both achievable and rewarding. Relying on each other's talents and strengths, strategizing together to counteract weaknesses, learning the fundamentals of how to work together successfully, meeting goals that strengthen and improve each team member—these are the elements of team-building that can lead to "winning" for many years to come.

One recommendation is that whether in sports, work, or marriage finding the right rhythm is important. Factor into your couple schedule all the ways you spend your time: work, household duties, sleep, children, sex, health needs, daily couple time, exercise, entertainment, and/or community involvement. Look together at these time expenditures and see where there is time to accomplish something you both want to do. Plan, prioritize, and collaborate. See how you can support each other with responsibility and cooperation. Never lose sight of the goal of building a strong "us" as you build your couple team. Be sure to include time for relaxing activities; they keep you refreshed and are important to the rhythm of performance.

Another recommendation is to avoid stress and frustration by giving attention only to whatever task is at hand. Or as a sports radio commentator said, "Be where your feet are." This allows for a focus of energy and avoids fragmentation. Your partner will welcome your full attention as a committed team member.

DAILY COUPLE TALK:
(EACH PARTNER RESPONDS)
*What is something important about
the rhythm of your couple-team?*

COLLABORATION

"Reframing" is the term for a kind of collaborative self-talk. It is taking an interpretation of another person's words or actions and casting them in a new light. It is putting an alternate spin on how we look at something, giving a more generous or optimistic definition to our first response--a negative reaction. For example, instead of thinking someone is "stingy," consider them "thrifty." "Bossy" talk could "show leadership." "Rigid and inflexible" ideas might also be "well-organized."

"Reframing" can also be done regarding actions. Bonnie told recently about her father-in-law, who seemed to her quick to find fault. Her objections were ignored. Because they lived in the same town, Bonnie decided that she would say nothing more and "just put up it." But as time passed and children were born, Bonnie became increasingly angry with lectures to her sons and criticism of her parenting skills.

"Reframing" allowed Bonnie to look at it a different way. "He really loves the children and wants them to behave well," she thought. "That's why he is so critical of me and of his grandchildren."   As she grew more gentle in her dealings with him, they were able to maintain a more enjoyable relationship. "Reframing" cannot solve every relationship problem, but it can bring a much-needed pause before we rush to judgment with only one interpretation.

DAILY COUPLE TALK:
(EACH PARTNER RESPONDS)
Reframe a scene with your partner that you might choose to regard differently.

COLLABORATION

A session with a local garden-center specialist yields applicable advice to marriage. The first question that day was from someone who wanted a recommendation for a fast-growing shade tree. "I need shade, and I don't want to wait," he said. The specialist said the terms were "mutually exclusive" because all the fast-growers have a short life-expectancy and are not resistant to "pests." How true for marriage. Growing a strong "us" takes time. Couples must log some time to see how best to make each other happy and how best to deal together with the "pests" that make us grouchy and vulnerable.

Another question was about which grass to grow in the shade. The specialist suggested switching to a variety of ground cover. That advice is also applicable to marriage. All couples are unique, like fingerprints. All couples come together from different backgrounds. Trying only one way to communicate, or one way to solve arguments, or one way to make love is as frustrating as the gardener who insists on growing grass where it lacks enough sun.

One gardener raised a curious question about holly bushes. He liked their durability and colorful berries but not their spines. "What can you suggest?" he asked. The specialist responded, "That's like saying to Willie Nelson, 'I like your music but do you have something without guitars?'" Compromise in marriage is necessary. We celebrate our partner's wonderful qualities, collaborate on needed changes, and accept everything else.

DAILY COUPLE TALK:
(EACH PERSON ANSWERS)
What is one thing you can celebrate
about your partner?

COLLABORATION

Why do some couples cope well in stressful situations? Several studies have been done on that, including Britton's dissertation on Family Strengths. When a crisis comes in the life of a couple, it creates an imbalance in the family. Things must change for a new balance to emerge. Face the various aspects of the dilemma, by examining each person's version of the facts of the situation and by sharing each person's feelings with each other, by suggesting options about what to do. Suggest the options without any editing or criticism, no matter how impractical they may sound. Choose one option and give it a chance to see what might work. Set a date to review it and decide together if it is working. Go back to the drawing board if it does not work for both.

Through this method of collaborative dialogue the couple will learn all the facts and feelings each partner has. Don't leave out the feelings. They can be a constructive part of resolution to the crisis. When stability is restored, the couple then finds themselves at a new level of balance and often with a new will to face other crises.

DAILY COUPLE TALK:
(EACH PARTNER RESPONDS)
*Name an issue that needs some collaborative
straight talk. Share the facts about the issue, as well as
the feelings. Then suggest some possible ways
to move forward on this issue.
If both feel comfortable with one of the suggestions
(or a combination of several),
choose one and try it.*

COLLABORATION

Sometimes a collaboration can lead to exciting ventures for the future. When Britton was almost 50 years old, he and Bobbye discussed what he wanted to do for the next 50 years. He told her that with good health he could live to be 100, and if he had needed education for the first part of his work life, he needed more education or retooling for a change of direction during the second part. They collaborated on this big step and agreed that he would go to graduate school for a Ph.D. It meant resigning his job and giving up a full-time salary plus insurance and benefits. But since their third daughter was about to complete her college work, financial needs would be lower. Bobbye would continue to teach English and they budgeted her salary carefully.

Then a surprising thing took place. The Woods had had a verbal agreement that neither would spend over $200 without first talking it over with each other. However, on Britton's 50th birthday Bobbye had a special surprise for him, a big-screen TV. He had been having eye trouble, needed cataract surgery, and loved football. A birthday card told him that this extravagant gift was a symbol of the faith she had in them and in their future. It was a true collaboration, a daring decision, and an important symbol. It allowed both to proceed according to the long-term plan they had decided on earlier, but it provided a daily extravagant reminder that sometimes couples need visible support in the endeavors of life.

DAILY COUPLE TALK:
(EACH PERSON DISCUSSES)
What are your long-term goals
both as individuals and as a couple?
Do you see ways to achieve some of these goals?
Collaborate.

COLLABORATION

Shifting the blame is an ancient technique. Supposedly Eve blamed the serpent when Adam asked her about eating the "forbidden fruit." Supposedly Adam tried a double shift as he blamed "that woman you gave me" when God asked about the same issue. Neither took ownership of their action, neither wanted to collaborate, both shifted the blame, and both lost the Garden.

Sometimes with our partner, we behave as though our subjective point of view is the only possibility, and all that is needed is explanation or justification. We do not want to listen to our partner's point of view; we do not want objective evidence. If we are pushed, like Adam and Eve, we will shift the blame. When we can come to the realization that there is NO one point of view in any situation, we can acknowledge that perhaps ours is only partial. Think of all the witnesses to a traffic accident who claim to have seen it clearly but who give differing testimonies to the investigating police, sometimes even giving differing points of view about the color of a car.

When we can listen to our partner's view without a challenge but without complete abandonment of our own, we are moving toward collaboration. We are admitting that truth is varied, point of view is subjective, and collaboration is desirable and very often helpful. Partners who avoid shifting the blame are moving their marriage to a new level of closeness.

DAILY COUPLE TALK:
(EACH PARTNER RESPONDS)
Discuss the issue of "point of view." Is it more important to be right or to work together? Why?

COLLABORATION

Intervention is a professional term for treatment of demoralized couples whose hope now lies in their therapist, pastor, or mediator—the last step before divorce. Prevention is the educational term for what happens to couples who are taught that their hope lies in themselves and in the resources already available within them._ Prevention is cheaper.

It starts with identifying and stopping to enjoy the good things about the relationship, the things that are working well and please both partners. Savoring the good parts is important, for it reminds both partners of the useful and beneficial connections already in place. Intervention cannot do this step because the couples do not see anything working and only feel the heavy emotional toll this has taken.

Another step in Prevention is to decide together on what could be improved. This can be as broad as "better communication" or as specific as who will do the vacuuming. What matters is a picture of a couple seriously and honestly engaged in a discussion of what would make them happier. Each partner's voice is being heard; each partner's ideas are welcomed; each partner's individual resources are going to be used. They are a team.

Partners in Prevention/Education honor each other, laugh with each other, share with each other, and make no unreasonable demands.

DAILY COUPLE TALK:
(EACH PARTNER PARTICIPATES)
What is one thing about your relationship that you are pleased with? One thing that could be improved?

COLLABORATION

Habits are easily formed and hard to change. Hold your hands up, palms toward each other. Bring your hands toward each other and intertwine your fingers, including thumbs. Check to see which thumb is now closest to you, left or right. Those with the left thumb closest are supposed to be smarter. No, that is ridiculous; it's just a matter of how you usually fold your hands. Now change the way you have your fingers folded. It may now feel awkward, and something inside wants you to change it back. Actually, it makes no difference how we fold our fingers. It is just a habit. It illustrates the number of things we do every day just because we got accustomed to doing them a certain way.

The same is true of relationship habits. Some of them began in childhood, and if we never think about them, they just continue. For example, if one partner's family-of-origin always greets each other with hugs, that partner wants to continue the familiar, warm greeting by giving it to both families. If the other partner's family-of-origin did not hug, the gesture may seem awkward and perhaps invasive to all members of that family. The family may regard the non-hugging partner as cold and reserved. All of these feelings about the hello hug go on under the conscious level; therefore, any changes will be hard to make.

Some habits are ineffective and destructive in close relations. Identifying these habits, discussing them, and working to make required changes can mean a more peaceful daily interaction.

DAILY COUPLE TALK:
(EACH PARTNER RESPONDS)
Collaborate about habits.

COLLABORATION

When gratitude and trust can collaborate within marriage, they become a gift that continuously gives, bounteously and with no strings attached. Their collaboration removes anxiety and what some have called "the paralysis of analysis." It opens hearts to the wonder of intimacy. It keeps commitment to growth in the forefront of our awareness. It gives meaning to our days.

Gratitude is the quality that helps us avoid looking at only the things we wish were different. Gratitude (or thankfulness) allows us to face life realistically but with a spirit of cooperation. It helps us laugh at the occasional craziness the punctuates our moments. It focuses our attention on what the partner is doing right and helps us to enjoy it. Gratitude speaks to us in the language of love.

Trust is a receptor. It keeps us receptive to the ways our partner is expressing positive regard and approval. It turns away the partner's words that might once have been considered critical or harmful. Trust helps partners believe that the daily discipline of practicing loving behaviors will reward us with unfathomable peace of mind and heart. Trust centers our hearts.

Gratitude and trust are words laden with meaning. Their collaboration gives couples safety and direction through the labyrinths of life.

DAILY COUPLE TALK:
(EACH PERSON ANSWERS)
Besides gratitude and trust, what are some other qualities couples need to stay on a steady course?

COLLABORATION

Whether you are planting an herb garden or training a rescue dog, having a plan is helpful. The garden will do better in a sunny area with some access to water; the dog will benefit from consistency and from positive reinforcement of good behavior. A plan provides a quicker route to success.

One evening our MEG program was on couple plans for dealing with illness. After a private time for individual couple reflection and conversation, the couples gathered in the family room. When it was their turn for dialogue, Sam and Judy talked publicly about the plans they made early in their marriage for dealing with doctors, medications, and convalescence. They even planned as young adults whether to use a cola or a ginger ale for stomach upsets. They had lived in Brazil and Mexico while their children were young, thus a clear medical plan was important in countries where a different language was spoken. Their early collaboration had guided them for years, they said, and had become very helpful in medical decisions.

Collaboration is high-quality couple-talk as partners move toward some decision that will result in a plan of action. It calls for clear communication, both talking and listening. It calls for honesty, respect, equity, and for living up to your word, once the plan is established. Collaboration is a kind of team-effort, like a double play in baseball or a halfback's run through the line in football. It is meant to produce a successful couple plan.

DAILY COUPLE TALK:
EACH PARTNER RESPONDS)
What is a subject you would enjoy collaborating on with your partner?

COLLABORATION

Whether you call it daily talk-time, couple dialogue, or huddle (Dr. John Van Eck's term), collaboration is an essential ingredient in a couple's growth pattern. Collaboration clears the air when there are ambiguities, allows understanding to flourish, and even leads to each partner's ability to filter messages with kindness. Collaboration causes what David Roth's song says:

❦ "I always find it surprising

❦ The way people say that they're falling in love

❦ When I always felt I was rising."

The closeness which collaboration brings motivates couples to share in the achievement of each other's goals. It inspires grateful hearts to give the partner appreciation and to graciously receive it. Collaboration builds useful listening skills and sharpens our focus on personal integrity. It helps partners sense that a shared life is a valuable gift. It gives direction to love, making sure it is "rising."

DAILY COUPLE TALK:
(EACH PERSON PARTICIPATES)
The folk song just quoted also asks, "How do you let love grow? You've got to give it a chance when you've found it." In what ways has your love grown since you got married?

COLLABORATION

"Rhinoceros" is a good word to help with accountability. Self-collaboration can keep us reminded of some of the things we believe are important to do in relationships—say what we want, suspend judgment, forgive easily, listen carefully, be available. Sometimes, however, self-collaboration needs to be goosed into action so that we stay accountable for the changes we are trying to make. We need ways to remind ourselves of what we really want to accomplish.

"Rhinoceros" is a mnemonic device like "spring forward, fall back" or "'I' before 'e' except after 'c'." It comes from an old saying: "You can keep a rhinoceros in the kitchen if you want to, but it WILL affect your cooking." Among other things the saying refers to the idea that in marriage we can hang on to old grievances, but it will affect our progress in couple growth and emotional closeness. Letting go of old negative habits and perspectives frees us to claim new attitudes and new skills.

Self-collaboration is an interior or mental conversation that we need in order to avoid laboring in old patterns of thinking (for example, "Why try? Nothing will ever change.") It keeps us attuned to the current ways our partner needs us to show our love, forgiveness, trust, and cooperation. And just to make ourselves accountable for the changes we are trying to make, keeping the word "rhinoceros" at hand may be helpful.

DAILY COUPLE TALK:
(EACH PARTNER RESPONDS)
What do you want to accomplish that would be a change in perspective? What is one step you could take to bring about that change?

COLLABORATION

The Woods' mentors, David and Vera Mace, have often said "Never waste a good conflict." David has also been quoted as saying, "Anger is the defense system of the ego." If anger is tied to one's ego, then how do couples learn to deal with anger issues better?

The "Love-Anger Cycle" helps to understand what is happening when one or both persons in the marriage get angry. Look at this illustration of what takes place in the cycle:

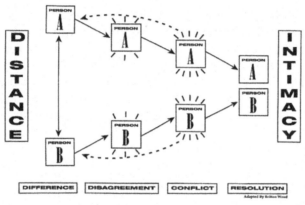

Notice that when the couple moves from the difference level to the heat of the conflict level, the dotted line shows that the tendency for most couples is to retreat to the safe difference level. What needs to happen instead is to share feelings <u>at exactly this point</u>. Once both listen to the partner's feelings, collaboration is more likely and resolution possible. Intimacy comes after resolution, but not before.

∞

DAILY COUPLE TALK:
(EACH PERSON PARTICIPATES)
Pick a low-level issue that each of you is interested in. Share your feelings about it. Doing this often makes it easier for more emotional subjects.

COLLABORATION

It is an old idea that a happy marriage is simply unattainable and can never deliver on the romantic images we continue in vain to cultivate. Think of all the disparaging jokes and cartoons picturing marriage as a thoughtless, limiting, boring, mean-spirited institution. We can choose to cling to the old idea that marriage is not supposed to be joyful, but that may just be our own rationalization to justify our lack of effort. It is far too easy to blame a ho-hum relationship on the old excuse that we simply did not pick the "right" partner.

Instead, today's new idea about marriage is that it can be designed to meet each partner's need, custom-made to ensure that each one gets a fair shot at developing whatever he/she feels is the kind of personal and couple growth needed for the future. It is very different from the past ideas of simply taking whatever happens as unchangeable and resigning oneself to make the best of a situation. That position kept many couples together, but it also kept them from applying new and different skills to resolve troubling issues.

The new idea takes honest conversation, open hearts, and willingness to collaborate with and support each other. It concentrates on what is happy in the relationship and seeks for ways to add more happiness and less stress. Marriage is the right place to invest in the new idea that in mutual love and respect we can experience both self-fulfillment and couple joy right here and right now.

DAILY COUPLE TALK:
(EACH PARTNER RESPONDS)
What is a major difference between your marriage and that of your parents? Grandparents?

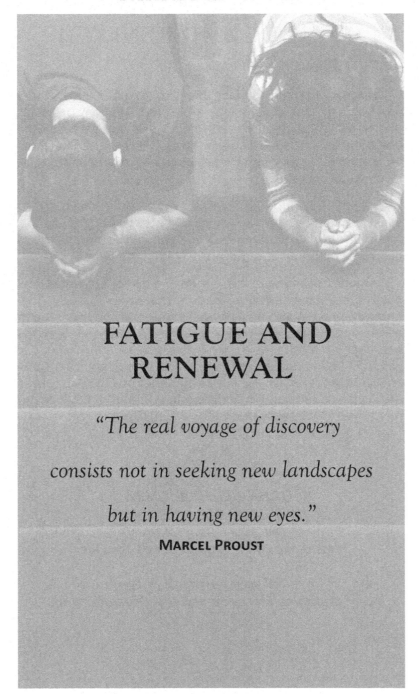

FATIGUE AND RENEWAL

"The real voyage of discovery

consists not in seeking new landscapes

but in having new eyes."

MARCEL PROUST

FATIGUE AND RENEWAL

Optimism is one of the first things to go when we are tired and frazzled. Our sleep may be disrupted. We may be eating poorly, just grabbing snacks and sugary drinks as we rush from one thing to another. Exercise? Hah! The result can be a major emotional letdown that keeps us cranky and reluctant to be loving and cooperative.

Yet a hopeful outlook is necessary to keep believing that personal and couple growth are not only necessary but rewarding. Joe and Michelle Hernandez of the Family Wellness Program describe an optimistic outlook as "finding the pony."

Everyone at times can feel buried in a pile of horse manure, but the optimistic outlook believes that where there is manure, there must also be a pony. Finding the pony consistently—personally and as a couple—can often determine how we approach each other as a couple and how we approach life in general. So in addition to the practical aids of good nutrition and sufficient exercise, tuning up our inner positivity may keep us on track. Looking for the good in a pile of difficult occurrences is a way to alert our minds and hearts to hope.

DAILY COUPLE TALK:
(EACH PARTNER RESPONDS)
Tell your partner 2 things
that make you feel good about your life.

Tell your partner 2 things
that make you feel good about your relationship.

FATIGUE AND RENEWAL

People usually find time to do the things they want to do. Avid bridge players can always find a game. Dedicated runners are on the track, even if dawn is the only available time in their day. If couples want renewal, big or small, it can happen.

Consider yourselves on a treasure hunt. You are looking for the gold that represents loving feelings. Time, trouble, and neglect has covered the feelings, but a treasure map unexpectedly comes into your possession. The map is old and dusty, and you half-way doubt it will work (probably more than half-way). But it clearly points out where the gold is, and having the gold would be nice. It might even be an exciting adventure. So.....

* Step One: Talk to each other about what you want. Do you want an orgasm every day? A love letter? A trip for just the two of you? More time together? Discuss it, with both partners contributing ideas about how to find the gold.

* Step Two: Practice doing at least one loving behavior for each other every day. Practice NOT saying or doing unloving behaviors. The map is very clear about this step.

* Step Three: Your map says you are at the right spot and advises you to dig in. You are already seeing signs that the map is correct.

DAILY COUPLE TALK:
(EACH PERSON PARTICIPATES)
Discuss Map Step One.

FATIGUE AND RENEWAL

Caring for self is a strong part of renewal. No one can love unselfishly, play wholeheartedly, or listen attentively who is depleted, mentally and physically. Taking care of your own health is an integral step in taking care of your marriage relationship. A strong "us" is made in part of a strong "me."

Caring for self requires finding and keeping a healthy physical balance. The obvious culprit in an unbalanced and physically draining schedule is a heavy work schedule. Work is not the only stressor on the body, but it is a common one. If work schedules cannot be changed, finding a gym or exercise class is a necessity. Caring for self is a pre-emptive strike for all balanced and healthy relationships.

Caring for self also requires finding and keeping a healthy emotional balance. If you find yourself sinking easily into rage, fear, or sadness, discuss it with your partner, who has probably already noticed the stress level, and get a medical check-up. Describe your feelings to a physician. New medications might help but so might building in more play together and more occasions strictly devoted to nourishing each other.

Renewal on its simplest level is energizing, both to the body and to the spirit. The personal feelings of emptiness and exhaustion begin to wane, as we allow ourselves to discover greater depths of intimacy and connection.

DAILY COUPLE TALK:
(EACH PARTNER SHARES)
*Describe a time when life felt unbalanced
and scary. How old were you?
What did you do about it?
What was the outcome?*

FATIGUE AND RENEWAL

Bobbye read a letter to the local Highway Department praising the responsible thinking that leaves tall reeds in highway roadside ditches. The reeds provide habitats for dragonflies which love to eat mosquito larvae. It is an environmentally sound decision, the letter said. A responsible and pro-active decision which can change the marital environment is the "renewal" of the mind. In other words, how we think about something affects our actions—voting, product purchases, volunteer work. Changing our thinking about our partner's actions can affect what we say and do.

"Renewing" our thinking can mean that we simply suspend judgment on something our partner says or does. Changing the tendency to look for and expect the worst motivation in others may be one of the best gifts we give our relationship.

"Renewing" the mind does not come easily and takes will and concentration. Suspending judgment is a mental discipline but like the local Highway Department's decision regarding the reeds, reducing negative assumptions creates a warmer and safer marital habitat.

DAILY COUPLE TALK:
(EACH PARTNER RESPONDS)
What is one world environmental issue that concerns you today? Is there anything you can do to help resolve that issue?

FATIGUE AND RENEWAL

Once a couple has mutually decided on renewal of their relationship, whether a big or small renewal, there is a common interest and common ground on which to meet. Fatigue, boredom, or bad habits may have crept in, but those conditions can be overcome when partners decide to take action. Renewal can move on several levels at the same time, some as visible as hyacinth bulbs bursting forth on a warm spring morning.

A good starting point is to renew giving loving behaviors to each other. Kind actions, gentle touches, and sweet words DO affect our attitudes. When we are concentrating on giving and receiving thoughtful deeds, we do not at the same time concentrate on malaise or the things that have gone wrong. Perhaps we may become better able to value both the gift AND the giver.

Another helpful relationship restorer is also simple: have some fun together. Whatever you used to enjoy doing together to relax and play, do some of those things. In addition, add some new activities. Work jigsaw puzzles together as you listen to favorite music. Take a cooking class to learn some new recipes and new kitchen techniques, then invite some couple friends to dinner. In other words, turn to each other for relaxation, not always to a blinking screen.

DAILY COUPLE TALK:
(EACH PARTNER RESPONDS)
Describe a beautiful place you have been to in the world. Share what you liked most about it. Would you want to return?

FATIGUE AND RENEWAL

A dilapidated, weather-beaten, but much-loved porch swing has been in the Woods' back yard for over 30 years. It was built and installed by a good friend, now deceased. Family photographs preceding Easter Egg hunts were always made in and around that swing. They serve as a record of grandchildren's growth over the years and as a reminder of happy family occasions.

Now the swing needs attention. The paint will have to be stripped, the wood sanded, the screws tightened, the slats repainted, and a protective finish applied. Renewal will take time and effort, but it is the preferred choice rather than merely throwing the swing away and buying a new one. There are too many memories simply to discard it.

Relationships too sometimes need renewal, when time, weather, and stress have led to a kind of fatigue. Effort will be needed to make repairs, but there will also be pleasure and satisfaction as two people work together to preserve something important.

∞

DAILY COUPLE TALK:
(EACH PERSON PARTICIPATES)
First, discuss together what you would want in a "renewed" relationship? Do you just want to recover some of the old happy times, or do you want to add some new dimensions? If so what?

FATIGUE AND RENEWAL

One summer afternoon our son-in-law Terry and grandson David took down a dead sweet gum tree in our back yard. The tree unfortunately was the home of a determined woodpecker, who had made himself an apartment deep inside the tree trunk. Later in the afternoon Bobbye heard distressed bird noises coming from the limb of another tree in the back yard. The woodpecker had returned and was expressing extreme frustration with not only the disappearance of his apartment but the whole apartment house. After pouring out his concerns, he left the yard. He has never returned.

No partner who is honest has not at some time felt frustrated or distressed over the perceived injustices of married life. Marriage is not only the legal joining of two lives but also the emotional melding of two different families, backgrounds, personalities, and outlooks. That there should be difficulties goes without saying, and like the woodpecker some partners see no alternative but to leave the yard.

There ARE reasons to end marriages, intolerable actions and/or addictions that make building an "us" impossible. Too many unions, however, make a decision too soon and fail to see that there are ways to survive frustrations, differences, and emotional fatigue. Renewal takes time, of course, but the rewards are worth it, especially measured against the hardships and expense of dissolving the marriage.

DAILY COUPLE TALK:
(EACH PARTNER RESPONDS)
If you were to discuss the subject of marriage with some of your friends today, what would you say?

FATIGUE AND RENEWAL

A baseball sports announcer recently said that a certain young pitcher had many expert pitches in his arsenal but what really mattered to his success was what was "between his ears." The announcer meant that too many concerns about batters, opposing line-ups, and expectations were robbing him of his ability to throw consistent strikes. What lies in our heads—our beliefs, fears, and goals—also affects our attitudes toward success in marriage.

Growth and change may be the rhythm of nature, but couple growth and renewal is sometimes thwarted by old habits and by a personal reluctance to consider new relational skills. Marriage is not a spectator sport. It calls for tough decisions, persistent efforts, and the practice of saying no to everything that crowds out couple growth. Here are some facets of the growing relationship worth considering:

1. It has to rely on what IS; it knows that it is not helpful to bemoan the blissful way the relationship felt in its early days.
2. It works best when partners see themselves as equals.
4. It knows that no relationship remains romantic "naturally."

3. It consistently practices empathy and compassion.
4. It makes a habit of loving behaviors.

DAILY COUPLE TALK:
(EACH PERSON ANSWERS)
Which of the five statements about a growing relationship do you find most difficult? Why?

FATIGUE AND RENEWAL

The award-winning TV mini-series called "Band of Brothers" follows a group of WWII paratroopers from their basic training until the end of the war. In one of the final episodes, one paratrooper, stationed in a small town in Germany, becomes bored with his mop-up duties and spends most of his time in a bar. He even cynically questions the meaning of the war. One day on patrol he is in a small group who go by an immense field with high walls around it. Puzzled they look for a gate, and when they find it and look in, they are shocked to see prisoners in striped pajamas, emaciated and ill. "Who are you?" the paratrooper asks. One prisoner who is holding a dead elderly man in his arms tells him that they are artists, dissidents, revolutionaries. This makes no sense to that soldier, so finally the prisoner says, "Juden. We are Jews." The patrol learns that as the Germans left, they had shot everyone until they ran out of ammunition. Then they left the rest to die of hunger. The tragic situation changes completely the paratrooper's cynical attitude.

Though definitions of and reactions to tragedy and loss may vary from couple to couple, there are some guidelines for getting through: collaborate on sharing respectfully and fairly. Recognize that people grieve in different ways. Give space and support to each other. Orchestrate times to talk honestly, reveal feelings, and discuss differences. Validate each other and get help when needed. Facing tragedy together can add a new dimension to the relationship.

DAILY COUPLE TALK:
(EACH PARTNER ANSWERS)
What difficulty/tragedy/loss have you encountered as a couple? What happened as a result?

FATIGUE AND RENEWAL

Couple fatigue can come from many sources: overwork, too many arguments that go around in circles, even the relatively new situation called "phubbing," when we snub our partner in favor of our phone, reaching for a virtual reality rather that who's right in front of us.

One way back to couple health and recovery is a renewed commitment to couple growth. Couple growth is hard to define because for each couple it will be different. But there are enough similarities to make it relevant. First, make a plan together about what each wants from and for the relationship. Then decide together some ways to bring about the desires. Be specific. "I'd like for us to be closer" is not as specific as "I'd like for us to take 15 minutes a day just for us to talk about what we want and what we are feeling."

Couple plans are goals to work toward and bring their own energy, but they also establish boundaries. For example, if your 15-minute conversation plan is to be enacted, it will mean that others must be informed about the need to respect your time together. Children are obvious intruders on boundaries, but suppose one of your elderly parents lives close and wants a visit every day just at the time you set. Staying committed to your couple plans means communicating difficult information, but it also means that the boundaries are established, fatigue is reduced, renewal noticeable, and that it happens in a surprisingly short time.

DAILY COUPLE TALK:
(EACH PARTNER RESPONDS)
What is one activity you would like to do (or do more of) with your partner?

FATIGUE AND RENEWAL

Research suggests that a new phenomenon will soon be apparent in the work force. For the first time ever, young women just out of university will be making more money than young men. This phenomenon can have an effect on marriage, as more and more couples will have to deal with what has long been an important issue: the division of labor within the home.

Of course, times have changed and with them supposedly for modern couples a much more equitable sharing of household tasks. However at a recent national conference on families, a break-out session on Marital Well-Being reported on two five-year studies of Mexican-American and African-American couples. The researcher stated that high rates of discord in the homes of these two groups centered around "home tasks and family responsibilities" and who should perform them. As more women worked outside the home, they wanted more cooperation from their partners. When they did not get it, there were problems or as the researcher put it, "marital dissatisfaction." Apparently our society still has some issues to address on chores and just at the time the new phenomenon is getting ready to add more stress.

DAILY COUPLE TALK:
(EACH PARTNER ANSWERS)
What are the shared household duties that work best for you? Which ones are yet to be worked out?

FATIGUE AND RENEWAL

Rebooting romance is a surprisingly easy activity. It is a celebration. It can happen at any time—on an evening with candles, music and flowers; during a trip to investigate National Parks; on a walk through the neighborhood; in the car after a football game. It is a warm recognition of the fact that marriage has found us and we are happy to be found. It takes two partners who are willing to talk honestly with each other about laundry and dreams, pets and hopes for the future, insurance policies and an ideal vacation.

One goal of this celebration is to produce the same effect on friends and colleagues as in the famous restaurant scene in the movie "Sleepless in Seattle." After a long look at the main character's enthusiastic and lengthy response to her partner, another diner told her waiter, "I'll have what she's having." Celebrations can be catching.

Rebooting romance is the time for enjoyment, marriage enjoyment. We are helpmeets, mates, friends, lovers, wives, husbands. We complement each other; we mesh; we share; we dovetail; we bond. We laugh and giggle; we are on a romantic adventure together; we are still attracted to each other; WE ENJOY. We celebrate what is right with this powerful incentive, this eternal invitation, this universal and primitive longing to be attached in a meaningful relationship with someone we love. Rebooting romance is a celebration of what's right with marriage.

DAILY COUPLE TALK:
(EACH PERSON PARTICIPATES)
Look at the last sentence and tell your partner something that you want to celebrate about marriage.

FATIGUE AND RENEWAL

In the closing scene of the Broadway show "Camelot," a fatigued and discouraged King Arthur is marshalling his troops to go into battle against the traitor Mordred. At the last minute he discovers a young boy dragging a sword he can barely lift. The boy has come to fight with King Arthur, he says, as an admirer of chivalry, the Round Table, and honor.

Arthur is touched by the boy's words, but he does not let him go into what he fears will be a losing battle, because Arthur believes there needs to be someone left to tell the story of Camelot. The play ends with a rejuvenated Arthur sending the boy away. "Run, boy, run!" are Arthur's last words as he straps on his armor and picks up Excalibur.

Some days partners are fatigued and discouraged. No one seems to care that marriage is a life-sustaining partnership. Threats abound against the peace and sanctity of the home. No one seems to care that children need its structure, even the children themselves. The ideal seems remote that love can prevail in a violent and cynical world. For just such days, the following practices are important. Commit to growth. Show loving behaviors. Share your feelings. Listen. Be affectionate. Stick steadfastly to conversation, at least 15 minutes a day. Give praise and compliments. Renewal comes when we stick to our ideals and to the practices that can bring the return of hope. Like Arthur, we are influencing the next generation.

DAILY COUPLE TALK:
(EACH PARTNER PARTICIPATES)
Name someone you know who seems to stick to his/her ideals. Give an illustration.

FATIGUE AND RENEWAL

Keeping marriage fresh, renewed, and entertaining stems from equal parts of realism and mystery. The realistic part is obvious. The other part cannot be overlooked, however, the sheer, inexplicable wonder and mystery that is also a part of the marriage relationship.

Recently a local kindergarten child was hospitalized with a rare form of cancer. The Make-a-Wish foundation learned that the child wished she could pet a cheetah. It was a formidable request, but they learned that a cheetah at an area animal park had just died giving birth to twins. The ailing child was allowed to visit the baby cheetahs in their nursery, to hold them, pet them, and give them a bottle. Soon her cancer went into remission and the child entered first grade. By second grade the cancer had returned.

Once again she wanted to pet the cheetahs. This time she could only stand at the chain-link fence and was warned that the half-grown cheetahs would not know her. But the adults were wrong. Miraculously the two cheetahs ran to the fence, let her pet them, and licked her hand. It was such a mysterious moment that the local newspaper did a story on it.

But it is no more mysterious and wonderful than a working, happy marriage relationship. Realism we can't do without, but for renewal, opening our hearts to wonder works.

DAILY COUPLE TALK:
(EACH PERSON PARTICIPATES)
Recall a moment of wonder the two of you have shared.

FATIGUE AND RENEWAL

It is not necessary to experience "April in Paris" in order to renew a feeling of romance in the relationship. Many couples say they are surprised at how simple, ordinary actions can lead to extraordinary feelings.

George tells about how much he likes to sit in the back yard in the late afternoon watching hummingbirds come to a big, red feeder. He enjoys their color, their movement, and their habits. He says he can feel himself "unwinding" after a busy day. One afternoon his partner Caroline came outside to sit with him. They talked, had lemonade together, and watched the birds. Soon they were holding hands, and both were convinced that this simple experience was a much-needed romantic interlude.

Other couples see the phone calls, texts, and lunch-box notes that they get from their partners as romantic connections saying, "I am thinking about you. I love you." One night a month Jenny cooks a dinner of special favorites for Mark. The dinner always has candles on the table, favorite music playing, and a note or card expressing something romantic. Terrence still sends roses after many years together, and there is always a card describing his partner's best body parts. Joy says she values the cards as much as the roses.

Being regularly assured that you are special can be as important as expensive vacations.

DAILY COUPLE TALK:
(EACH PARTNER RESPONDS)
What is a romantic experience you have enjoyed recently with your partner?

FATIGUE AND RENEWAL

Sometimes no matter how strong and prepared you are, life's storms get you down. It's more than fatigue; it's between numbing shock and stressful pain. Getting through the day is the only goal manageable. Here is the time when a strong "us" can make a crucial difference in couple health and in renewal.

Many couples who have endured tremendous losses (children, jobs, health, houses, businesses) say that the one tool that helped them to remain intact (and sane, as one said) was their earlier development of A SUPPORTIVE WAY OF TALKING TO EACH OTHER. When the crisis came they were already adept at sharing their feelings with each other and at listening carefully to each other's sorrows and frustrations. Leaning on the "us" in a supportive conversation became not just a means of survival but a means of growth, both for the individual and for the marriage.

One couple at the tragic death of their son eventually designed and installed a small garden at their church with a bench bearing a favorite quotation. Together they chose the flowers and shrubs that would insure something is colorful there at any time of the year. In this way they were able to bring beauty out of sorrow. The joint approach to grief and restoration worked because they had made a habit of using the simple healing properties of supportive conversation.

DAILY COUPLE TALK:
(EACH PERSON PARTICIPATES)
Share one joy you experienced recently.
Share one concern. Listen.

FATIGUE AND RENEWAL

Unfortunately for many couples the time spent getting to know each other in courtship gets reduced in marriage. An activity like dinner, movie, or tennis was really just an excuse to get together to talk and to explore the ways they were beginning to care for each other. Changing this process in marriage also changes some of the reasons they were interested in each other initially. Avoiding conversations is not a direct intention. It is more a response about what can be left out of a debilitating day of long hours and hard work. Yet talking together is what both partners need for growth and connection.

Even a 15-minute conversation a day about feelings provides needed information. Here is where you learn what's going on in both worlds, both the events and the feelings they aroused. Here is where you learn what support is needed and what mutual affirmations need to be exchanged. Without the discipline of engaging in a pre-arranged conversation, much of this needed information does not get exchanged until there is some kind of a conflict.

If there are unresolved issues that need to be faced, set an appointment to deal with them. If there are schedule items that must be discussed, find a way to deal with them outside this conversation time. Remember that you fell in love during intimate conversations and you are more likely to stay in love if you make time to continue them.

DAILY COUPLE TALK:
(EACH PARTNER RESPONDS)
So, what happened today that made you feel good?
What happened that made you feel bad?

FATIGUE AND RENEWAL

Someone has said that insanity is doing the same thing over and over yet expecting a different result. Perhaps that is true in general of many couples who try to use the same inadequate solutions for reoccurring problems and issues.

One strength of marriage education is that both partners learn the skill-building at the same time, whether it be conflict management, new ways of communication, or better methods of dealing with family-of-origin issues. Both pick up new ways to relate and one does not become an authority telling the other, "YOU need to try this!" The new skill is available to both and the couple explores together whether or not it (or something like it) would be beneficial to them.

Bobbye and Britton's early struggles with conflict management is a good example. Both looked at conflict differently. Both grew frustrated when often-repeated arguments failed to reach resolution because different skills were being used by each partner.

When they were both trained at the same time by the Association of Couples in Marriage Enrichment (now called Better Marriages. Org,}, they learned a new way to deal with anger and conflict and almost immediately were able to use the technique together to find a resolution to an old, nagging issue. The important thing was not the technique; it was that they learned it together and used it together.

DAILY COUPLE TALK:
(EACH PARTNER PARTICIPATES)
What is one issue in your relationship that you would like to resolve? What kind of skill-building would be most helpful?

FATIGUE AND RENEWAL

Happily married couples treasure the stories and images of how they first met, how they felt, and how they courted. It is their private history, set apart from everyone else's, and re-counted with fondness and pleasure. These moments are what toasts celebrate-- our history and by extension our future. They show our pride in possessing such a wonderful partner, blessed in our choice and blessed to have been chosen.

Drawing on happy memories gets us through times of deprivation, helping us to believe that the future can be more fulfilling. It is keeping a firm and realistic hold of the present while drawing from the wells of memory and symbolism. It is acknowledging both partners' flaws and mistakes, seeking to fix what is possible, and all the while holding on to the eagerness we felt in our hearts when we first began our re-lationship. It is allowing the marriage to be reshaped and refurbished and renewed.

Marriages can be custom-made by the couple in ways that their grandparents never dreamed possible. A good marriage can give strength after a troubled childhood and adolescence; it can meet needs for a stable family life; it can fulfill sexual needs and build self-esteem. It is an exciting adventure and gratifies our need for friendship, affection, and understanding. It is greater than the sum of its parts, but one of those parts has to be the joyful and imaginative memories of our beginning.

DAILY COUPLE TALK:
(EACH PARTNER RESPONDS)
*Describe what you felt when you first
knew this was "the one."*

FATIGUE AND RENEWAL

As the old song says, "Little things mean a lot." Suppose the big things that trouble couples are largely settled:

- 🐝 You maintain equal power and concentrate on couple growth.
- 🐝 You talk daily with each other.
- 🐝 You have made it safe to handle differences and conflict.
- 🐝 You collaborate on decisions with respect and careful listening.

Now it's the "little things" that can add spice and flavor to the every day. Pay attention to Dr. Gottman's 5:1 Ratio. If negative statements or criticism have happened, keep the positive statements coming until there is a balance. Use terms of endearments, private nicknames, and gestures of affection. Welcome Home and Good Morning hugs and kisses should not be perfunctory. Write cards and post-it notes with expressions of regard and/or sexy suggestions and leave them in unusual places, just for the surprise-and-delight factor. Perform some task usually done by the partner, such as unloading the dishwasher or putting gas in the car. Dance in the kitchen as you prepare dinner.

All of these are "little things," and are not of great significance if each is taken only for itself. But the "little things" can easily add up and have a way of burrowing into our hearts and shining up a drab day.

DAILY COUPLE TALK:
(EACH PERSON PARTICIPATES)
Reread the next-to-last paragraph. Choose one of the "little things" and use it as a surprise.

FATIGUE AND RENEWAL

Most couples not only know what their "trouble" is but also know that most of it lies within the relationship itself. True, sometimes in-laws, children, or a difficult job situation intrudes from the outside in a way that upsets couple closeness. But dealing with this kind of intrusion is sometimes easier than facing the relationship "trouble" that can fester and lead to emotional weariness.

Perhaps Cameron Mackintosh, producer of musical theater such as "Phantom of the Opera," "Les Miserables," and "Cats," has some helpful suggestions. As each of these shows entered their third decade, Mackintosh reworked each show to make a new production, quicker, livelier, and of more interest to younger audiences. "I'm not interested in being the Madame Tussauds of musicals," Mackintosh said. "Musical theater is a living creation, and they [should be] always contemporary and relevant." Mackintosh could have been talking about couples as well.

Confronting "trouble," especially the kind that has been around for a while, can be a way of renewing the relationship and keeping it "contemporary and relevant." Whether the "trouble" is not listening, leaving out necessary time for couple recreation and play, having too many expectations, avoiding arguments, or demonstrating a lack of trust—to name a few—confronting the trouble together can reduce clutter and complications. Success leaves a kind of simplicity that is timeless.

DAILY COUPLE TALK:
(EACH PARTNER RESPONDS)
What is one decidedly relevant
thing about you as a couple?

FATIGUE AND RENEWAL

An advertisement for a new concept in restaurants announced that it would be "farm-to-table." The menu would feature the freshest ingredients available, with no latent pesticides or growth hormones. The menu would feature tried-and-true family recipes, and the public was requested to get ready to "open your palate to new flavors." That culinary request could also be true for couples—those who want an exciting relational experience, a different perspective on couple closeness, and an opportunity to add the "new flavor" of nurturing.

Although the process works best with mutual couple participation, it also can work when one partner chooses to be the catalyst for change. Get clear on what you want for yourself and for your relationship, and be specific. "We never have any fun" sounds accusative and is not as clear and achievable as "I want us to take swing dance lessons." Expect occasional setbacks. Enjoy the "new flavors" of added information about your partner's opinions, daily experiences, and personal feelings gleaned from the conversation.

After ample time for adjustments to a simple change, see if a mutual plan for other changes might work. A date night? A joint project, volunteer activity, or exercise program? A discussion of an acceptable way to deal with disagreements? Adding just one more change to your routine will add the "new flavors" and bring more zest to the relationship.

DAILY COUPLE TALK:
(EACH PERSON PARTICIPATES)
*What is one change in your relationship
you would like to try?*

FATIGUE AND RENEWAL

Renewal can come at any time. Britton and Bobbye have been married for 60 years. For most of their married life they tried to practice the skills learned through marriage education. They considered themselves adjusted, still in love, and accepting of each other's limitations. They were happy, had a loving family, and helped others practice the social skills that they knew "worked."

One day recently with a joyful reaction they came together physically and emotionally in a new way. The closeness and enthusiasm in the relationship suddenly bubbled to the surface and astonished both of them. They have tried to analyze what comprises their new connection. They cannot overlook years of effort, of course, but here are the component parts that comprise "renewal":

1. They deliberately make a space in every day for what they now call "our time." This is done no matter what else is happening.
2. They include in "our time" an intimate conversation without fail, talking not about things outside the relationship but about the "us" and its construction.
3. They give each other plenty of physical signs of affection.
4. They laugh together, lightening the cares of the day and celebrating the happy "renewal."

DAILY COUPLE TALK:
(EACH PARTNER RESPONDS)
Different couples prize different component parts of closeness. What parts of your relationship give you the most joy? Try to get those parts into every day, and every day can be a "renewal."

FATIGUE AND RENEWAL

Studies show that we can improve our health and keep it longer if we pay attention to what we eat (and don't eat) and how diligent we are about exercise. Even walking for 20 minutes a day, they show, has a remarkable effect on blood pressure, circulation, digestion, and attitude. Smoking, of course, is too dangerous and destructive.

Studies also show that reading bedtime stories to children produces great and measurable benefits. It gives valuable bonding time with parents, teaches that reading is important, and stimulates kids' creative thinking. It even helps children calm down and fall asleep more easily.

Studies also show that when couples learn and practice new relational skills that enable them to address their divisive issues, the benefits are immediate—not just for the couple but for children, job performance, and extended family. When one partner begins to change and have more self-control—and not devote energy to try to control, fix, and change the other partner—both partners experience the growth of trust, healing, and the ability to forgive.

Too many couples get caught in the worry-web of rehearsing what is wrong with their couple relationship and never get to the point of being responsive to each other. Listening, seeking to meet needs, and celebrating the good things in the relationship brings renewal. Learning and practicing heart-healthy skills can be your gift to your relationship.

DAILY COUPLE TALK:
(EACH PERSON PARTICIPATES)
One gift I bring to our relationship is _____ .
One gift you bring is _____ .

FATIGUE AND RENEWAL

A plan for couple renewal takes some effort, but it also can have exciting benefits for both partners. Start with an informal discussion about what you want to accomplish. When the precise goal is identified, talk at length about the desired couple result of the goal. Picturing what you want often provides the energy to actually do it. Even if just one partner is pushing for the goal, it at least gives helpful information to the other about what one thinks the relationship needs.

Do you want more equality? Is one tired of always riding in the passenger seat? Do you want more fun, perhaps even including a week-end trip for two? Do you want a 15-minute intimate talk-time every day? Do you want more sex more often? Do you want a weekly couple-walk in a nearby park? The point is, both partners need to be involved in the goal-setting. It's what the business world calls a "merger-deal."

After discussing the renewal result you want, craft together the steps you might take to make it happen. Keep it simple. It's like learning to drive, where what you are experiencing teaches just as much as what you have already learned. Couple renewal plans should be exciting, even talking about them.

DAILY COUPLE TALK:
(EACH PARTNER RESPONDS)
*Identify a wished-for couple goal that
you can discuss later.*

FATIGUE AND RENEWAL

The Woods have a big back yard, perfect for Easter Egg hunts held at family gatherings over many years. The hunt originally had real eggs dyed in bright colors. Then it changed to plastic eggs stuffed with candy. Today the plastic eggs hold more money than candy, and food, toiletries, gift cards, and batteries are also included as children have become young adults. Change is the one constant families can expect.

One beautiful benefit of couple renewal is that it's often done in the midst of change. When couples can keep their focus on their own closeness and connection, even while life swirls around them, every change is an opportunity for couple growth. As time goes by and family changes occur, rather than wearily hanging on to accomplishments of the past, a couple needs to constantly evaluate its relationship, its "us," toward steady improvement and mutual growth. Communication skills rarely stay in place without attention. Negotiation and decision-making need exercise. Couple closeness is fleeting without effort. Giving loving behaviors can wither without constant reminder of why they are needed.

Family changes call for a couple's relational renewal, and the fatigue of life's pace is easily alleviated by the excitement of shaping society's most basic and important social relationship to fit the demands of that pace.

DAILY COUPLE TALK:
(EACH PARTNER PARTICIPATES)
Examine the changes around you over the last few years. Which ones have most affected you? Which couple skills do you need to renew in order to stay current?

FATIGUE AND RENEWAL

Renewal often comes when together partners can face some tragedy or loss in their lives and deal with it. Grief can be elusive and sneaky, returning long after a person thinks he/she is "over" the sad occasion.

Robert Frost has a poem called "Home Burial" that illustrates this truth. A New England farming couple experience the loss of their first baby. The farmer had dug the grave in his family graveyard, buried the infant, and expected to go on with farm life. He resents his wife's tears, in case some neighbor should come by, and wants to discuss the weather with her, where too much rain is rotting his fences. His wife is furious with what she considers his lack of emotion, spends time every day looking out the window at the baby's grave, and threatens to leave. Both partners are grieving in their own way even though it is a couple loss. Symbolically at the poem's ending their front door is left open, perhaps suggesting some hope for resolution.

Renewal after loss does not come with one candid conversation, perhaps not even after several. But if partners give each other time, are quick to listen and not criticize, and continue to exchange their thoughts and feelings, renewal can at least begin. Neither partner will ever get back to where they were before the loss, but with time they can share a place together that neither has ever been. As that place becomes familiar, trusted, and shared, the fabric of life suddenly has new threads and designs not noticed before.

DAILY COUPLE TALK:
(EACH PARTNER RESPONDS)
Describe a loss you have experienced in your life and tell what you learned.

FATIGUE AND RENEWAL

Although not as historically decisive as Martin Luther nailing his 95 theses to a church door, partners in the holy bonds of matrimony regularly bring each other hopes, concerns, apologies, wishes, and needs for nourishment. This demonstrates the trust partners have that in love one special person can ease aching hurts and worried minds. It shows the confidence that in honestly sharing with this one person, the partner can count on having someone in his/her corner, someone who both understands and accepts. It is one of the great benefits of marriage.

Whatever else happens, surely this sweet exchange fulfills some of the pledges we made to each other at our wedding, for example, promising our support "in sickness and in health, "for richer for poorer." In the emotion of the wedding scene, we probably had no idea of the healthful benefits we would later get from a faithful openness to each other. That so many couples remain unaware of this life-giving exchange is one of the tragedies of married life.

Want help for loneliness or stress? Want someone who will listen to your funny experience at work? Want an apology for what the partner said that hurt you? Want to extend forgiveness for an acknowledged pinch? Want to deal with anger situations rather than let them accumulate?

Life can be a daily renewal experience when each partner makes sharing a priority. And like Martin Luther's action, the sharing becomes part of life's rich history.

DAILY COUPLE TALK:
(EACH PARTNER ANSWERS)
What is one hope, need, apology, or experience you would like to share today?

FATIGUE AND RENEWAL

A radio ad had a dramatized roll-call of the first day of school. After calling a few names, the teacher paused and asked tentatively, "Tara Dactyl?" A very weary voice said, "Here." There are many painful things from the past that none of us had control over, including our names. Getting over them can sometimes be harder than we expected.

That's where a 75-year, $20 million dollar study conducted by Harvard University can be helpful. 268 undergraduate men from all walks of life allowed researchers to study their lives over 38 years. The study was to find out what made these men happy and to present those "secrets to happiness" with a combination of statistics and anecdotes. The study culminated in a book written by Harvard psychiatrist George Vaillant, who says the whole thing can be summed up in a five-word conclusion: "Happiness is love. Full stop." While most people theoretically believe that love is important, acting it out in the everyday can be challenging. Because of the past experiences some people labor under and the attitudes these experiences have engendered, giving and receiving love for some can be a life-long renewal task.

The task can be made easier by facing the issue, discussing it with your marriage partner, and planning a few steps for the future. Together you make it happen. Who knows? With a loving partner and a new name, maybe Tara Dactyl is somewhere happily celebrating right now.

DAILY COUPLE TALK:
(EACH PARTNER RESPONDS)
*What is one accomplishment for the future
that you would like to undertake?
What might be a reasonable first step?*

FATIGUE AND RENEWAL

Renewal can be celebrated many times over the years as the relationship grows and the "us" develops. From the euphoric honeymoon experience to the relaxed comfort of retirement, loving partners at many ages and stages of life can feel the impact of the connection between them and the power it brings. As the "us" grows over the long-term, most couples notice that there are fewer meltdowns and more use of relevant strategies to address the differences that all couples have.

This is different from merely tolerating differences and slowly developing a truce to handle them. One partner tacitly agrees to say nothing about annoying or frustrating actions if the other partner will do the same. Both live in a kind of bitter détente. They do not share each other's hopes and dreams, and they never discuss what they would like to achieve in their marriage or what future goals could make each one happier.

Renewal can happen every time a couple chooses to be honest instead of indifferent or ambiguous, to trust each other instead of warily watching for a mistake, and to cooperate instead of ignore. As the "us" settles into a steady growth pattern (a process that Marcel Proust once called having "new eyes"), couples of all ages and stages are able to see new horizons and new perspectives.

DAILY COUPLE TALK:
(EACH PERSON PARTICIPATES)
Renewal is worth the effort. It keeps the relationship current and fresh. Celebrate renewal by reviewing something you have worked on together that has nourished the "us."

MARRIAGE FOR THE EVERDAY

GIVING AND GETTING

"We make a living by what we get;

we make a life by what we give."

WINSTON CHURCHILL

GIVING AND GETTING

According to Joe and Michelle Hernandez of the Family Wellness program, the five most challenging areas for couples are money, sex, children, use of time, and division of tasks. Notice money is first. A surprising number of people, young and old, who participated in the Woods' informal survey about marriage stated that talking about financial issues was the answer to the question, "What advice would you give a friend who is getting married?" Linda put it, "Get all the financial advice you can get." Monica advised, "Set a budget together." Tony felt that "financial responsibility" was an imperative. They all talked about the need to understand each other's ideas about money and to do so as early as possible.

Getting enough money to be comfortable, making a budget together, agreement on a personal spending ceiling for big purchases, decisions on separate or joint accounts at the bank, donations to worthy causes, paying off credit cards each month—these are practical issues that couples can work together on, and when they do, a surprisingly high number of financial disagreements disappear.

DAILY COUPLE TALK:
(EACH PARTNER RESPONDS)
Of the common subjects listed in the last paragraph, which one have you spent the most time discussing? What did you decide? Why?

GIVING AND GETTING

In Shakespeare's <u>Macbeth</u> young prince Duncan is being encouraged by McDuff to return to Scotland and rightfully assume the throne. After a period of testing each other, Duncan tells McDuff the attributes he believes a king should have. He includes magnanimity as one of them. The dictionary defines this word as "generosity of spirit," "noble in soul or mind." It is an attribute greatly needed in a growing relationship.

A generous spirit looks for ways to be helpful to the partner. Rather than waiting to be asked to share in a task, a generous spirit volunteers. That willingness is not lost on the other partner even if he/she is perfectly capable of performing the task alone. Thus magnanimity concerning daily tasks abundantly creates good feelings, which are also extended to other parts of the relationship. This can happen even if the partner does not accept the offer to help.

A generous spirit does not waste time thinking of "if only." There of course will be things in the past that we regret doing or saying, for both partners, but dwelling on them cannot change the results. Letting them go and concentrating our efforts on accomplishing loving behaviors in the present is much more practical.

DAILY COUPLE TALK:
(EACH PARTNER ANSWERS)
Name one thing your partner has done for you recently that you know took extra effort on his/her part.
Express your appreciation.

GIVING AND GETTING

Accepting words of appreciation is hard for some people. It is typical to hear someone on the tennis court compliment an opponent on a really good serve. Then that complimented person is likely to say, "Yeah, one in ten serves is not bad." Appreciation sustains our self-worth and sweet words feed our hungry hearts. Yet so often we choose to minimize the compliment, make a joke about it, or to toss it back quickly with something like, "Oh, YOU'RE the one who should be thanked!"

Learning to say a simple "thank you" to a word of appreciation is a special skill. The fact is that everyone thrives in a generous and sincere relationship. When the partner offers a compliment, try to avoid asking yourself, "What does he/she really want?" or "How much is it going to cost me?" Don't worry about whether you "deserve" it or not. Let the compliment be freely given and freely received with openness and good will.

Then concentrate on how you can return the words. One way is to use what you have learned about the things your partner would like to be appreciated for. Affirming the partner is easier when you know the ways he/she likes to be noticed. In this way getting and receiving compliments builds a warm atmosphere of encouragement that fills the lonely places in our lives and at the same time builds the relationship.

DAILY COUPLE TALK:
(EACH PERSON PARTICIPATES)
What are three things you really appreciate about your partner?

GIVING AND GETTING

John D. Rockefeller once said, "Don't be afraid to give up the good to go for the great." Many marriages are still legally intact because the partners are coasting, just waiting for the children to grow up, or because they regard divorce as a costly failure, or because they see no better options, or because they have settled for what they already know about each other as enough. There is emotional distance between them and probably has been for some time, yet if someone asked about their marriage they would both classify it as "good."

Giving up the safe, the familiar, and the easy can be difficult, especially if most couples you know are not doing it. Learning to believe that a couple can make changes and that those changes can bring a new excitement and energy to both partner takes some getting used to.

Great marriages do not happen by chance. They grow over time as couples regularly talk to each other about personal things. They are carefully built as couples speak their minds to each other and begin to fight fairly. Great marriages are full of freely expressed affection and joyful intimacy. Great marriages happen because two people want them and are willing to do the things that produce understanding, growth, and enduring love.

DAILY COUPLE TALK:
(EACH PARTNER RESPONDS)
Getting a great marriage is a great adventure of knowing another person really well. What have you learned about your partner recently that you did not know before?

GIVING AND GETTING

One long-held difference between Britton and Bobbye is about punctuality. Bobbye grew up in a family that valued it and taught her, "Never be late!" Britton's family-of-origin did not value it and neither did he. He was once even late for a flight at the airport, a thing that makes Bobbye shudder just to think about.

One morning after 59 years of struggle over this issue, Bobbye had to go to a meeting at 9:15. Britton was to be in the same place a little later and did not want to take two cars. They agreed the evening before to leave home together at 9:00. At 8:40 Britton remembered their deal and dressed in record time. By 8:55 he was ready to go. It was a "gift" to the relationship, he said, and was thanked profusely. How did this old issue get resolved?

First of all, the difference was acknowledged. Both views regarding the subject had been presented many times. Both partners knew that one partner found the subject to be important and one did not. On this occasion the Woods went with the partner who cared most about the subject. Punctuality is a small issue in the grand scheme of things, and choosing to honor it as a "gift" to Bobbye was also small. However, it made a big difference to Bobbye."

Britton did not "give in" on this issue, sounding like a petulant adolescent who in frustration says, "Oh, have it YOUR way." He did not "give up," as though he were surrendering a strategic position on the battlefield. He simply gifted Bobbye's need to be punctual and joined her.

DAILY COUPLE TALK:
(EACH PARTNER RESPONDS)
What "gift" has your partner given that was important to you? What "gift" have you given?

GIVING AND GETTING

Zucchini can be grilled, baked, fried, and sautéed. It can give body to muffins, soups, and breads. It can appear in dips, fritters, and pasta. It is gluten-free and low in calories.

Giving and receiving physical affection, like using zucchini, offers variety. Hugs, for example, should come often, from the perfunctory hello-and-goodbye hug to the lingering one-Mississippi, two-Mississippi, three-Mississippi, four-Mississippi, five-Mississippi embrace whose long count frees the mind and allows partners to concentrate on each other's bodies.

Kisses too need to have variety. Pecks on the cheek are for family and high school reunions. Kisses on the mouth are for lovers. They can be tender, inquisitive, passionate, welcoming, awakening, or re-assuring. They should be used often. Hormone challenged teen-agers know little to nothing about kissing compared to a seasoned veteran of marriage who has explored all kissable places and has learned which ones give the maximum pleasure.

Giving and getting attention to the body's so-called "pleasure centers" is important . Getting in touch with the body's amazing chemistry is more than a marital routine, and like cooking with the zucchini, needs variety and innovation.

DAILY COUPLE TALK:
(EACH ONE PARTICIPATES)
*Britton and Bobbye once won a bottle of
champagne on a cruise marriage show for being the
contestants with the most original place
to have made "whoopee."
Where has been one of your unusual places?
How did it make you feel?*

GIVING AND GETTING

Finding a balance between work and play does more that keep Jack from being "a dull boy," as the old adage says. It also equips Jack (and Jill) to keep their relationship running smoothly.

GET plenty of rest and exercise. Overworked and over-stressed people have no interest in building anything, including relationships.

GET along. Learn to compromise, to deal with "pinches," and to be the appreciative partner who is watching for all the partner's endearing and amusing qualities that need complimenting.

GIVE quality time to each other. Too often we talk briefly on our way to somewhere else or can only give each other the left-overs of our busy schedules. Make a priority of the 15-minute daily conversation where you talk about yourselves. This keeps you current.

GIVE gifts. These do not have to be monetary. Listening attentively can be regarded as priceless. Saying even one comment that shows understanding and empathy is of great value. Not saying something critical or demeaning can be just as rewarding.

Achieving a balance in life can sometimes be the difference in maintaining energy for important tasks. Like Jack, we need to take it seriously.

DAILY COUPLE TALK:
(EACH PARTNER RESPONDS)
What is one adjustment you could make in your schedule to build in more play time?
How could the partner help?

GIVING AND GETTING

In a helpful pamphlet called "Have a Great Conversation" Bea and Jim Strickland, longtime Marriage Enrichment friends, discuss some turn-offs in conversations.

One such turn-off for couples is MONOPOLIZING, taking control of a conversation so that the other person does not get to talk. Probably the partner has long since stopped listening to these long monologues, but an easy technique can be a remedy for both. The monopolizer must say no more than three sentences, before stopping to allow the partner to paraphrase what was said—and no interruptions. Then the partner gets three sentences to respond to the original information, with a paraphrase from the other partner. In this way both partners begin to see conversation as a 2-way street.

A second conversational turn-off for couples is NAYSAYING. This person has slipped into the conversational habit of taking the negative side of every topic. No matter what the partner says, the naysayer quickly refutes or negatively reframes the statement. To change, the naysayer should listen carefully and then paraphrase what he/she heard. Once this part is mastered, he//she should begin to make only positive or upbeat responses. It may feel awkward or phony at first, but replacing this turn-off style with a more relaxed give-and-take will eventually make both partners happier in conversation.

DAILY COUPLE TALK:
(BOTH PARTNERS PARTICIPATE)
What's your favorite holiday and what do you enjoy about it? Pay attention to how you talk and listen.

GIVING AND GETTING

Bringing about change in a relationship may work, and it may not. But three principles about giving and getting make change more likely to happen.

First, both partners need to say what they want, not just what they don't want. Having a clear goal in mind is much easier to accomplish. Often, other side subjects have to be cleared out (or shelved until another time) before partners can come to the one definite change one or both are seeking. Avoiding being specific merely puts added obstacles in the way.

Second, in order to get the change you want, you may have to give up a portion of what you are proposing to change. Granddaughter Leslie once suggested that in marriage you have to pick the battles that are most important to you, because one person cannot win on every part of every issue without doing damage to the relationship. Maybe she is right. Say what you want, listen to your partner's ideas, and be prepared to compromise on some part of the proposed change.

Then both partners need to do whatever they agreed to do. Failing to do so will only make the next change harder. The more our partner sees us trying to keep our promises, the more cooperation we are likely to get. Giving is contagious.

DAILY COUPLE TALK:
(EACH PERSON ANSWERS)
When you were growing up, how was negotiating change handled in your family of origin?

GIVING AND GETTING

A sign Bobbye saw recently said, "Courage is being scared to death—and saddling up anyway." Many couples go into marriage scared of failure. If the family-of-origin had examples of divorce and separation, those models are already in mind as a possibility. If there were painful relationships that have left scars, the fear that it could happen again is a very real awareness.

The fact that someone who is scared has "saddled up" and said "I do" is at the very least hopeful. Hope can keep partners looking for the good ways things are working out. Sometimes that's enough to ease our concerns. After all, it's just as easy to see the respectful, the kind, or the humorous things the partner says and does as to see the rude and unreasonable. Loving behaviors add a layer of contentment to the many ways we can overcome our fears. Give loving behaviors, watch for them in return, and suddenly we have created a beautiful picture of exactly what we had hoped for.

Plenty of couple-talk about what each wants from this relationship makes some goals clearer. As couples talk together about their lives, describing what they are getting and what they are willing to give, they are gaining crucial knowledge about the specific and special "us" that is their relationship, unique as a fingerprint. Courage, hope, loving behaviors, and plenty of honest and candid couple talk—all are ways to enrich the daily ride through life.

OO

DAILY COUPLE TALK:
(EACH PARTNER RESPONDS)
What was something you thought you wanted from marriage when you were much younger? What is something you want now?

GIVING AND GETTING

PART 1

Giving up the marriage myths we grew up with is unexpectedly hard, but in many ways marriage is where fantasy and fact have to accommodate each other. When that accommodation happens, we can feel disillusioned or relieved, but at that point of self-awareness we become able to make responsible choices about living together with real understanding.

One popular marriage myth is that the partner will always be available and agreeable. Many fairy tales, in fact, end with the line, "and they lived happily ever after," as though the wedding is the portal that insures a permanent state of contentment. The person who believes in this marriage myth suffers more disappointment than usual. Seeking a more mature definition of happiness—one that includes the partner's goals and ideals as well—is one step toward the great blend of romance and reality that marks a successful marriage.

Another marriage myth is that all needs will be met by the partner. Granddaughter Leslie thinks this myth is the most important subject a new partner has to deal with. Becoming responsible for oneself and one's choices is part of becoming a real member of a couple-team.

Giving up our myths is hard. But getting a view of ourselves as a contributing factor in a real relationship gives a boost toward achieving a goal worth celebrating.

DAILY COUPLE TALK:
(EACH PERSON PARTICIPATES)
What myths do you think many modern couples have?

GIVING AND GETTING

PART 2

"Love is all we need" is another marriage myth that sooner or later will have to be addressed. Most people come to marriage having been "in love" with someone else, probably feeling at the time that this one was Mr. Right or Miss Perfect. But that couple did not get married. Obviously something else was needed.

Making a good marriage involves personal effort, which this myth does not suggest. If we are expecting to maintain a "loving feeling" through all of life's frustrations and anxieties with little or no effort, we may be doomed to failure without knowing why.

Learning together to deal with our conflicts sounds strange if we have told ourselves that being "in love" would mean no disagreements. Learning to deal with different bathroom habits, different ideas on food preparation, or different laundry procedures sounds ridiculous to those who secretly thought "love" would cause all adjustments to happen automatically. Little things not dealt with can stack up like bricks and build a wall.

We are expanding our definition of "love" and also putting it into action daily when we acknowledge that words such as friendship, courtesy, cooperation, and teamwork are also a part of "love." Rather than giving up the myth, we find that we have got the best part of it.

DAILY COUPLE TALK:
(EACH PARTNER RESPONDS)
What is one "little thing" that you feel good about having dealt with as a couple-team?

313

GIVING AND GETTING

Donna Leon, a Venetian author of twenty-one novels featuring Commissario Guido Brunetti, ends one book with the Funeral Mass for a beloved local veterinarian. When Brunetti gets to the church, he is surprised to see such a crowd of people. There are two formal wreaths of flowers by the coffin, but there are also many home-made bouquets from local gardens, tied with string or simple ribbons. As he takes his seat, Brunetti realizes with some surprise that there are also cats, dogs, rabbits, and even parrots in attendance and that the priest is not at all bothered by this curious congregation of family, friends, and patients or by the noise it makes.

When the Mass is finished, the organ begins to play. From the front of the church comes an agonized howl that is louder than the organ. The howl is from a golden-brown dachshund who is expressing love and grief for the loss of their gentle friend. It seems to Commissario Brunetti a fitting conclusion to a sweet service, an appropriate goodbye.

Couples often have the chance for a sweet, sincere, home-made time together perhaps at the end of a long, busy day. Drawing together of an intentional "us" gives hope to each partner that his/her "gift" of work and effort is noticed and his/her "gift" of love is welcomed. As Marcel Proust observed: "Let us be grateful to people who make us happy. They are the charming gardeners who make our souls blossom."

DAILY COUPLE TALK:
(EACH PERSON PARTICIPATES)
Tell your partner 3 things that he/she has done recently that you really appreciate.

GIVING AND GETTING

Three gifts can make a big difference in the everyday practice of an important relationship like marriage. The gifts cost no money and earn the giver great rewards.

The first is the gift of repair. When there is a couple misunderstanding or disagreement, being the partner who first pitches the idea that you both have an agreed-upon strategy which you both will now use is being the partner initiating repair. That someone intends as well to hang in with the strategy until an understanding and/or resolution can be reached. The partner knows who made the effort first and that knowledge can affect both the process of the disagreement and its outcome. Win/Win/WIN.

Another gift is what Dr. John Gottman and his wife call "leaning toward." This means that when your partner expresses an interest in something and wants to tell you about it, you take the time to listen. The more times you "lean toward," according to the Gottmans, the closer your relationship grows.

The gift of connection is why some people get married. One side of connection is purely physical and is a universal form of communication all by itself. Take kissing, for example. Kissing can be affectionate, friendly, affirming (you're my sweetheart), inquisitive (ready to go on?), or passionate. Whatever the intent, kissing is an intimate gift that couples should never do without. Definitely a Win/Win/WIN.

DAILY COUPLE TALK:
(EACH PARTNER RESPONDS)
Which of the three gifts would you value most today?
Explain.

GIVING AND GETTING

A long-term happy marriage is both a goal and an opportunity. Much modern research shows that the long-term marriage produces better health for the partners, fewer illnesses and faster recovery from them, a better income, better sex, and a more specific and measurable contribution to the future. With rewards like that it's hard to believe that our national statistics for divorce hover around 50%.

On a radio broadcast Bobbye recently heard about the 100 % Rule and thought it could apply to a happy long-term marriage. When we only give some goal a well-meaning 99%, the radio speaker said, we spend energy without producing results. We feel that we have failed and have fallen short of our goal. We worry about it at odd times and feel a vague sense of guilt. The procedure for following the 100% Rule is simple: identify what one thing needs 100% of your attention, put in the effort, and repeat (for other goals).

For example, in the relationship if the identified goal is to have at least a 15-minute personal conversation with your partner every day, it means we put in the effort to do it until that conversation time becomes a comfortably established habit and we know we have succeeded. Then we turn our attention toward another small but clearly identified goal and make the effort to accomplish it.

DAILY COUPLE TALK:
(EACH PARTNER RESPONDS)
If you were choosing a small relational goal to make a 100% effort to accomplish, what would it be?

GIVING AND GETTING

When the giving and getting of forgiveness becomes a daily commerce in a close relationship such as marriage, both partners have an unexpected freedom. It is a weighty task to keep score and to remember all injustices. No wonder, according to The Journal of the American Medical Association, 13% of Americans now use anti-depressants to combat tension and anxiety.

A happy marriage relationship gives many benefits, but surely learning to trust, to forgive, and to understand is one big gift.

The sweet story is told of an elderly farmer in another century who never missed evening prayers at his local village church. One day he went into the forest to cut wood and broke a wheel on his cart. By late afternoon it became clear that he could not get back on time, and he was distraught because he had forgotten his prayer book with the exact prayer to be said on that date. Finally, he knelt in the forest and said, "OK, God, I am going to say the alphabet through two times very slowly. You put those letters together into the words you want for tonight's evening prayer."

It is a quaint solution to the farmer's dilemma but one many couples understand. Sometimes we can't find the right words of apology or explanation but in trust we offer them, confidant that in the partner's love we will find the freedom and solace of forgiveness.

DAILY COUPLE TALK:
(EACH PARTNER RESPONDS)
Share with your partner a time that you gave or received forgiveness. What happened?

GIVING AND GETTING

PART 1

Getting a firm handle on dealing with conflict is often a way of giving juice to a tired relationship. The only way to stop having disagreements is to keep the relationship static and stale, and staying in a constant upheaval is exhausting. So the ideal is to work together as a couple to find a way to deal with anger and conflict.

The first step in what they called their Anger Agreement was for Bobbye. It says, acknowledge your anger. Most people do not need this step, but for those who have spent years suppressing or denying their anger or artfully disguising it, it can be very helpful. Acknowledging that what you feel is anger—and that it is ok to feel that because nothing bad is going to happen—frees you to face the fact that you have options about how you will behave. This one step can get you ready to participate fairly and honestly.

The second step is to let your partner know you are angry. Using "I" talk to communicate means you are simply sharing feelings— "I am angry because _____ and I want us to talk about it." It does not try to blame anything on anybody, merely to clarify a position. Starting the process in this way gives an order to the argument and reduces frustration and fear. It is a gift.

DAILY COUPLE TALK:
(EACH PERSON PARTICIPATES)
In what way could an orderly and agreed-upon beginning to an argument affect its outcome? Explain.

GIVING AND GETTING

PART 2

Designing an agreement that gives a structure to dealing with conflict is a useful tool for couples and a gift to the relationship. When both partners are in agreement about procedure, the outcome is reached more economically and amiably.

Be sure you both know the definition of the issue dividing you. Verbally adding in other things blurs the focus and makes it harder to reach resolution. If necessary, make a list of the other issues needing attention and set them aside for later.

After identifying the issue, share feelings about it. At first this step seems awkward and unnecessary, but since feelings are often a part of the issue (hurt, unfairness, being discounted), stating them gives important information to both partners. It also reduces tension and serves as a bridge between "I am angry about . . . ." and "What can we do about it?"

Then both partners share ideas about what might resolve the issue. What you choose might be a combination of ideas, but both partners need to know exactly what they are choosing. Then set a time to review your choice. If it is not working, you can revise it.

This Anger Contract (or one like it) gives a structure to most arguments and over time can be an invaluable gift.

DAILY COUPLE TALK:
(EACH PARTNER RESPONDS)
Look at the steps of the Woods' Anger Contract.
Which one seems the most helpful to you?
What would you want to change?

GIVING AND GETTING

Gus Portokalos, father of Toula in the movie "My Big Fat Greek Wedding," had a simple solution for most problems, Windex, which could be sprayed easily to cure almost anything. The simple solution worked for Mr. Portokalos, even if his family had trouble applying it, especially to family relationships.

Getting what you want from your relationship has some simple steps. It starts with a frank, positive conversation with your partner, with clear statements about what is good about your marriage. Each partner participates and each partner listens to the other. Then add one or two simple things that could be improved. Each partner is expressing an opinion so no lecturing or analyzing. The goal is to get what you want from and for the relationship; therefore, these improvements need to be stated precisely. "I want to be happier" is a bit broad even if it is true. Finally, each partner states one or two specific things he/she will do in order to bring about the improvement. Getting what you want involves giving. It is an exchange of cooperation and good will.

The more you use this conversation format, the easier it becomes to (1) stay positive, (2) say what you want, (3) be cooperative. As together you move toward more intricate subjects, the simple solution moves with you, because you know that you are giving and getting something valued.

DAILY COUPLE TALK:
(EACH PARTNER RESPONDS)
Name one thing you like about your relationship. One thing that could be improved. One thing you can do to bring about improvement.

GIVING AND GETTING

PART 1

Give some attention to your investments in a new company called Couple Growth, Unlimited, and watch the dividends roll in. For some couples, trying new investments in the "us" is putting themselves in a vulnerable position, but it's a position infinitely worth the risk. As hockey player Wayne Gretzky once said, "You miss 100% of the shots you don't take."

MAKE AN INVESTMENT IN A NEW PERSPECTIVE ABOUT GROWTH. Hit the pause button often in your next few day's activities and think about what you really want from a partnership in life's most important human relationship.

When you have decided on two or three things that matter to you, share them with your partner. If they are realistically achievable (and they are if you have stated them aloud and both of you agree), you now have a share in the new company. The dividends will start right away.

Believing that you can reach the goals that you have set for yourselves individually and as a couple helps you look for ways to accomplish them. Every day's words and actions become important to your new company, Couple Growth, Unlimited. Every day's words and actions become important when you "take the shot" from a new and optimistic perspective.

DAILY COUPLE TALK:
(EACH PERSON PARTICIPATES)
What is a couple goal that would make you happy to accomplish? What can you personally do to reach the goal and reap the dividends of the new company?

GIVING AND GETTING

PART 2

For the progress and solvency of your new company Couple Growth, Unlimited, MAKE AN INVESTMENT IN DECLUTTERING YOUR RELATIONSHIP. Over time some relationships have issues that have never been resolved. Avoiding the issues merely causes them to burrow deep into both partner's minds and can distract from the new perspective of reaching goals and growing the company.

Getting to work discussing one such issue could be the first board meeting of the new company. Remember that you are a team. The goal is to face the issue together and not let it divide you. Resist the temptation to make it only one partner's problem. Once the issue is stated, it belongs to the relationship. Whatever progress you make, even if it's minimal, celebrate the accomplishment and do something fun together. Set a time to confront the issue again. Even Wayne Gretzky did not make 100% of his shots.

MAKE AN INVESTMENT IN LOVING BEHAVIORS TOWARD YOUR PARTNER. Harsh words and moody silences can cut down on the company's dividends, so at first you may have to double your efforts for creatively showing affection. But "take a shot" at it anyway. Investing in loving behaviors toward your partner enriches your company and others as well.

DAILY COUPLE TALK:
(EACH PARTNER PARTICIPATES)
Your new company, Couple Growth,
Unlimited, is looking for a new mascot.
What would you suggest? Why?

GIVING AND GETTING

Give at least as much attention to relational fitness as you do to your individual programs of nutrition and exercise. Just as preventive habits can work toward producing better health in the future, giving attention to couple relational skills reduces stress in the relationship, the "us," and adds an easy confidence to the daily commerce of life together. The future looks more secure and interesting when both partners are joined in practicing

- ❦ Daily expressions of affection

- ❦ Generous amounts of compliments and encouragement

- ❦ Practical (that means what works for both of you) ways of discussing divisive issues

- ❦ Positive attitudes toward growth

- ❦ Daily conversations about what you think and feel.

Think of these practices as relationship vitamins and/or exercise programs aimed at keeping every part of the relationship as strong as possible.

Giving to get, getting to be motivated to give more—it's a productive cycle that leads to better understanding of each other, better sex, better conversation, better expressions of appreciation, and better relational fitness in general. And just like adequate nutrition and regular exercise, you feel and see the results.

DAILY COUPLE TALK:
(EACH PARTNER PARTICIPATES)
What are some of your beliefs about physical fitness?
About relational fitness?

GIVING AND GETTING

Seldom does anyone benefit when families break up, reform into other patterns, break up, and degenerate into fragments. It happens, but it has more liabilities than assets. It is a disturbing social trend. Getting married is important and giving up with too little effort diminishes its importance for everyone.

One way to maintain the relationship is to commit to it. Most complications short of abuse or addictions can be handled with patience and determination. Hanging in is one way to demonstrate to your partner that you are serious about learning to live together. Hanging in also equips you to look for the good things in the relationship, not just concentrate on those you dislike. An honest discussion about what each one wants and needs benefits both partners and gives direction about some things you both can do. If even one of you begins to demonstrate a willingness to cooperate, things begin to look better. When both try, the situation improves immediately.

Remember that it takes time to get what you want from the relationship and it takes time to learn how to give what your partner says he/she wants. We are a quick-fix society and do not like to wait for satisfaction. But quitting too early just means neither one will get the satisfaction that marriage should provide.

DAILY COUPLE TALK:
(EACH PARTNER RESPONDS)
If a good friend asked you what you value most about marriage, what would you say?

GIVING AND GETTING

Assume you get $86,400 in your bank account every morning, but it all has to be spent every day. What a bonanza! Think of the ways you could enrich your lives together and the good you could do in a needy world. The truth is, that is the exact number of seconds in a day—86,400—but it's gone at the end of the day. Putting it in that perspective encourages us to be more responsible about our loving, our spending, our giving, and our getting.

If we want to get a good night's sleep, going to bed surrounded by electronics and with a chocolate bar snack is probably not helpful. If we desire a resolution of some of the divisive issues in the relationship with our partner, continuing to fight in ways that have proven ineffective will not get the closeness that could be ours.

What works is figuring out what we want, what we need, what is reasonable, what makes us happiest, what makes us angry, what makes us want to be cooperative, what makes us want to be loving. It is quite literally self-awareness. Tell this information to the partner. Then learn from the partner this same information and listen carefully. This is the prescription for getting and giving that can make the next few years a great adventure—or not. The next step is to take those 86,400 seconds a day and make the most of them. We all have equal opportunity before Time.

DAILY COUPLE TALK:
(EACH PERSON ANSWERS)
What do you most want to accomplish today? What do you most want to share with your partner?

GIVING AND GETTING

Giving and getting love is a worthy endeavor that can last a lifetime. Speaking in the love language of those whom we value insures that our intent matches the impact.

Bobbye's primary Love Language is communication, especially words of affirmation. Nothing feels real to her until it is spoken or written. Words are the Love Reality. Britton, on the other hand, feels that acts of service best show love. He likes both to give and get kind and thoughtful actions.

One Saturday afternoon while Bobbye was running errands, Britton changed the light bulb in her closet, which she told him had burned out. He was excited about this special surprise and sure that she would be pleased, but he said nothing about it. Eventually Bobbye noticed the light worked but assumed it had been some problem with electricity. She said nothing about it. Britton was disappointed and Bobbye did not know why. Both felt a sense of unrest.

This scene or one like it is repeated often because partners do not give or receive love in the same way. Learning what each other expects and feels is the kind of marital education that smooths the way to understanding.

DAILY COUPLE TALK:
(EACH PARTNER RESPONDS)
According to the research of Dr. Gary Chapman,
there are five primary love languages:
Words of affirmation, Acts of service, Touch,
Gifts, and Quality Time spent together.
Which language do you prefer to give love?
To get love?

GIVING AND GETTING

According to Barbara and Bob Zelinski of Marriage Management, none of us plan to get sick, but it happens. When it does, it can impact our partner and our marriage. It is important to give and get information about how we want to be treated when we are ill. Like sex, money, and in-laws, this is a subject that couples need to be clear on.

As with most subjects, many of our feelings and opinions about illness are born out of past experiences. Perhaps we experienced a lack of medical attention when we were growing up, and it left us fearing that our partner won't want to help us. Perhaps we were taught that useful work should be our most important priority and illness is to be avoided because we can't accomplish what we need to do. Perhaps we do not even want to mention illness because of former family skepticism about a relative who was a chronic complainer and often cried "wolf." Perhaps we were caretaker for a loved-one who had a lingering catastrophic illness and the legacy of heartache makes us wary of involvement.

Whatever the feelings, the marriage relationship needs to prosper and grow "in sickness and in health." In discussing each partner's attitudes, we gain helpful information.

DAILY COUPLE TALK:
(EACH PERSON ANSWERS)
How do you feel about being ill? How do you feel when your partner is ill? What do you want from your partner when you are ill? What are your feelings about a long-term illness for either of you?

GIVING AND GETTING

Some days everyone's self-esteem takes a battering; every day someone's self-esteem takes a battering. It's just life. Many people work in cubicles with only technical equipment as company. Others commute long distances, either alone in their car or surrounded by strangers on a train. Quite a few couples live far away from friends and family. The upshot is that we often end our days feeling fragmented and bruised.

Here is the opportunity for partners to give each other a great gift. Consistent and genuine words of affirmation and appreciation have a powerful way of helping the partner to be centered and to feel a sense of being recognized as worthwhile. Getting these words not only binds up emotional wounds but also motivates us to live up to the words. Giving and getting loving behaviors, praise, and compliments works toward building and restoring self-esteem. In fact, a marriage that does not regularly give and receive these words and actions may be causing a kind of emotional malnutrition. It is entirely possible that partners who drift into affairs do so far more often because of flagging self-esteem than because they are looking for sexual adventure.

For the days that we have taken a battering that no hot shower, glass of wine, or favorite TV show can alleviate, it can be a life-saver to get a vote of confidence in the form of expressed appreciation from someone whose opinion we value.

DAILY COUPLE TALK:
(EACH PARTNER RESPONDS)
What is a quality in your partner that you especially value?

GIVING AND GETTING

What do you get if you choose to develop a long-term relationship like marriage? Not what do you have to do, or do without. Not what you have to give, or give up. What do you GET? Being clear on this one point offers some incentives for investment.

It's an opportunity to develop gifts and dump heavy baggage. Everyone who says "I do" brings prettily wrapped packages of gifts to the relationship. These are personality attributes such as optimism or patience, sense of humor or ability to work hard. These are habits such as punctuality or telling the truth. A long-term relationship is the place to develop these gifts and habits and to use them for the good of others.

But everyone who says "I do" brings baggage also, sometimes a heavy backpack that weighs on the shoulders and restricts movement, baggage such as childhood trauma, former incarceration, prejudice, or a hair-trigger temper. Baggage does not get dumped immediately, but with effort to identify it and create new patterns (with someone cheering on the sidelines), the odds are good that we can eventually lighten the load. A supportive and loving relationship is part of the strength we need to make changes. The partner who thinks he/she is not getting something valuable from giving the gifts, exercising the habits, and exorcising the baggage is the partner who has not yet attempted to claim this benefit.

DAILY COUPLE TALK:
(EACH PERSON PARTICIPATES)
What is a "gift" that you give to your relationship?
What "baggage" are you working on?

GIVING AND GETTING

What else do you get from a long-term relationship such as marriage? Researchers are only beginning to gather and publish information about the benefits, such as having more money over a longer period of time, getting and staying healthy, having better sex, and enjoying a wide network of extended family and couple friends. The children of long-term relationships are more secure and confident in the world and tend to do better in school.

Chip and Joanna Gaines, stars of HGTV's monster hit "Fixer Upper," credit their marriage with giving them a successful real estate company, a home furnishings line, and a remodeling business that buys, fixes, and flips houses. "We seem to give each other energy," says Joanna. "We function better together than we do apart." Many partners get the same boost from each other's support and encouragement. It may not lead to a business venture, but it certainly is a factor in counteracting loneliness and inspiring unselfish living.

Finally, we get to be a valuable part of a team. We are wanted. We are needed. Team-building takes time but in also keeps interest high while we work. It is what we gave ourselves to when we said "I do."

DAILY COUPLE TALK:
(EACH PERSON ANSWERS)
Our couple-team is poised for a new season. What does our team have that can help us reach the play-offs?

GIVING AND GETTING

Giving loving behaviors to your partner is a decision. Giving loving behaviors does not depend on feelings, which someone has said are notoriously "flighty." Giving loving behaviors puts you AND your partner in a place where gratitude and trust combine.

Suppose partners are taking a Time Out because emotions are high in the midst of a disagreement. Both need time to calm down before destructive things are said or before a silent and arid distance emerges. A loving behavior at that point may simply be choosing, deciding, to consider the partner's good qualities. It might be choosing, deciding, that both partners have a valid point of view and a further discussion might reveal the thoughts and feelings that lie behind them. The loving behavior is a decision NOT to use the Time Out for self-pity or for mentally trashing the partner. It is an important decision.

Like the comic book action figures, Spider-Man, Wonder Woman, or the Incredible Hulk, for whom action itself is the sought-for reward, loving behaviors put us in a more stable emotional place, better able to meet the partner on equal ground. Giving loving behaviors thus helps us grow as individuals.

DAILY COUPLE TALK:
(EACH PERSON ANSWERS)
*What is something your partner does or
says that you really like?*

GIVING AND GETTING

Getting on the Resilience Ladder and standing on the rung of sharing feelings helps couples get over the wall of conflict between them. The whole concept of resilience deals with the re-establishment of balance. Resilience, as Froma Walsh describes it, is "the capacity to rebound from adversity strengthened and more resourceful."

Britton spent 20 years working with college students and single adults. What he observed time after time was the lack of effort most of them put forth to resolve conflicts. It is a world where many people have jobs designed to solve problems. An auto mechanic relishes some problem to be repaired. He even gets paid for it. The IT person in a business is there to fix what is not working. Yet in relationships there seems to be a reluctance to get on the Resilience Ladder and try a technique to restore balance.

Britton remembers specifically the first time he and Bobbye chose to stand on the "sharing feelings" rung of the Resilience Ladder and confront a re-occurring conflict. He was scared and uncertain about where it would go. Yet he was willing to explore the possibilities. As they began to share their feelings, they also began to see ways the conflict might be resolved. It brought a new day to them. Sometimes a new technique brings new energy as well.

DAILY COUPLE TALK:
(EACH PERSON PARTICIPATES)
Share three feelings about this day and what you must do (or already did). Stay away from information about the activity and concentrate on the feelings. It is good practice for the times you stand on the Resilience Ladder.

DOLLARS AND SENSE

"The most important things in life

are not things."

DOLLARS AND SENSE

What the world of business values in an employee may not be the same for how the partner views the same traits. Doing more than one thing at a time at work makes you look skilled and adept; at home the partner may feel you never listen. In the workplace, you may be considered a perfectionist, valued because you can force others to work at a high level; at home your partner may be alienated by criticism and manipulation. At work, you may be praised for stoicism and control; at home, you merely cut off all sharing. In other words, there are different standards appropriate for different places.

There are two skills which work at either venue, and the first is communication. If you make a habit of saying what you mean and meaning what you say, others will trust that you are sincere and that you will present facts accurately. If you are also able to listen to the other person carefully enough to be able to paraphrase what they say, you are exhibiting respect and empathy.

The second complementary skill is the ability to manage your emotions and at the same time work toward understanding those of others. This control allows you to deal with stress and disagreement and to formulate equitable deals that make others happy.

Valuing and improving communication skills and responsibly managing your own emotions improve relationships both at work and in the family.

DAILY COUPLE TALK:
(EACH PERSON PARTICIPATES)
In dealing fairly with an error made by the grocery store checker, what are some skills needed to resolve the situation?

DOLLARS AND SENSE

Having a transparent financial plan is a strong step toward reducing conflicts about money. When both partners know the same information, and are moving together toward a shared goal, trust is also operating and smoothing the way to greater success.

On this subject, it is imperative to be realistic. Knowing each other's exact income and living within it is important, whether or not you have joint bank accounts. If either of you is in debt, it is important to work together to pay it off as quickly as possible. All financial counselors see debt reduction as a high priority. Know all of each other's investments and insurance policies and know how to access them. One moment of financial recklessness by either partner can weaken ties of connection and closeness. Pay attention to financial reality and both of you will grow in appreciation for and trust in each other.

The easiest way to know the weekly or monthly expenditures is to prepare a budget together. Keep a careful record of what comes in and what goes out. Doing so can help you see the difference between things you want and things you need. It can help you plan together how to move toward major purchases so that you both have a sense of what is possible and what is not. Making a budget needs to be a joint activity that expresses both personalities.

Sound money planning and budgeting makes a big difference in the everyday commerce of your relationship.

DAILY COUPLE TALK:
(EACH PARTNER RESPONDS)
Discuss a plan for developing an emergency fund.

DOLLARS AND SENSE

Winning in our competitive world becomes important to each of us. Getting the most sales, the top grades, the top raise, or the most gold medals translates into accolades, money, and high self-esteem. It is therefore natural to want to "win" arguments, whether in the courtroom or the bedroom.

One problem is that in the relationship at home the "winning" of the argument does not bring accolades. BOTH partners must leave the encounter feeling heard and understood. BOTH partners should leave the encounter with a healthy sense of their own self-worth. And the relationship has to leave the encounter being strengthened and improved. Only in this way can the process and outcome of the argument benefit everyone involved. This is very different from typical procedures of winning in the business world.

Conflicts are inevitable and if handled fairly can even be helpful in airing feelings to each other that need to be brought to light. Think of the disagreement as a yellow caution light, announcing that a deep feeling may be underlying the issue and needs to be addressed. With attention to this one skill, this one attitude shift, partners move to a new level of interaction and trust. That is worth more to your "us," your relationship, than winning a raise at work.

DAILY COUPLE TALK:
(EACH PERSON ANSWERS)
Complete this statement: Both businesses and marriages could be improved if we

_____.

DOLLARS AND SENSE

Bobbye's paternal grandmother gave her some advice when she was just a small child: "Try to be savin'." The advice stuck. To this day Bobbye thinks it is important to have some money tucked away, just "in case." She always puts away a portion of her monthly $100 "allowance"—an agreed-upon monthly amount to do whatever she wants with no accountability to anyone else. It is important to her to be "savin'."

Growing up in a family that frequently had "too much month at the end of their money," Britton decided as a boy that to avoid embarrassing situations he always needed to have some cash with him. Credit cards or a check book will of course cover most purchases, but in case there is any problem, it is still important to Britton to have cash in his pocket, no matter what.

The point is, we all have attitudes and beliefs about money, many of them brought with us from childhood. Some of them are helpful, like avoiding unnecessary debt or paying off the total balance of our credit cards every month. Some of them need to be reviewed in the light of our partnership to make sure they produce logical financial decisions that both are happy with.

DAILY COUPLE TALK:
(EACH PERSON PARTICIPATES)
*What is an attitude toward money that
you consider important?*

DOLLARS AND SENSE

So many comedians and professional speakers make jokes about marriage and money that it's easy to see why this one subject is controversial with many partners. Here's a typical joke told by James Holt McGavran: "There's a way of transferring funds that is even faster than electronic banking. It's called marriage."

And as if our strange and cynical attitudes about money were not enough, many partners keep secrets, according to <u>American Express Spending and Saving Tracker.</u> As many as 27% say they have misrepresented the amount of a purchase to their partner, and over 30% say they have hidden purchases from their partner. Fifty-six % of couples say they have made an unreported financial mistake.

Money talk apparently makes us uneasy, so if we can, we avoid talking about finances, debt, and household expenses. Some couples say they are more likely to know their partner's weight than their salary. With these taboos and secrets no wonder money is the number one subject couples fight about. What we need is Couple Dialogue about the subject because before you can ever realistically discuss or plan what to save, invest, or give, you need to know the literal numbers you will be working with.

DAILY COUPLE TALK:
(EACH PARTNER RESPONDS)
Describe the financial habits of your family-of-origin.
What take-aways have you carried into your adult life?

DOLLARS AND SENSE

The joining of two people in marriage is the joining of two different educations concerning money. This is relevant because money to most people represents important things like security, status, independence, trust, or power. It is a multi-layered subject.

Suppose one partner grew up in a family in which money was a symbol of status. Every purchase, every monetary decision, was carefully measured as to its effect on others. This attitude does not automatically go away, even if you did not agree with it. Discussing the money-as-status symbol helps both partners deal with current issues in their own relationship. Candid information about attitudes toward money is the key to prudent joint financial choices.

Suppose one partner grew up in a family where money was regarded as a means to enjoyment. Having a good time outweighed paying bills, and credit cards were often maxed out. Like money-as-status, this attitude does not automatically go away and can affect the expectations one or both have currently. Again, candid discussions lead to an examination of attitudes as to what money represents to each partner.

DAILY COUPLE TALK:
(EACH PARTNER PARTICIPATES)
Discuss the following statements
(designed by Life Innovations, Inc.)

1. Having high quality things reflects well on me.
2. Having some money in savings is important to me.
3. I look up to people who are financially successful.
4. People who have money have more fun.
5. Money can't buy happiness, but it sure helps.

DOLLARS AND SENSE

Dealing well with differences makes life easier for partners who value their relationship and do not take it for granted. Some differences are amusing. Some do not matter, like preferences for food or colors. Some cause problems, and these are the ones we need to deal with. Differences regarding money seem to bring the most drama to the relationship.

As with dealing with any divisive subject, the goal is growing the relationship. Bullying, crying, shaming, threats, avoiding— none of these techniques enhance the relationship. How we discuss the differences regarding money is as important as arriving at a workable solution to the issue.

Suppose one partner wants to clear up all debts promptly, and one sometimes spends over the level of income. Finding the fair and honest way to discuss the issue is the way for both partners to feel good about the outcome and abide by agreed-upon decisions. It is the way to keep the relationship strong AND to protect the financial future. It is a goal worth celebrating.

DAILY COUPLE TALK:
(EACH PARTNER RESPONDS)
What is one decision regarding money that we should be making soon?

DOLLARS AND SENSE

Allen and Jeannie are typical of many couples who had no idea where their money was going each month until they were forced to see that they were making far too many credit card purchases. This recognition led to a joint decision to use only cash until they could regain control of their finances. It was a major change, but for them it was the right step.

Allen and Jeannie's strategy has released them from the stress of looming financial problems. As a sports radio commentator observed about an NFL team, "It's hard to build a team when you're strapped for money." So, with the couple-team. Few things upset our marital equilibrium as much as the unwise use of money. So, three pieces of financial advice:

1. Commit to achieving debt reduction, even it if means a temporary sacrifice in standard of living.

2. Put nothing on your credit cards that can't be paid off in 30 days.

3. Limit all credit debt to 15-20% of monthly income, except for the mortgage.

DAILY COUPLE TALK:
(EACH PERSON ANSWERS)
Which one of the pieces of financial advice might be most helpful to you? Why?

DOLLARS AND SENSE

Positive ways of interacting are critical to the well-being of the relationship, the "us." Being good to ourselves—adequate sleep, good nutrition, and exercise—is a start to better health, but we also need to do the things that boost self-confidence. When we can count our blessings and not dwell on failures, we are more likely to be able to see and celebrate the good qualities in ourselves and in our spouse as well. It sets up a positive cycle of regard that comes back to us. As the old saying goes: "There is a destiny that makes us brothers. None goes his way alone. All that we send into the lives of others comes back into our own."

Making a budget together can be a positive way of interaction. It gives both partners a sense of control of their money. And when partners view money in this perspective, it feels like they are directing where the dollars go and not the other way around. Seizing control of the income—and doing it together—is a positive action that cuts down on the stress and friction that the subject of money sometimes causes.

Seeking the support and encouragement of other likeminded couples is another positive way of interacting. Avoid couples who tend to drag you down with their own destructive ways of relating. Concentrate instead on those couples who value growth, intimacy, honesty, fun, and happiness. In the long run, they will be the most helpful.

DAILY COUPLE TALK:
(EACH PERSON ANSWERS)
*What is one positive interaction with
your partner that you value?*

DOLLARS AND SENSE

Arguments over money are common for couples. Money is as a strategic part of our everyday life, so whether we are arguing over gas money or an unexpected expense at work, it is not surprising that this is a subject that brings out strong opinions.

But arguments over money have other sources. Power struggles of various kinds may be the real issue, or one partner may not feel sufficiently appreciated in what he/she contributes. One partner may have had a scary financial loss in the past and now sees every expenditure as a potential disaster. One may believe gender should determine who makes financial decisions. One may be fearful of the future unless money is handled in a certain way.

Keeping the lines of communication open—especially about money—is one way to show commitment to the relationship. Planning a simple budget together is helpful in bringing to light habits and attitudes toward money, if both partners feel it is ok to have differences and that those differences are important. Honest discussions about money not only allow us to manage our finances better but to make connections relationally despite differences. Being aloof, evasive, defensive, or irritable will not help. The goal is building the relationship, and it overshadows any other goal.

DAILY COUPLE TALK:
(EACH PARTNER RESPONDS)
*If you were given $500 to be spent next week-end,
what would you want to do with it?*

DOLLARS AND SENSE

Sometimes dealing with money issues seems so overwhelming that it threatens the health and stability of the couple. For these times, many couples point out that COMMITMENT TO THEIR RELATIONSHIP steadied their resolve enough to allow them time to get through a crisis and to work together to set achievable goals.

When practices of commitment are decided on and a few goals are considered, both partners feel more in control of what is happening, even financially. That is the time to make some short-term goals together about money. Let them be simple and achievable so that completing them is relatively easy.

When those easy goals are reached, move to a goal that can make a real difference financially. Decide together on the goal AND the plan for achieving it. Even though one partner may be more adept at money management, choose to pay each bill together so that you are making joint decisions. Do this until each feels more comfortable about money and its impact on your relationship. Commitment to the health and growth of the couple is more important than money, and a kinder approach to each other can unexpectedly reveal new financial abilities.

DAILY COUPLE TALK:
(EACH PARTNER ANSWERS)
*What is one idea about commitment
that is important to you?*

DOLLARS AND SENSE

In all money conversations think hard about the following. In fact, pause and discuss the following word by giving your ideas and feelings about it:

RETIREMENT

The sad fact is that many couples do not give attention to this word and the realities it stands for until the time has come to face it. AARP statistics report that up to 60% of the population over age 65 have made no preparation for retirement and are trying to live on their social security alone. Poorly equipped for a future that is now stretching two decades past 65 for many people, the end of life issues for many couples are grim to consider.

Just as grim to consider is a marital future in which little efforts toward skill-building have been made. Having ignored opportunities to grow closer, suddenly there is no dependable person who makes a positive difference, who gives eagerly and generously, who raises spirits just by being present. Simply logging time with someone is different from developing a deep and intimate relationship in which friends and lovers have worked together over time. Planning for the future is essential.

DAILY COUPLE TALK:
(EACH PERSON PARTICIPATES)
What plans should we be making for retirement?

DOLLARS AND SENSE

Most couples can begin to resolve their money issues not by earning more but by spending less. Some financial planners recommend making two budgets. One is a NEED budget, covering only the necessities; the other is a WANT budget, which can have the things you think would bring you pleasure and still be within your price range.

The NEED budget has the monthly expenses that must be paid: housing (which financial planners say should not exceed 25% of your after-tax income), food (which should not exceed 20%), and a certain amount for non-monthly expenses such as auto repairs, clothing, home improvements, entertainment, or medical expenses (which all together should not exceed 30%). That leaves 20% for gifts and charitable donations.

The WANT budget takes the remaining 5% of the NEED budget every month and uses both partners to plan how to save for the miscellaneous larger items you want. Planning together gives both partners a sense of ownership of their future. The two budgets give tangible form to what is happening financially and as you work together to live within that form, you become aware of what are the real assets of marriage.

DAILY COUPLE TALK:
(EACH PERSON RESPONDS)
*If you could devote 5% of your
monthly NEED budget
to planning for a major expenditure,
what would you want to buy?*

DOLLARS AND SENSE

Britton has always felt he would be able to earn needed funds for the family, but this was severely tested in the early years of marriage. During seminary, he also worked in retail sales with a good salary plus commission. Upon graduation and appointment to his first college campus ministry, things changed abruptly. Now his salary was only half of what he had formerly made, and there was no commission to rely on. The obligations were the same, the credit card payments that had accumulated needed to be paid off, and appliances for the home needed to be purchased. It was a new experience and forced the Woods to take a serious look at how they were handling their dollars and whether they were using good sense.

Thus, they closed all credit card accounts and slowly paid them off. They paid cash for food, auto expenses, clothing, and utilities. They revised their eating and entertainment habits, and when the expenses came down, immediately paid off all student loans. What did this young family learn from their financial dilemma? They learned that they could deal with adversity by "tightening their belts" during this difficult time. They also learned by talking it over and by being very specific on using dollars sensibly. How each couple addresses issues and shares concerns will make a great deal of difference in how they handle tough times.

DAILY COUPLE TALK:
(EACH PERSON PARTICIPATES)
What does "good sense with money"
mean to you?

DOLLARS AND SENSE

Financial advisor Dave Ramsey said on a radio show that people should pay off their debts as soon as possible and concentrate on building an emergency fund equal to at least two month's salary. Only when that is done should they make plans for future expenditures. The key to accomplishing this, Ramsey said, is intentionality. Without it people are likely to make only half-hearted efforts. With it they will "lay back their ears" and put their plans into immediate action.

A Biology professor brought into his class one day a jar, several good-sized rocks, some pebbles, a little bucket full of sand, and a big bucket of water. He asked his students if all of these items would fit in the jar, and they said no. He then showed them the ONLY way it could be done. The rocks had to go in first, because they were biggest and took up the most room. Then the pebbles fit in around the rocks. The sand was small enough to sift into the tiniest crevices and soaked up the whole bucket of water.

Beginning with the largest or most important financial task and arranging everything else in a logical order is a way to arrive at the desired destination of financial solvency. And to start the task at all, there must be some mutual plan that both partners agree will work. And behind the plan, according to Dave Ramsey, is intentionality. Then "lay back [your] ears" and go for it. Your future will thank you.

DAILY COUPLE TALK:
(EACH PARTNER RESPONDS)
If you were to choose one thing in your life to be more intentional about, what would it be? Why?

DOLLARS AND SENSE

One part of money trouble exists because we are married. If one is making and spending his/her own money, what happens to it is that person's business. But when we go into our marriage partnership, protests are going to be raised if one buys something the partnership can't afford. So, unless you have unlimited financial resources, you simply need to find a way to organize your household business life in some rational and orderly fashion. This includes (1) knowing all your assets and ALL your debts, (2) deciding how the bills will be paid, (3) working out a budget, (4) deciding on personal allowances, (5) deciding on insurance (life, home, automobile), (6) making plans for future expenditures, and (7) planning for savings accounts and investments.

The other part of money trouble is a reflection of issues in your relationship not yet resolved. Don't be satisfied with solutions in terms of money policy alone. Money usually symbolizes our emotional attachments to inanimate things and at the heart of many arguments about money is some form of need for security and protection. The concerns are as real as those of people in 3rd World countries who have the fear of starvation chilling their spines and making them careful.

What Dr. John Gottman calls "turning toward each other" works with money discussions just as with other subjects important to marriage. Partners who practice it, he says, "are building up an emotional savings account" that gives comfort and relaxation.

DAILY COUPLE TALK:
(EACH PERSON PARTICIPATES)
What is one concern you have about money?

DOLLARS AND SENSE

Sometimes money is used to exert control in the marriage. It is no longer widely accepted that the partner who makes the most money should control the finances. Still, there are some partners who try to use money as the issue that symbolizes or establishes their authority in the relationship. Those controlling partners may also:

1. Limit or monitor the activities of the other.

2. Make a unilateral definition of roles or appropriate actions.

3. Control the partner during arguments.

4. Demand compliance on all issues, including sex.

Equality has to be a guiding principle in the marriage. No relationship can grow in healthy ways otherwise. From equality radiates out trust, respect, fairness, shared responsibility, and support. Equality keeps partners negotiating together, sharing through communication, listening non-judgmentally, and being truthful. Equality keeps the marriage playful and light-hearted. It encourages self-development and time with friends. It is the only way that self-disclosure can happen, and self-disclosure brings intimacy and emotional closeness. Equality engenders confidence in the future and establishes an environment of safety for children.

Using money as a form of control leads to one partner's isolation from the other. Working together builds bridges.

DAILY COUPLE TALK:
(EACH PARTNER RESPONDS)
How is equality shown in our relationship? In what ways could we increase equality between us?

DOLLARS AND SENSE

Working to improve the marriage relationship makes sense. The dollars expended in dissolving marriage and the loss of money trying to live separately are not worth the trouble. Except in cases of addictions, incest, or abuse, couples who give relationship growth a chance can gain enough satisfaction to put them on a firmer footing—and keep them there.

The following chilling statistics show why it makes financial sense to work for improvement:

> Three/fifths of American children (some 15.8 million children) live with a single divorced parent who cannot adequately support them. It is becoming the new American norm.

> As high as 85% of women who divorce receive no alimony or child support. Being awarded child support is not the same as getting it.

> Health studies report that being divorced puts people at a higher risk for expensive physical ailments. The National Institute of Healthcare Research reports that "being divorced and a non-smoker is only slightly less dangerous than smoking a pack of cigarettes a day and staying married."

For the marriage relationship to improve, grow, and make both partners happy, it takes education and effort but the rewards are infinitely worth it.

DAILY COUPLE TALK:
(EACH PERSON PARTICIPATES)
If someone were going to give you $500 for one improvement in your relationship, how would you use the money?

DOLLARS AND SENSE

The Woods once had a Siamese cat who hated Hallowe'en. Poky was ordinarily a very calm and loving cat, but once a year the constant ringing of the doorbell, strangely costumed children at the door, and unusual noises and lights upset her so much that she resorted to howling out her frustration.

For some couples, any conversation about money is like Poky at Hallowe'en. Just paying the monthly bills is stressful; add to it planning for retirement, dealing with end-of-life issues, deciding on insurance, and evaluating investments and the whole process leads to frustration. Neither partner may actually howl, but they want to.

One Hallowe'en we put Poky in a cardboard box in the kitchen with a dishtowel covering the box. The cat let us know this was helpful by howling every time we removed the dishtowel. Eventually calm was restored as Poky allowed her "family" to work with her on an issue made of many stressful parts.

Partners can help each other deal with any stressful issue, including money. The key is being a team and using the same honesty, cooperation, planning, practice, and rule-keeping that any team needs—athletic, business, or couple. Your couple-team may never like dealing with this issue, but with a reciprocal reliance and practical strategies you can move toward a win/win/WIN.

DAILY COUPLE TALK:
(EACH PARTNER RESPONDS)
What are some of the strengths of your couple-team?

DOLLARS AND SENSE

Marriage counselors say that when a couple insists that their problem is money, sex, or in-laws, the underlying issue is communication. Work on communication skills that build bridges, and the ability to talk about hot subjects like money improves also.

First, making derogatory comments of any kind (even those where one partner insists he/she is only "kidding") will never produce a healthy conversation. Barbs may be ever-so-witty, but the partner who is their target will be turned off before the important talk begins. If partners are to address a touchy subject together, there needs to be courtesy and security or there will be only withdrawal.

Second, "you" talk (YOU always spend too much, YOUR family did not teach you right) is not as productive as "I" talk (I'M sorry I forgot to pay that bill, I'D like us to make a budget). "You" talk puts the partner on the defensive since it is tinged with blaming. "I" talk tends to level the playing field and sounds like it's asking for an equal partnership.

Third, both partners get to talk. If one partner dominates or constantly interrupts, it's harder to get to any point that both feel good about. Equality of speaking and listening is important. Once partners find that they are beginning to enjoy their conversations and to participate in them jointly, they often find it easier to discuss money, sex, or in-laws.

QC

DAILY COUPLE TALK:
(EACH PARTNER PARTICIPATES)
Of the three points listed above,
which is NOT an issue for you?

DOLLARS AND SENSE

Like it or not money is essential to our sense of well-being; therefore, how we handle money in marriage is part of the well-being of our "us." The amount of money has little to do with it. Plenty of low-income families have strong, stable marriages, and many well-to-do couples struggle with financial stress.

One reason for how we handle money is its association with status and success. Partially this is due to our consumer-driven culture that tries to persuade us that having more "things" will meet our emotional needs for approval. When couples can come to regard a strong relationship as the provider of real happiness and well-being, they not only blunt the force of the consumer-driven society but give a living testimony to that same society of the value of a thriving "us."

A second reason for how we handle money also is rooted in our attitudes. Couples need to work together in trustworthy ways. If one uses money as a way to control the other, the "us" will never prosper. Money can be a threat if partners grew up with very different attitudes toward it, but those differences need to be discussed and respected, as with differences in other areas of relationship. For one to dominate the other slows down the coping strategies needed for this issue and hinders the sense of well-being necessary to both.

DAILY COUPLE TALK:
(EACH PARTNER RESPONDS)
*On a scale of 1-10 (with 10 being high)
how satisfied are you with how
money is currently being handled?
Explain.*

DOLLARS AND SENSE

A mattress company recently announced the results of a survey about sleep position preferences. It seems that a whopping 41% of us like to sleep on our sides, with knees drawn up and arms folded as in a fetal position. For sleeping we like to "get back to the basics."

Although most people agree that it is important to have enough money to be comfortable, a surprising number feel that it is basic to happiness. A common illustration of this fact happened when Britton and Bobbye were in Taiwan on a speaking engagement. At the end of one program, a sweet lady from the audience gave them two felt mice, blue with red ears and whiskers. The mice were creatively made, but Bobbye asked about their significance. The giver said the mice were supposed to "up the money." When Bobbye asked what that meant, the reply was, "You want to be happy? Money is the way!"

The real basics of couple satisfaction is how they talk and listen to each other, how they resolve disagreements, how they give each other support and encouragement, and how they lavish loving behaviors. The money mice sit on a kitchen shelf as a reminder to the Woods that "getting back to the basics" calls for a different emphasis.

DAILY COUPLE TALK:
(EACH PERSON PARTICIPATES)
What is something you would like to accomplish with your money? What keeps you from accomplishing it? What can you do personally to help?

DOLLARS AND SENSE

Money is sometimes the factor that separates a good relationship from a great one. If partners in a committed relationship like marriage cannot figure out a way to handle reoccurring arguments over money, they likely will not ever reach the loving plateau where intimate conversations, pleasurable sex, restorative playtime, and wise decision-making combine to create "close companions" that take pride in their relationship, their "us."

In his famous book <u>The Essential Humility of Marriage</u> Dr. Terry Hargrove offers this suggestion. There is no one "right" way to handle money, he says. To spend time correcting and criticizing the partner's shortcomings will seldom get a workable plan. Both partners need to take responsibility and both need to have ownership of the problem and the plan to fix it.

Individual differences and interests will stay problematic until the "us" asserts itself and confidently says "let's work together on this." A couple's "us" is "like a child that both spouses have created. It will define its identity by how it is loved" and trusted. When the "'us" gets involved in financial decisions, the couple is moving to a stable level of satisfaction.

DAILY COUPLE TALK:
(EACH PARTNER RESPONDS)
What are some characteristics of your "us" that have been developed during your time together?

DOLLARS AND SENSE

Early Christian philosopher and apologist Augustine once said:

In necessary things, unity.

In uncertain things, freedom.

In everything, charity.

Augustine's ideas apply to money as well as other important facets of couple experience.

UNITY is imperative for sound financial planning. One partner may become the main money-manager, bill payer, electronic banker, or investor, but without transparency of information, the other partner may not feel fully and equally responsible for choices and decisions. Regular couple conversations help maintain balance and unify the financial decisions about the future.

FREEDOM is also important. Whatever the monthly budget requirement, both partners need to have some discretionary money available, money not dedicated to bills and for which they are not accountable.

In marriages that value the growth of the relationship, CHARITY (or love as it's called today) directs money decisions just as it does other decisions that affect the health of the couple.

DAILY COUPLE TALK:
(EACH PERSON ANSWERS)
*How can you use unity, freedom, or charity
in your daily money decisions?*

DOLLARS AND SENSE

Our attitudes toward money often impact the way we save it, spend it, invest, go into debt, give it away, donate to charity, hoard it, or borrow. Daily Couple Talk: From the following list choose several statements you believe. Then discuss them with your partner.

❦ I will buy something that is on sale instead of getting what I really want.

❦ It is sometimes important to seize the moment and not worry about the cost.

❦ I have more freedom because I have a budget.

❦ I would not want the responsibility that comes with inheriting a large sum of money.

❦ I would not want to borrow money from friends or family.

❦ It's important to have money set aside for an emergency.

❦ I like to research costs of expensive items.

❦ I like to give gifts that are a name brand and expensive.

❦ It is important to give to charitable organizations.

❦ Expenses should be limited to only the necessary.

❦ I feel like a failure when I don't have enough money.

❦ I like to live modestly and think others should too.

❦ If I had a lot of money, I would use it to help others.

DOLLARS AND SENSE

A tee-shirt boldly announcing "When the going gets tough, the tough go shopping" may be amusing, but the sad truth is that material goods and comforts do not provide the deep satisfaction of a loving relationship, and we all know it in our hearts. Nevertheless, we are a society of spenders—

- ❦ With shopping electronically soon turning into a business netting $100 billion in the next five years,

- ❦ With 83% of disposable income going to pay off debt,

- ❦ With the average person carrying as many as 9 credit cards.

Making couple financial changes takes careful communication, much as with any other important subject. Judgmental talk, accusations, or threats slow down the process; using "I" statements gets to the subject faster. Take time airing feelings before moving to negotiation. For example, if the last tax refund went into a CD with no consultation, feelings may still be hurt at the lack of financial trust. Getting as much information as possible will end up helping final plans seem more realistic to both partners. The goal is to become allies, not enemies.

Maybe wearing a tee-shirt saying "Yea us!" would remind couples that getting on the same page financially can make a huge difference in over-all couple health.

DAILY COUPLE TALK:
(EACH PERSON PARTICIPATES)
If you were going to create a couple tee-shirt, what would you put on it?

DOLLARS AND SENSE

Bobbye and Britton once spent the night at a bed-and-breakfast out in the country, sure that they would have a quiet experience different from the noise of city life. Early the next morning they sat drinking coffee at a pretty table under tall trees. Suddenly a firetruck went by, with loud sirens. This woke up the dogs in a boarding kennel across the road, who all began to bark and howl. This woke up the geese in a nearby farmhouse, who honked in protest at the noise. Then two donkeys in a nearby field joined in. There was nothing to do but laugh, relax, and try to enjoy the unexpected panorama.

When reality meets expectations and they do not match, as in the country scene at the bed-and-breakfast, flexibility can often bridge the gap and help a person adjust. What IS doesn't mean what will always be and that fact can be encouraging, but facing the truth of the moment is also important. This is also true for the subject of money, where reality and expectations often collide.

Numbers have a reality of their own which for fiscal sanity must be accepted. But the acceptance and flexibility of the adjustment is just as important and has a lot to do with whether in the future we look back with laughter or frustration.

DAILY COUPLE TALK:
(EACH PARTNER RESPONDS)
What is something you hope to do financially in the
next five years? How could it be paid for?

DOLLARS AND SENSE

"Partners who characteristically turn toward each other rather than away are putting money in the bank." This statement by marriage counselor, teacher, and researcher Dr. John Gottman helps us picture relationship rewards by using a commodity society cannot do without—money.

Putting money in the bank in our name brings security and confidence. It allows us to pay bills, buy necessities, and occasionally do something so special that we remember it for years. That same security and confidence is what most couples hope is going to be theirs in marriage. That it is entirely possible is surely one of modern life's greatest discoveries, right up there with plastic and antibiotics.

Notice that someone must do the "putting"; someone needs to make the deposits. When couples are intentional about "turning toward" each other, they are making emotional deposits that build the relationship and fulfill the desire for security that lies deep within every psyche. Feeling loved, feeling accepted, feeling understood—these are the emotions which couples have the power to produce in each other as in love they add to the bank account in the name of "us."

DAILY COUPLE TALK:
(EACH PERSON ANSWERS)
What is one way your partner "turns toward" you that makes you feel emotionally secure and builds up the bank account of your "us"?

DOLLARS AND SENSE

There are at least three styles of marriage. Each style also sheds light on the way the marriage is practiced by the couple. Note the examples of these styles:

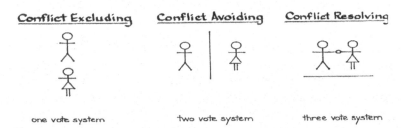

The *Conflict Excluding* style is a one-vote system with only one spouse taking the leadership in most decisions in the marriage. This will include how the couple chooses to spend and invest its funds. The one-vote system works only if both spouses agree to it.

The *Conflict Avoiding* style is a two-vote system with both spouses dealing with their respective roles. Some funds are allocated to one spouse (groceries, household expenses) and other funds are with the other spouse. This system works if both do their part and are fully responsible for their roles in the marriage.

The *Conflict Resolving* style is a three-vote system with each spouse getting one vote and the relationship receiving one vote. Each person considers what is best for each and for the relationship and discusses it with the partner.

DAILY COUPLE TALK:
(EACH PARTNER RESPONDS)
Discuss with each other which style of marriage is more accurate for your marriage. Do you move from one style to another? If so, in what ways?

WHAT WORKS?

"When love and skill work together,

Expect a masterpiece."

JOHN RUSKIN

WHAT WORKS?

PART 1

Marriage Enrichment is a positive, solution-oriented process designed to help couples find more satisfaction in their relationship. The more effort couples put into their relationship mutually, the greater the satisfaction. In baseball, a batter who gets a hit three times in ten at-bats can become a multi-millionaire. Partners who try to apply the Marriage Enrichment techniques can experience a similar success in feelings of well-being.

Which parts of the process produce the most success? By far an improved communication system makes the highest impact. Start with 15 minutes a day of quality conversation, keep it up for at least two weeks, and begin to feel some of the jagged edges of the relationship soften. Sprinkle the conversation with compliments and the sharing of feelings, and like sprinkling a plant's pollen, new things begin to grow. If you can't manage 15 minutes face-to-face, use the telephone. But make a verbal connection. It takes time to replace bad habits such as not listening, being critical, or not taking time for couple interaction. You are aiming for both partners wanting more.

DAILY COUPLE TALK:
(EACH PARTNER RESPONDS)
If improved communication has the highest impact on couple success, on a scale of 1-10 (with 10 being high) where do you rate your current communication satisfaction? Explain.

WHAT WORKS?

PART 2

A second recommendation for more couple satisfaction is simply the couple's attitude toward what it wants to achieve. If you

1. want couple growth and more happiness,

2. miss the days when you talked easily, laughed often, flirted over dinner, or just enjoyed being with each other,

3. are hopeful that the two of you will once again exchange loving behaviors enthusiastically,

4. then you are already on the way to looking for opportunities to get what you want. The actions spring from the attitude.

Marriage Enrichment calls this mutual commitment to growth, and it means that both are trying to view everything that happens—even arguments—as a way to fairly provide the relationship with the healthy ingredients it needs to grow. Insults, ridicule, criticism, and demeaning do not bring about growth. Choose words and actions that will bring about a dynamic and radiant "us."

DAILY COUPLE TALK:
(EACH PARTNER PARTICIPATES)
What could be one nutrient that would bring about growth in your relationship?

WHAT WORKS?

Strange as it may seem, getting a MUTUALLY satisfactory way of handling arguments brings with it a concord that defies logic. In fact, according to many couples just the lessening of stress in the relationship by knowing there is a way to deal more productively with divisive issues is a help. Less stress, more confidence, fewer hard feelings, greater enjoyment of time together—hmm.

It is at this point, however, that old habits can stand in the way of progress. One yells; the other retreats. One uses reason; the other uses tears. One avoids; the other tries to dominate. To continue the same habits when they are not working well is to continue a process doomed to fail.

Instead, make a plan together for handling arguments. Stick to it. Keep working the plan long enough to change old, familiar habits that do not fit with the new plan. After a while (and when you are not angry) review the plan and discuss any needed changes. It may be a strange approach to reaping marital benefits, but it works.

DAILY COUPLE TALK:
(EACH PERSON RESPONDS)
If you could change just one thing about the way you deal with arguments and misunderstandings, what would it be?

WHAT WORKS?

Dr. John Gottman's extensive research with couples leads him to conclude that "a lasting marriage results from a couple's ability to resolve the conflicts that are inevitable in any relationship." Thus very early in his famous career he reported four warning signs, which he called the Four Horsemen of the Apocalypse."

The first Horseman is CRITICISM. Criticism differs from complaints in that complaints are about deeds and asked-for actions that didn't get accomplished. Criticism is about the person. Criticism has a way of becoming pervasive and according to Dr. Gottman's research "corrodes the marriage." CONTEMPT is a similar Horseman but goes one step past criticism with name-calling and an intent to insult or wound. Both criticism and contempt happen because an issue has not been dealt with, and both are attempts to blame the other person.

Another Horseman is DEFENSIVENESS, an effort to avoid an argument by long explanations and repeated excuses. Responsibility is denied. The final Horseman is STONEWALLING. This has several manifestations, including not listening, not responding, maintaining a disapproving distance, retreating in silence, and refusing to engage with the partner.

Dr. Gottman has found that these Horseman are warning signs that a more effective method of dealing with arguments is essential. These Horsemen can sabotage anybody's relationship.

DAILY COUPLE TALK:
(EACH PARTNER RESPONDS)
Which of the Four Horsemen is the most destructive and why?

WHAT WORKS?

PART 1

On a recent drive around a downtown city center, these ambiguous signs appeared on buildings: Collaborative Transystems, Rosedale Pharmacy Compounding, Gold Medal Metro Services, and End-Products, New and Used. There was no clear way to discern what those businesses offered. And just in case there is a similar problem with terms recommended to couples by marriage educators, here are some explanations.

Win/Win/WIN is both concept and technique. It is an attitude toward building (and keeping) a strong "Us," as well as a technique for doing so. It gives to each partner a voice, a vote, and a "win" in the daily commerce of life. The couple also considers the third element in their relationship, the "us," which also is given a voice, a vote, and a "win."

There are some actions or words, for example, that each refrains from doing or saying to each other simply because it would damage the "us." Whether the couple is together or away at separate work sites, respect for the "us" guides their words and actions. Even in the midst of attempting to resolve divisive issues, this formula must be considered. Win/Win/WIN means each partner treats the other fairly and both honor the voice and vote of their relationship.

Commitment to this formula both as concept and technique is "both the fuel and the essence" of a great marriage, according to Dr. Scott Stanley's book The Heart of Commitment.

DAILY COUPLE TALK:
(EACH PERSON PARTICIPATES)
What are some characteristics of your "us," your relationship, that continues to give you satisfaction?

WHAT WORKS?

PART 2

Another marriage education term that might need explanation is the MEG, or Marriage Enrichment Group. This is a group of couples who agree to meet once a month for an agreed-on period of time in order to discuss issues common to marriage. To learn more about it, access Better Marriages. Org. One purpose of the MEG is the practice of skills needed for better communication. Plenty of opportunity is given to private couple dialogue, free from phones, children, or other distractions.

As many marriage educators have said, among them Dr. David Olson in his book Empowering Couples, "the most important area distinguishing happy and unhappy couples is communication." In all his research Dr. Olson has found that a reliable predictor of happiness for couples was their satisfaction "with how they talk to each other." The MEG is a safe place to improve communication skills, along with other couples who are doing the same.

The monthly MEG also gives opportunity to practice desired skills. Routine is the goal here, much as athletes need a routine in order to improve their skills. The same energy for building physical muscles builds the required relational muscles couples need. Change takes time, but the effort of practicing good communication skills at home plus the MEG format of couple dialogue offers a fast-track to achieving couple goals.

DAILY COUPLE TALK:
(EACH PARTNER RESPONDS)
Which of the following is more important to you for the future: teamwork, deeper attachment, better communication, more quality time together? Why?

WHAT WORKS?

We have friends who love their sailboat and insist there are parallels between sailing and marriage, mostly at the point of confusing romance and realism.

There are sailors, they say, who look only at sunsets, dolphins playing, and puffy white clouds. They prefer not to discuss hurricanes, backed-up bilges, engine tune-ups, overflowing commodes, sounders that do not avoid the shoals, or navigation tools that do not work. There are also those who insist that in marriage if you "love" each other, everything else will take care of itself. You'll always agree, never get sick, and the wedding day will last forever.

Sailing can be relaxing and invigorating, whether you're ghosting along on a gentle breeze in Long Island Sound or watching colorful fish off the Bahamian out islands. Marriage also can be relaxing and invigorating, whether you're arm-in-arm on a walk through autumn leaves or laughing together on a rug in front of the fireplace. What makes both sailing and marriage work is keeping a heady blend of romance and realism. One focuses on the beauty of the ideal; one focuses on the beauty of daily detail. Both are necessary.

DAILY COUPLE TALK:
(EACH PERSON PARTICIPATES)
If you could take a paid-for trip to somewhere beautiful in the world, where would you want to go? Why?

WHAT WORKS?

Stephen Covey says: "Nothing great and durable has ever been produced with ease. Labor is the parent of all the lasting monuments of the world, whether in verse or in stone, in poetry or in pyramids." And the same is true of marriage. No happy and successful marriage relationship happens by accident but is the result of couple labor to achieve what each partner wants and needs.

In the past couples stayed together because stability was their priority. Modern couples value happiness and a sense of fulfillment most and will not stay in a relationship that does not seem likely to meet those needs. Millennials are willing to cooperate in actions and efforts likely to produce happiness and fulfillment but only up to a point. The emphasis is on WORKING. Unless it is perceived as a mutual effort, with both partners equally involved in the endeavors, the fuel and motivation run out quickly.

The shortest path to a goal is a direct line. Wherever you are in the number of anniversaries you've spent together, stop right now and find out what three things the two of you could work toward that would make each person happier. You are building a lasting "us," a unique relationship, a "monument" that society will thank you for. "Labor is the parent of all lasting monuments."

DAILY COUPLE TALK:
(EACH PARTNER RESPONDS)
Talk about the three things.

WHAT WORKS?

Britton once participated in a workshop identifying Family Strengths. Carefully researched, the strengths eventually became a book called <u>Secrets of Strong Families</u> by Dr. Nick Stinnett, at that time a professor at the University of Nebraska. As the heart of the home, the couple leads the way in introducing and practicing those strengths.

One strength is COMMITMENT. If the partners are dedicated to promoting each other's welfare and happiness in their relationship, the whole family benefits. The children develop a sense of belonging and identity and are interested in supporting each other's interests. Through the family, the schools are also enriched, and through them the community and society in general.

Another strength is COMMUNICATION. Family members who can be open and honest with each other become valuable members of society, and it starts with the couple, the heart of the home. According to many educators, the one thing more important in a marriage than sex is communication. Developing a workable and satisfactory model for speaking and listening to each other is crucial.

A third strength is APPRECIATION. Here is where family members affirm each other's good qualities and decisions. New granddaughter-in-law Grace has even incorporated this strength in her first-grade classroom, finding that it motivates her students better than criticism.

DAILY COUPLE TALK:
(EACH PERSON ANSWERS)
Which of the listed three strengths do you think is most important for YOUR relationship?

WHAT WORKS?

A major resource in the long-term happiness of couples is their determination to keep fun in their relationship. Hardly anyone gets married in order to solve problems efficiently, get along with in-laws, or make realistic budgets. But lots of people marry to continue friendship and fun with one special person.

One problem is that as we become involved in more activities at work and in the community, time seems to rule out fun. Relaxation and spontaneity get lost, and even adequate sleep seems hard to come by. This is the moment when playtime becomes most important.

Like keeping track of what we are eating, it's important to make a record of how we spend our time. This makes it easier to see that there IS a way to make better time choices. For personal fitness, squeeze in time for exercise, even if it's just 30 minutes a day; for relational fitness, save at least one evening often to do something together that you both like. Strategize together as a couple. Protect this time from conflict and the tyranny of cell phones. Your relationship, your "us," will thank you for it.

DAILY COUPLE TALK:
(EACH PARTNER RESPONDS)
Look at your typical week together. When could you have a "date" together and what would you like to do?

WHAT WORKS?

Drs. Charles and Elizabeth Schmitz were the speakers at a Better Marriage Conference. The Schmitzes have traveled to 7 continents, 49 countries, every state in the U.S., and seven provinces of Canada. They interviewed couples who have been married for at least 50 years and asked them what makes a successful marriage. What works?

The top answer about success was finding a way to talk to each other without harming with words; talk often; talk honestly; talk without discounting the partner; talk about health; talk about money; talk about sex; talk with respect. This is the one piece of advice that cuts across all continents, the Schmitzes said. It was also the one thing that the interviewed couples thought all newlyweds should know.

A second answer about marital success (what works?) was that the happiest couples were those who supported and encouraged the partner. They acted as "cheerleader" for each other, and conversation with those couples was sprinkled with "we" and "our." Both partners felt strong as individuals because of this support, and both felt they had a "voice" in all decisions and conflicts. A sturdy and flexible "us" built by conversation and support was evident.

⚭

DAILY COUPLE TALK:
(EACH PARTNER FILLS IN THE BLANKS)
I try to show you that you are a very
important person in my life by _____.
I try to give you encouragement
in our relationship by _____.

WHAT WORKS?

Everyone has a backstory. Some of these stories are associated with increased chances of divorce and are impossible to change, such as personality differences, parental divorce, or abuse. This means that couples with difficult backstories have to work harder for stability and happiness. They also should be encouraged by knowing: all couples have problems; IT'S HOW YOU HANDLE THEM THAT COUNTS MOST FOR THE FUTURE.

Abolish negative patterns of communication immediately. It seems like a small step, but it is the essential beginning that every couple must pay attention to, according to all counselors, therapists, and marriage researchers. It is the one most rewarding thing you can do for your marriage and the greatest predictor of trouble. There can never be a strong "us" when disturbing ways of talking threaten every good feeling for each other.

Find a way to talk that feels safe and comfortable to both. Many therapists say that developing a structure both partners trust is the best way to improve communication in general. Emotional safety is the goal here. When both partners feel good about the chosen structure, that is the way to communicate safely and clearly. Practice it regularly so that you can use it when either partner slips into old negative patterns. This will eventually be like giving a present to your relationship: the removal of anger, disappointment, frustration, and sadness.

DAILY COUPLE TALK:
(EACH PERSON DISCUSSES)
What can make talking with each other easier?

WHAT WORKS?

A well-stocked relational toolbox is a must for every couple. Keeping relationships in good repair frees both partners to be at their best and to have ample energy for life's demands.

One handy tool is the Time-Out. If an argument is escalating to the point where some rash comment is likely to cause damage, call for a Time-Out. Either partner can do it, but it will work better if one says, "WE need a Time-Out" instead of "YOU need a Time-Out," according to Dr. Scott Stanley of PREP. Use the time apart to calm down so that the argument can deal logically with the issue at hand. If there is not enough time left for a productive discussion, set an appointment to get back to the issue. This way both partners know it will be addressed, and both can plan for it.

Tantamount to having an all-purpose screwdriver is having a reliable communication tool. If one partner does not like criticism, or does not like sarcasm, or does not listen, these issues need to be cleared up. Talking should be for pleasure, exchanging information, self-disclosure, and growth. Making it so for both partners is using the communication tool skillfully.

Other needed tools are a plan for resolving disagreements, for expressing affection in the way the partner appreciates, and for living with a can-do attitude about the relationship. Having the relational tool box well-stocked gives assurance that partners can handle issues.

DAILY COUPLE TALK:
(EACH PARTNER RESPONDS)
What other tools should be in your relational tool box?

WHAT WORKS?

Blueprints in hand, the contractor began the initial inspection of the land that would eventually hold the office building. For months he had been planning, and now the beginning work on the foundation was just days away. The building's shape was already in his mind.

The contractor's blueprints are similar to wedding plans, which are also detailed and specific. Granddaughter-in-law Grace even posted an on-line schedule for a 3-day period, so that the wedding party knew the exact time and place they were supposed to be and what each should bring.

Yet many couples make no plans for the business of putting their lives together. It's not too surprising that right around 50% of couples do not stay married, many of them separating around the first anniversary. It is a testimony to the longing in the human heart for coupling that marriages continue to be performed, even knowing these alarming and expensive odds.

So what to do? One of our prime needs today is for extended marriage horizons. We need an enlargement of our vision of what a strong and happy "us" does for society. When this happens, we will also see the need for a reliable plan, a blueprint that equips couples for facing together all of life's ups and downs, sorrows and celebrations, failures and triumphs, a deliberate plan for success.

DAILY COUPLE TALK:
(EACH PARTNER RESPONDS)
If you were making a plan for your future, what would you consider to be most important?

WHAT WORKS?

In the best-seller <u>Seven Habits of Highly Effective People</u>, Stephen Covey says the first habit is to write a mission statement. It should state what we want to accomplish during our time on earth. It should state how we want to be remembered and what is important to us. When we have made a thoughtful mission statement, Covey says, we then have the beginnings of a clear plan of action for reaching those wishes and goals. It is here that many people have a problem. There is a disconnection between their goals and the efforts they plan to make in order to achieve them.

Many couples come to marriage wishing and hoping for a happy experience, a loving family, and a respected presence in some community. It is a noble goal and a needed one. But if couples do not perform the actions that make marriage a happy experience, they are short-circuiting the process and then will be disappointed because their early hopes and wishes did not work out. Unfortunately many of these same couples (or at least one of them) repeat the same process again and again with different partners.

The mission statement of this book is "to build a better future for couples, families, and the community." Toward that end are recommended and time-tested actions, attitudes, techniques, and practices that help flesh out the mission statement. They are presented to help couples preserve their love through the years.

DAILY COUPLE TALK:
(EACH PERSON PARTICIPATES)
Write a BRIEF mission statement about your marriage.

WHAT WORKS?

Saying what you want or would like has many benefits. It allows the partner to know the subject and your opinion on it. It avoids the indirection of many conversations, where one partner tries to test the other's feelings without risking rejection. It does away with the hints that often leave the partner confused or unaware of the real meaning of the message.

Saying "I've heard 'Sully' is a good movie" is not the same as saying "I want us to go see 'Sully' sometime soon." If your partner does not respond to the first statement and thinks you are just making an observation, it would be unfair to feel that your request has been rejected. Saying what you want just puts a subject on the table for further discussion and planning. It does not mean that you are a selfish and demanding person, and it does not mean that you will get everything you want.

It does mean that when communication is open and frank, partners have more trust and are more likely to be relaxed and attentive. They think they are getting accurate information, and this leads to an even greater degree of interaction and connection. It all starts with saying what you want and would like.

DAILY COUPLE TALK:
(EACH PARTNER RESPONDS)
Think ahead to whatever holiday season comes up next.
What is something you want to do?

WHAT WORKS?

The couple is the "heart" of the home. It's an awesome responsibility but one that has to be in good working order for the rest of the parts of the family to function smoothly. Thus the couple must constantly strive to strengthen and improve their relationship, just as the human heart needs to be kept strong and healthy.

In J.D. Robb's novel <u>Apprentice In Death,</u> Lieutenant Eve Dallas is shocked when after three years of marriage her wealthy husband Roarke proposes remodeling her home office. In order to help her feel more secure in his fabulous New York mansion, before they married Roarke had rebuilt a replica of her former office, right down to the same flooring and battered desk. She had really appreciated the sweet understanding that she needed her place. It takes a while and many discussions, but Eve finally realizes that an agreement to remodel would be tacitly saying, "I do not now need MY place; I want it to be OUR place because my life now is with you." It is a way of strengthening their couple relationship, their "us," their "heart."

Whether a first marriage or a blending family (yours, mine, and ours), the couple is the "heart" and needs to assume that role for the good of all others involved.

DAILY COUPLE TALK:
(EACH PERSON ANSWERS)
*How can we show others that we
value our relationship?*

WHAT WORKS?

Marriage at its best is a joyful voyage of love and adventure. It helps us mature; it often produces children; it provides a helpmeet to face life's problems. But unless we keep it exciting and transforming for both partners, it never reaches the potential possible.

To keep the voyage rewarding for both is to KEEP A STRONG COUPLE CONNECTION. This may be in the form of physical touch—holding hands, hugging, snuggling, kissing, massaging, or embracing. The connection may be in verbal form—having a 15-minute conversation every day just about the two of you, regularly giving compliments and words of appreciation, using words to show admiration and support. With a connection that both partners sense comes the built-in confidence that this is an important voyage.

To keep the voyage rewarding for both is to KEEP A STRONG COMMITMENT. When we believe that the voyage is important, we stick with it even through inconveniences and problems. We give time to making the voyage safe for both. We figure out what our partner wants and seek ways to make it happen. We talk honestly to each other and we don't talk trash. We focus on strengths and tolerate shortcomings. We are committed to growing a strong "us."

Connection and commitment lead to a joyful voyage, as we love and let ourselves be loved, care and are cared for, discover and let another discover important things about us, learn and are known.

DAILY COUPLE TALK:
(EACH PARTNER RESPONDS)
What relational voyage would you like
to take with your partner?

WHAT WORKS?

A balanced and heart-pleasing marriage can be a breathing space for a society that increasingly holds its breath for the assault of the next bad news.

A happy marriage can be the safe place where bucket lists are accomplished and where someone really cares about the answer to the question, "How was your day?" A warm and accepting marriage develops a strong and healthy "me" and "you" and works steadfastly to develop a strong and healthy "us" that reflects the best that both partners put into it. A long-term and growing marriage works at life-skills that mutually satisfy both partners and establishes a reputation that attracts others. A life-enhancing marriage maintains a balance of personalities, values, and respect. A marriage on a firm foundation helps each partner reach his/her potential, whatever happened in growing up or in past relationships. A truly distinctive marriage recognizes that this is a unique relationship and as such needs to establish its own goals and boundaries.

This kind of union, this kind of relationship, this kind of growth as a couple leading a family, this kind of commitment, this kind of intimate connection that blesses the heart and warms the psyche—this does not happen without effort and time. But this is the breathing space in the midst of violence and strife. This is the kind of marriage that makes the beautiful music others sing.

DAILY COUPLE TALK:
(EACH PERSON PARTICIPATES)
Our "us" is made of some valuable insights,
among them _____ and _____.

WHAT WORKS?

Raising a family and making a living are major life-goals of many married couples. The qualities necessary to reach these goals successfully are sometimes the reason couples stay together.

Yet many couples meet those life-goals by adding to them shared laughter and a sense of humor. The ability to make each other laugh, to share jokes and puns, to tease and develop funny secret code words—this quality may be overlooked as a contributing factor to marital success. Laughter and playfulness are a treasured kind of interaction that amuses, entertains, and reduces stress. They can add the electricity that makes marriage more than a business partnership, more than a strong friendship, more than a helpful support system, although all these things enhance the quality of married life.

A major benefit of laughter is fending off boredom, a sneaky enemy of growth in marriage. Humor keeps things interesting by keeping partners ever-open to the liveliness of a good relationship. Laughter at the incongruous, the silly, and the annoying; laughter at spontaneous wit; laughter at paradoxes— laughter quite simply can enliven the relationship.

Perhaps laughter and a sense of humor cannot measure up to the important goals of raising a strong family and making a living. But it can become an oasis in the daily round of effort necessary to reaching those life-goals.

DAILY COUPLE TALK:
(EACH PARTNER PARTICIPATES)
*Think of an amusing situation in your
relationship and tell about it.*

WHAT WORKS?

Marriage is always a work in progress because people and circumstances are dynamic and change over time. The challenge therefore for every couple is to stay connected. Those who believe that the relationship will just rock along naturally by happenstance often wait until too late to make substantive changes. Still others merely live side by side, united by habit or their shared history. When marriage succeeds in making both partners happy, it is because it grows with the changes and attends to the many ways connection (and reconnection) happens.

Several identifiable periods of transition can break the connection for couples. The transition to becoming parents is a well-known trouble time, as is midlife (usually considered ages 35-55), with its psychological and physiological changes in adults. Another troubling transition is when the children leave home and the couple is suddenly alone and no longer defined by being parents. Another transition occurs at the time of retirement, with today's added concerns of aging parents.

Staying connected through these transitions is imperative. Connection is maintained when we: keep an intimate talk-time, help each other with tasks, discuss plans for handling new ventures, encourage each other, stay friends and lovers. These can infuse new life into the marriage at any stage.

DAILY COUPLE TALK:
(EACH PARTNER RESPONDS)
We are a "work in progress." Fortunately, we have the following tools: _____ and _____.

WHAT WORKS?

PART 1

"When love and skill work together, expect a masterpiece," British philosopher John Ruskin once said. Here are some commonly heard questions regarding marriage as the Mona Lisa or the "Halleluiah Chorus" of relationship.

Question: Our parents and grandparents stayed married until they died. They just loved each other. Isn't that enough?

Answer: Yes and no. Both our parents and grandparents did also, and they never heard of Marriage Enrichment. But times are different, and stability alone is no longer a goal for marriage.

In addition, people can expect to be healthier longer because of new medical practices, new and better medicines, and wider knowledge of the impact of preventive health habits (no smoking, regular exercise, more fruits and veggies). Taking care of your marriage is like taking care of your health, by using all available resources. Doing so gives a NEW meaning to "just loving each other."

Question: Isn't being good parents most important?

Answer: Parenting is important, but children will grow up and found their own homes. It therefore impacts the future directly if parents provide children with a healthy model of two adults working toward equity, respect, tenderness, and good communication skills. Having a happy marriage gives joy to the partners AND gives security to the children about relationship. The roles complement each other.

∞ DAILY COUPLE TALK:
ACH PARTNER RESPONDS)
What is one way that love and skill works together for you?

WHAT WORKS?

PART 2

Marriage as the high point of human relationships brings out many questions.

Question: What skill is best to improve the marital relationship?

Answer: It will be different for every couple, depending on what you most want to accomplish. If your arguments leave you with wariness and resentment, practicing a new skill here will probably be most noticeable. Others say their single most effective skill was affirming each other; criticisms were reduced and cooperation multiplied. Still others credit the 15-minute personal daily dialogue as revitalizing their relationship. Also regularly mentioned is sharing feelings and making "I" statements. Making a plan together is a good start.

Question: We already have a good marriage. We don't need therapy or counseling.

Answer: Marriage education does not assume anything is wrong; instead, it seeks to build on what is good and what works. Think of it as Spring Training in baseball. These are athletes who already know how to play the game and who often make millions of dollars doing so. But they all go to Spring Training hoping that by reviewing and practicing their skills they can have a winning season and perhaps play in a World Series.

∞ DAILY COUPLE TALK:
(EACH PERSON PARTICIPATES)
What is one skill whose development would create an improvement in your relationship?

WHAT WORKS?

Marriage is a complex relationship. Two people begin their lives together vowing to support each other "in sickness and in health," and "to forsake all others." Those are lofty goals and high expectations, as should befit one of life's most important relationships. But accomplishing them is a daunting task for some couples. Other than a general resolve to "love each other," many couples do not have a clear plan as to how living together might be a great adventure over the years, bringing out the best in each partner and the best in their relationship, their "us."

An early, relaxed, and candid talk about what each partner values establishes goals and exchanges information about core beliefs. It shows areas where there may have to be compromise. A "values conversation" suggests ways to make each other happy and gives each spouse the freedom to meet needs in a realistic but individually purposeful way.

One exciting thing about a "values conversation" is that it can happen any time. Our values may change as we do and as our family expands and puts new pressures and expectations in place. Sharing with each other in a clear way about what we need to be fulfilled is only fair and reasonable. It keeps our relationship current. It gives information that COULD be acted upon and both partners know it.

◐◑ DAILY COUPLE TALK:
(BOTH PARTNERS RESPOND)
Perhaps this "values conversation" has not happened for a while. What would be two things you would want your partner to know about what you believe?

WHAT WORKS?

The theme of a recent Better Marriage conference was "Gourmet Love in a Fast-Food World." The speakers, Greg and Priscilla Hunt, admitted that both kinds of "dining" were necessary and had their advantages. For those couples interested in having a "gourmet" relational experience, here's what the Hunts recommended.

Start by recognizing the satisfactions and pleasures you already have. It "tastes good" to both spouses to hear the things that are right, so take plenty of time over this part of the "meal."

Second, become partners in building self-esteem. Each partner already knows where the other could use confidence. Having a partner affirming your efforts and not pointing out your mistakes is helpful in savoring the "tastes" of success. Affirm each other sexually also. If "studmuffin" or "sugar britches" used to be in your lexicon of sweet names, bring those out to enhance the meal.

Finally, search for ways to express love, even in the way you talk to your partner. Instead of "you" statements that can create defensiveness, use "I" statements that only convey YOUR feelings and point of view. Taking the time to speak clearly and also lovingly makes both partners want to linger over the meal.

DAILY COUPLE TALK:
(EACH PARTNER ANSWERS)
What does your partner do (or say)
that makes you feel loved?

388

WHAT WORKS?

To help a marriage grow, you have to make an effort: be present emotionally, validate your partner, be affectionate, talk and listen empathetically, give compliments, be honest. To break a marriage apart, it doesn't have to be an affair or too many unproductive arguments. Just make no effort, and even if you do not do anything wrong, according to most marital advisors, the results will be the same; the relationship declines and dies.

Laura wants to talk about her pleasant evening out with friends; when she gets home, she tries to tell her husband Jim about the evening. He asks no questions. He looks up once from his magazine when she asks him if he wants to hear any more about it, but he doesn't answer. Then he is surprised when she gets angry and leaves the room. All he did was make no effort.

Joanna forgot to go to her partner Keith's award party, where his firm honored him for making the top sales. When he got home and reminded her about it, she did not apologize or congratulate him. Keith assumed that Joanna was not interested in his work. Neither made the effort to talk about it and both went to bed unhappy.

These common examples could so easily be changed. All they needed to do was make a response. Instead, both left with low-level stress, a widening distance, and a kind of chronic resentment. To help a marriage grow, you have to make an effort; to help it waste away, just do nothing.

DAILY COUPLE TALK:
(EACH PARTNER RESPONDS)
*Why are courtesy and active listening important
in a relationship?*

WHAT WORKS?

"Too many marriages go down the drain because each spouse is waiting for the other to change first," says Dr. Michele Weiner-Davis in her book <u>Divorce Busting</u>. She goes on to say that most marriages can be saved "simply because most problems are solvable."

During a marriage education course several years ago Britton and Bobbye met a couple who said they can't talk to each other without "negatives," so they have stopped talking. In a communication exercise about saying what you want, one partner told her husband that she "didn't want to be late for this course" (not what she DID want) and "you make us late every time" (no "I" talk, only accusing and blaming.) Here was a good place to suggest to the wife a possible change, which she immediately made. Then the husband practiced reflective listening with her, matched her tone, and when it was his turn to speak, told her that he didn't know it was so important to her, that she had never told him about it, and that he would get ready in plenty of time for the next meeting. She paraphrased his words so that both knew that both had heard the same thing.

It was a simple lesson and would have been unremarkable except for what happened afterward. The couple began to smile. The wife laughed at something he said. Their facial expressions relaxed. Sometimes it's just reassuring to learn that "most problems are solvable."

DAILY COUPLE TALK:
(EACH PERSON PARTICIPATES)
Give the details about something you want to do, including the reasons why it might not be a good idea. Let your partner paraphrase your statements. It's good practice.

WHAT WORKS?

Police hate to respond to domestic 911 calls because of the erratic and sometimes violent behavior. Couples who started their married lives with the usual expectations of harmony have instead let their relationship decline to the point that they attack each other (and sometimes those who try to help). When couples run out of ideas about how to solve their problems, they often react with frustration, even rage. The distress they feel very often spills over into their families. Helping couples cope with divisive issues is not just enabling a better outcome for one moment in time but for developing a pattern for the future.

Disagreements are inevitable for every honest couple. It's how disagreements are handled that makes a difference. Avoid blaming or being defensive. Softening the beginning of the argument makes an amicable outcome much more likely. If one or both partners cannot be calm, use a Time Out. When you continue, limit the discussion to ONE issue. Each partner offers some feelings about the issue and some ideas that might solve the problem, with no criticism or analysis. Choose one idea that seems practical and set a date in the future to review the solution and evaluate its success. Abide by your chosen solution until time to assess it. Then change solutions, if you need to.

As you begin, think of the result you want above all. If you want a good marriage more than you want to "win," you are already in a better place to discuss the issue fairly.

DAILY COUPLE TALK:
(EACH PARTNER PARTICIPATES)
Name an issue that needs talking about in your relationship. Set a time to discuss it.

WHAT WORKS?

Sometimes all that is needed is just to listen.

Let's assume Mary has just got home after an exhausting day. With a glass of iced tea in hand, she and her husband Mark are sitting on the back porch. Mary tells him she has no time for herself because work is so demanding. Mark tells her she could quit her job and explains how they could manage without her income. She says she forgot to call their daughter and is worried. He admonishes her to quit worrying because it's making her too unhappy. She argues that she is NOT unhappy, tells him he never listens, and angrily goes in the house.

Here's what Mark might say if he "listened." Mary says she has no time for herself because work is so demanding. Mike pats her hand and observes that it sounds like she had a busy day. Mary tells him she forgot to call their daughter. Mark says, "Hmmm." She says she is worried about the daughter's new house. He smiles and tells her she is a loving mother. Mary gives him a hug and tells him he is SUCH a good listener. He thanks her and hugs her back.

One conversation offers advice and lectures, and at one point even high-jacks the subject and talks about money management. No wonder Mary was angry at the end of it. The other conversation matched the speaker's emotional tone, was patient, and showed empathy about the fast pace of life. It gave compliments to the speaker and offered gestures of affection. No wonder it ended in hugs. Sometimes all that is needed is just to listen.

DAILY COUPLE TALK:
(EACH PARTNER RESPONDS)
What essentially happened here?

WHAT WORKS?

Those who have never experienced marriage education are sometimes skeptical of its value. In Perth, Australia, on a speaking tour, Britton and Bobbye told a pastor that they would be asking couples to share with each other in a dialogue. The alarmed pastor said that Asian couples would find that experience outside their cultural comfort zone and would not do it. Yet on the evening that the Woods introduced the exercise, the Asian couples participated along with everyone else. And just before the Woods left Perth, an older Asian couple gave them a thank-you card expressing appreciation for the tool of Couple Dialogue. In the card was $100 in American currency.

In Madrid, Spain, the announced subject was Conflict Management, and the worried pastor of the international church where the Woods were speaking nervously watched couples packing into the room. After some preliminary ice-breaker exercises, the Woods modeled the steps for resolving a conflict. It was a spirited discussion because the conflict they chose had happened that afternoon as they toured El Escorial. The large audience was absolutely silent during an authentic dialogue dealing with real issues and real solutions. It was a beautiful sight when couples all over the room began to practice healthy communication skills in many languages as they worked through their own issues. At the refreshment time many proud couples wanted to share their results with us, and an astonished pastor had to admit the experience had been valuable.

ᴏ⦁ᴏ

DAILY COUPLE TALK:
(EACH PERSON ANSWERS)
*What new skill would you want to try
with your partner?*

WHAT WORKS?

Many people—not just millennials—have concerns and fears about living with the same person for decades. Adjustments can be handled, they expect; misunderstandings can be negotiated; children bring any number of changes, but those can be dealt with. It's just the sameness of watching the years go by in our most basic social institution that sets up anxiety for some.

A <u>Time</u> magazine article called "Staying Married" offers some interesting insights into what researchers have discovered about long-term marriage. Along with the usual reports about more health, sex, and money, the statistics report that marriage today can "achieve an unprecedentedly high level of marital quality." This is true, the article states, in spite of today's elevated expectations about what marriage partners should be able to accomplish.

"Couples who have made it all the way later into life have found it to be a peak experience, a sublime experience to be together," says Karl Pillemer, a Cornell University gerontologist who did an intensive survey of 700 older marriages. All the couples agreed it was "really, really hard," Pillemer found, but all—100%--said that their long marriage "was the best thing in their lives."

This is a book on "what works" for a marriage to flourish in good times and bad. For those anxious about the "humdrum" times, it's encouraging to hear that there really IS a pot of gold at the end of the marital rainbow.

DAILY COUPLE TALK:
(EACH PARTNER RESPONDS)
What is one exciting memory of the time you have spent with your partner?

REFERENCES AND RESOURCES

AARP Bulletin, October, 2016, Vol. 57, No. 8, p. 9.

Arp, David & Claudia, *The second half of marriage.* 1996. Zondervan Publishing House, Grand Rapids, MI.

Covey, Steven R., *The 7 Habits of Highly Effective Families,* 1997, Golden Books, New York.

Fort Worth Star-Telegram, Article, *"Team-building could improve unity, record.",* Carlos Mendez, Tuesday, August 23, 2016. p. 4B

Fort Worth Star-Telegram, Article, *"'Phantom' production coming to Bass Hall is a little faster, a little darker,"* Mark Lowry, Thursday, October 20, 2016, p. 14B.

Gottman, John, *Why Marriages Succeed or Fail.* 1994. A Fireside Book, Simon & Schuster, New York.

Hargrave, Terry D, *The Essential Humility of Marriage.* 2000. Zeig, Tucker, Theisen, Inc., Phoenix, AZ.

Harley, Jr., Willard F. *His Needs, Her Needs. 1986. Fleming H. Revell Co.*

Howe, Reuel, *The miracle of dialogue.* 1963. Seabury Press.

Karon, J. *Come Rain or Come Shine.* 2015. G. P. Putnam's Sons, New York.

Leon, Donna, *Beastly Things.* 2012. Atlantic Monthly Press, New York.

Dr. Nicholas Long, Pediatrics Professor, University of Arkansas for Medical Sciences, Presentation: *"Looking into the Future: Anticipated Trends in Parenting Education,"* Texas Council on Family Relations Annual Conference, 2016.

Luscombe, Belinda, *"How to stay married,"* June 13, 2016, pp. 36-40, Time, New York.

Lyubomirsky, Sonja. *A conversation with...,* AARP Bulletin/Real Possibilities, June, 2016

Mace, David R., *Getting Ready for Marriage (Revised).* 1995. Abington Press, Nashville, Tennessee.

Markman, H., Stanley, S., Blumberg, S. *Fighting for Your Marriage* 2001. Jossey-Bass, San Francisco, CA.

McManus, Michael J. *Marriage Savers.* 1995. Zondervan Publishing House, Grand Rapids, Michigan.

Mellan, Olivia and Christie, Sherry, *Overcoming Overspending, a winning plan for spenders and their partners.* 1995. Walker and Company, New York.

Miller, S. and Miller, P., *Couple Communication II, Thriving Together.* 2000. Interpersonal Communications Programs, Inc. Evergreen, CO.

Olson, David H. and Olson, Amy K. Empowering Couples. 2000. Life Innovations, Inc., Minneapolis, MinnesotaRoth, David, "Rising in Love," Maythelight Music, P.O. Box 1174, Old Chelsea Station, New York, New York 10011.Perrine, Laurence & Arp, Thomas R. *Sound and Sense, an introduction to poetry.* 1992.

Harcourt Brace Jovanovich College Publishers, Fort Worth.

Robb, J. D., *Apprentice in Death.* 2016. Berkley, New York.

Roth, David, "Rising in Love," 1988 Maythelight Music, P. O. Box 1174 Old Chelsea Station, New York, NY

Sotile, Wayne M. & Mary O., *The Medical Marriage, A Couple's Survival Guide.* 1996. Birch Lane Press, New York, NY.

Stanley, Scott, *The Heart of Commitment.* 1998. Thomas Nelson Publishers, Nashville.

Stanley, Scott, Markman, Howard, Blumberg, Susan, *Fighting for* your Marriage. 2001. Jossey-Bass, San Francisco.

Stinnett, Nick & DeFrain, John, *Secrets of Strong Families.* 1985. Little, Brown & Company, Boston

Vaillant, George E., *Triumphs of Experience, The Men of the Harvard Grant Study.* A 75-year study of Human Happiness.

Wallerstein, Judith S. and Blakeslee, Sandra. *The Good Marriage.* 1995. Warner Books, New York.

Walsh, Froma, *Strengthening Family Resilience.* 1998. The Guilford Press, New York.

Watzlawick, Paul, Bavelas, Janet B., Jackson, Donald D., *Pragmatics of Human Communication, A study of Interactional Patterns, Pathologies, and Paradoxes.* 1967. W. W. Norton & Company, New York.

Whiston, Lionel A., *For Those in Love.* 1983. Abington Press, Nashville.

Wood, Bobbye, *Building Lasting Marriages.* 2004. Britton Wood & Associates, Fort Worth, Texas

Wood, Bobbye & Britton, *Marriage Readiness. 1983.* Broadman Press, Nashville, TN.

Wood, Britton, *The Experience of Grief, Reluctant Learning and Forced Growth.* 2009. Britton Wood & Associates, Fort Worth, Texas.

MARRIAGE FOR THE EVERYDAY

365
Conversation Starters
Designed to Deepen
Couple Relationships

BOBBYE AND BRITTON WOOD

MARRIAGE FOR THE EVERDAY

CPSIA information can be obtained
at www.ICGtesting.com
Printed in the USA
BVOW03s1311080217
475602BV00004B/4/P